Cultural Diversity for Virtu

Cultural Diversity for Virtual Characters

Birgit Endrass

Cultural Diversity for Virtual Characters

Investigating Behavioral Aspects across Cultures

With a foreword by Prof. Dr. Elisabeth André

 Springer Vieweg

Birgit Endrass
Augsburg University
Germany

Dissertation Augsburg University, 2012

ISBN 978-3-658-04909-6   ISBN 978-3-658-04910-2 (eBook)
DOI 10.1007/978-3-658-04910-2

The Deutsche Nationalbibliothek lists this publication in the Deutsche Nationalbibliografie; detailed bibliographic data are available in the Internet at http://dnb.d-nb.de.

Library of Congress Control Number: 2014931022

Springer Vieweg
© Springer Fachmedien Wiesbaden 2014

This work is subject to copyright. All rights are reserved by the Publisher, whether the whole or part of the material is concerned, specifically the rights of translation, reprinting, reuse of illustrations, recitation, broadcasting, reproduction on microfilms or in any other physical way, and transmission or information storage and retrieval, electronic adaptation, computer software, or by similar or dissimilar methodology now known or hereafter developed. Exempted from this legal reservation are brief excerpts in connection with reviews or scholarly analysis or material supplied specifically for the purpose of being entered and executed on a computer system, for exclusive use by the purchaser of the work. Duplication of this publication or parts thereof is permitted only under the provisions of the Copyright Law of the Publisher's location, in its current version, and permission for use must always be obtained from Springer. Permissions for use may be obtained through RightsLink at the Copyright Clearance Center. Violations are liable to prosecution under the respective Copyright Law. The use of general descriptive names, registered names, trademarks, service marks, etc. in this publication does not imply, even in the absence of a specific statement, that such names are exempt from the relevant protective laws and regulations and therefore free for general use. While the advice and information in this book are believed to be true and accurate at the date of publication, neither the authors nor the editors nor the publisher can accept any legal responsibility for any errors or omissions that may be made. The publisher makes no warranty, express or implied, with respect to the material contained herein.

Printed on acid-free paper

Springer Vieweg is a brand of Springer DE.
Springer DE is part of Springer Science+Business Media.
www.springer-vieweg.de

dedicated to my parents

Foreword

With the proliferation of virtual spaces, more and more people come across avatars or autonomous conversational agents that rely on gestures, body postures, facial expressions and speech to interact with each other or the human user. It has often been emphasized that cultural influences have a great impact on how users respond to embodied conversational agents. Nevertheless, research into agent architectures that parameterize the agents' behavior by cultural factors is still rare. In most cases, culture-specific behaviors are not explicitly modeled, but the cultural background of the system designer is implicitly coded in the system. While some people might find it inspiring to converse with an agent that reflects a cultural background different from their own, others might have the impression that the system developers indirectly impose their own cultural values and norms on their users.

The thesis by Birgit Endrass goes beyond previous behavior modeling approaches for embodied agents by including empirically grounded cultural factors into an agent mind architecture. For the first time, a theoretically and empirically grounded model of culture was integrated within a multiagent system to simulate a wide range of multimodal behaviors considering cultural-specific differences in aspects of verbal, non-verbal and communication management behavior. The thesis successfully integrates research on behavior modeling conducted in the agent community and work on cultural models by social scientists.

The collaboration with partners from two Japanese Universities funded by the German Science Foundation (DFG) and the Japanese Society for the Promotion of Science (JSPS) gave Birgit Endrass the chance to acquire data in an international context and validate her approach with the German and the Japanese culture. In addition, Birgit Endrass was able to successfully transfer her approach to the Arabian and the American culture sponsored by a grant for an internship from the Institute for Creative Technologies. These achievements demonstrate in an impressive manner the universality of her approach that is not limited to selected cultures only.

In sum, the thesis opens up new research directions in the field of multiagent systems by giving agents cultural identity. Among other things, the approach provides an excellent basis for the realization of a simulation environment for future cultural training systems. Furthermore, the work bears high potential for agent-mediated decision-making and negotiation that should take culture-specific factors into account. While there has been some work on the generation of behaviors for synthetic cultures, the approach by Birgit Endrass bears the advantage that it can be applied to and measured against existing cultures. The chances are high that the approach presented in the thesis will be used by others as a method of choice for the development of agents with culture-specific behaviors.

Prof. Dr. Elisabeth André

Acknowledgments

First and foremost, I would like to thank my supervisor, Prof. Dr. Elisabeth André, for her constant support during this dissertation. Her helpful comments and suggestions certainly were a valuable input for this thesis. I also want to thank her for the help in establishing research collaborations and international contacts. Without her encouragement during the years I would not have become a researcher.

My special thanks go to Prof. Dr. Matthias Rehm, my co-supervisor, for his constant help throughout the years, and for initiating the Cube-G project, in the scope of which this dissertation was conducted.

Further, I would like to thank Prof. Dr. Franziska Kluegl for her quite spontaneous agreement to serve as a third reviewer for this dissertation.

I would like to express my gratitude to all colleagues of the Cube-G project. In particular, I want to thank Prof. Dr. Yukiko Nakano and Prof. Dr. Toyoaki Nishida for their cooperation in the corpus recordings, annotations and evaluation studies. Additionally, I would like to thank my former student workers Ionut Damian and Peter Huber for their support in graphics and simulation.

Furthermore, I thank the National Institute of Informatics (Tokyo, Japan) and the Institute of Creative Technologies (Los Angeles, USA) for the possibility to conduct internships at their labs, which not only gave me the opportunity to learn from their knowledge, but also to develop an open mind and to experience other cultures myself.

I am also thankful to the Elitenetzwerk Bayern (Elite Network Bavaria) for the scholarship which allowed me to follow my own ideas.

Above all, I thank my parents for their encouragement, understanding and unconditional love which have helped me throughout my whole life. Without their support, this thesis would not have become a reality.

Last but not least, I want to thank my dear friend Hilkka Uschkoreit for the discussions, life support and her belief in me during the past years.

Birgit Endrass

Summary

In human conversation, meaning is transported through several channels such as verbal and nonverbal behavior. Certain of these behavioral aspects are culturally dependent. Mutual understanding or acceptance is thus, amongst others, dependent on the cultural background of the interlocutors. When designing virtual character behavior, culture should be considered as it may improve the character's acceptance by users of certain cultural backgrounds.

In this dissertation, the simulation of culture with virtual characters is investigated. Thereby the focus lies on the generation of different culture-related behaviors by integrating culture as a parameter into the behavioral models of virtual characters, rather than simulating obvious differences such as outer appearance or language.

In the scope of this dissertation, aspects of verbal behavior, communication management and nonverbal behavior were explored and exemplified for the German and Japanese cultures. These aspects are of special interest, since they are dependent on culture, and address different modalities of a virtual character's behavior. For the integration of culture into computational models, a hybrid approach was developed that combines the advantages of a model-based approach and a corpus-driven approach. The hybrid approach enables us to model the causality of culture and corresponding behavior in a generalizable manner while concrete behaviors can be extracted from empirical data.

For the generation of culture-specific behaviors, methodologies from Artificial Intelligence were applied, in particular distributed behavior planning and Bayesian networks, and simulated in a 3D virtual environment. To evaluate the culture-related behaviors, perception studies were conducted in both targeted cultures. Results indicate that human observers tend to prefer character behavior that was designed to resemble their own cultural background. For the behavioral aspects where our hypotheses were confirmed, we consider their attention when designing virtual character behavior as promising. We aim on contributing to the field of intelligent virtual agents by providing our findings that can help improve a character's acceptance by users of certain cultural backgrounds.

However, the integration of cultural background into the behavioral models of virtual characters can not only enhance their acceptance, but also be used for cultural training in virtual environments, for the localization of computer games, or for cultural heritage by preserving and transferring culture-specific behaviors. Although the workflow has been applied to two national cultures, it is of a general nature and can serve as a guidance for other culture-specific generation approaches.

Contents

1 Introduction

Culture plays a crucial role in our lives. Mainly on a subconscious level it influences our behavior, decisions and judgments on everything we encounter. Although most people instinctively know what the term culture means, it is hard to formalize and even more difficult to explain what drives people to feel they are a member of a certain culture.

Language is the most obvious barrier when people from different cultures communicate. But even if both communication partners speak the same language fluently, misunderstandings may occur due to different cultural backgrounds. Human communication includes a lot more than the content of speech, e.g. a vast part of our communication happens nonverbally. In addition, *how* we communicate, e.g. through politeness strategies, can sometimes be more crucial than the semantics of the communication. Thereby, aspects such as personality, emotional state and cultural background influence our behavior. How this behavior is interpreted, vice versa, does also depend on the listener's social and personal background.

In the domain of virtual characters, the influence of human factors, e.g. emotional state or personality, has been widely researched. Although culture as a social factor influences our behavior crucially, it has hardly been investigated so far. In this dissertation, different culture-related aspects of behavior are simulated with virtual characters including verbal as well as nonverbal behavior (see Figure 1.1 for the virtual characters used for this approach).

Regarding cultural background, two different layers of culture can be investigated in principle when building computational models. The inner layer of culture

Figure 1.1: Virtual characters used in this dissertation.

explains what happens on the inside and reflects on why certain behaviors are shown. This can be formalized in a cognitive model that determines an agent's mind. In contrast, the external layer of culture investigates what happens on the surface through observable behaviors. This dissertation takes into account the external layer of culture and, thus, models culture-related aspects of human behavior. Virtual characters are very well suited for that aim since through their embodiment, they are able to express verbal as well as nonverbal behaviors and hence observable culture-related behaviors.

This dissertation was developed within the Cube-G project [Aug09] that is based on a theory of cultural dimensions and investigates whether and how the nonverbal behavior of agents can be generated from a parameterized computational model. Using an empirical study of communicative behaviors, it is further investigated how to interpolate behavior along different cultural dimensions. To integrate culture-specific aspects, Cube-G thus envisions a combination of a model-based approach and a corpus-based approach to automatically generate culture-specific behavior for virtual characters.

1.1 Motivation

Living in the 21th century enables people to travel to foreign countries quite easily. The big dos and don'ts of behavior are usually summarized in travel guides for a particular country. These are useful hints that help avoid to drop a clanger. However, there are more subtle differences across cultures that are not as obvious and easy to avoid.

An example of such a behavioral difference includes the style in which conversations are managed. Interrupting the conversation partner, for example, is perceived as impolite in many cultures such as Germany. Controversially, it is judged positively as an increased interest in the ongoing conversation in other cultures, such as Hungary. A conversation where two people of contrasting cultures meet, is bound to cause trouble. While one communication partner might feel offended because of being interrupted during the conversation, the other might have the impression that the interlocutor is not interested in the conversation. In either case, a negative impression of the conversation and, in particular, the communication partner might be the result. However, as non-experts in intercultural communication, interlocutors might not be aware of the reason for their impression, but just feel a general dislike for that particular person. This way, people might be confronted with being refused in another culture without knowing the reason, which in turn can lead to frustration or even culture shock.

The example given above demonstrates how easy a cultural misunderstanding can occur. In a similar manner, computer-based systems can be misunderstood due to the cultural background of the user. If, for example, the programmer of a software intends to make a certain impression on the user, the user might not necessarily understand this intention and perceive it otherwise. This could easily happen with a programmer and a user from different cultural backgrounds. Marcus and Alexander [MA07], for example, describe the different perceptions of a homepage by users with different cultural backgrounds. Regarding virtual characters, these differences can play an even more crucial role, since they are designed to simulate human behavior in a natural manner. If cultural differences are overlooked when modeling the communicative behavior of a virtual character, a certain group of users may fail to accept the model. This risk has been taken into account by the furniture company IKEA. Their consultant virtual character Anna shows different appearances on websites of different countries. The German agent, for example, is blond, while the agent on the UK website is brunette (see [IKE12a] and [IKE12b]).

Adapting a virtual character's appearance can enhance its acceptance by certain user groups. This effect can be explained by the similarity principle [Byr71], which states that interaction partners who perceive themselves as being similar are more likely to like each other. However, the example of culture-related differences in communication management described above suggests that more subtle differences need to be modeled to reach a higher degree of acceptance than simply changing a character's appearance.

Not too long ago, the privilege of traveling to foreign countries was reserved to a very selected group of people. Well-paid managers, for example, who were sent to another country were often prepared for their task and the contact with members of the foreign culture by means of role plays with professional actors who behaved in a culture-specific way. However, this approach is too expensive and time-consuming for today's travelers. At this point, another advantage of integrating culture into the behavior of virtual characters comes into play. By meeting a different culture in a virtual world, a first contact can be experienced in a save environment, without the risk of making a fool of oneself or embarrassing a member of the other culture.

The domain of research studies constitutes another application spectrum. The virtual representation of culture-related behaviors can be used as a test bed for conducting studies which test the impact of certain behavioral patterns on the perception of human observers. In comparison to studies with humans, aspects of behavior can be shown in isolation or in an exaggerated manner by virtual characters. As a result, the observer's focus is directed to the target behavioral aspect and side effects are avoided.

1.2 Approach

The aim of this dissertation is to integrate culture-related differences in human conversational behavior into the behavior models of virtual characters. Through evaluation studies with human observers, we want to find out which of the aspects of behavior actually have an impact on their perception.

In principle, there are two approaches that might be taken to integrate social aspects such as culture into virtual character systems: top-down and bottom-up. For the top-down approach, definitions of culture and in particular, descriptions of culture-related differences in behavior are extracted from literature and integrated

Figure 1.2: Workflow of this dissertation.

into a computational model. Thus, it is a model-driven approach where schemes that are already established in the social sciences are transformed into a computational model. In contrast, the bottom-up approach is data-driven. Human behavior is analyzed with regard to behavioral differences. Observed tendencies are then integrated into the simulated behavior of virtual characters.

The approach taken in this dissertation combines the two approaches described above. Descriptions from the social sciences are sometimes abstract and describe tendencies of behavior rather than clear rules. By analyzing the differences described in literate by means of concrete examples of human behavior, statistical data is extracted that serves as a basis for the resulting computational models. Thus, for our approach, social sciences teach us which behavioral aspects are of interest when building a model that describes culture-specific behavior, while we learn from empirical data how differences in these aspects manifest themselves in a concrete manner. Figure 1.2 outlines the steps that were taken for the approach.

Literature Study As a first step of the approach, literature from the social sciences is studied in order to extract culture-related differences in behavior for the targeted cultures. The resulting behavioral expectations serve as an input for the empirical study.

Corpus Analysis As a next step, the tendencies extracted from literature of social sciences are grounded in empirical data. Therefore, a video corpus recorded in the two target cultures is analyzed taking into account the expectations on behavioral differences.

Scenario Integration Using the findings from literature and corpus studies, computational models are built that generate culture-specific behaviors. For simulation, a demonstrator is designed including a virtual world as well as virtual characters that perform culture-specific behaviors.

Evaluation   Finally, the culture-related differences in behavior of the virtual characters are evaluated to investigate their impact on the perception of human observers of the target cultural backgrounds.

Cassell suggests that the evaluation results of simulated agent behavior can be used to refine the underlying computational model [Cas07]. Thus, she presents a development cycle that can be iterated several times. We appreciate the value of this idea and will consider a refinement of our models based on the results of the evaluation studies for our future work. Due to the extensive amount of data required for the integration of culture-related behaviors, however, for this dissertation, the steps described above are executed only once. To exemplify the approach, the workflow is carried out for the German and Japanese cultures.

1.3 Problem Statement and Significance

The aim of this dissertation is to integrate culture-related behavior into the behavioral models of virtual characters. Therefore, several tasks have to be carried out:

1.3.1 Identify operationalizeable Models of Culture and Behavioral Differences

In the social sciences, a huge amount of scientific literature is available that, in principle, can be used as a basis for culture-specific models for virtual characters. However, most theories are rather abstract and hard to formalize computationally. Thus, theories that qualify for the operationalization in computer science need to be identified.

Similarly, aspects of behavior have to be determined that are suitable to express cultural differences using virtual characters. Descriptions from the social sciences constitute a good basis for this purpose. Since there is a large amount of possible behavioral aspects in human behavior, it is helpful to include literature from computer science and related work on virtual character behavior. In particular, aspects of behavior that have been proven already to successfully simulate behavioral differences for other human factors are of special interest.

1.3.2 Extract concrete Behavioral Differences from a Video Corpus

Descriptions from literature of the social sciences are helpful to understand different cultures and are a good guideline to formulate hypotheses. For the implementation of computational models, however, they are sometimes too abstract and do not provide enough data to design specific behavioral differences. To overcome this shortcoming, empirical data can help support the hypotheses derived from literature. To ground the expectations derived from literature into empirical data, a video corpus is recorded in two different cultures and analyzed in this dissertation.

Recording such a video corpus is a challenge, since a huge amount of data is required to explain culture-related differences in behavior for at least two different cultures, while all participants need to face the same conditions.

Analyzing the large amount of data is a time-consuming task. In particular, the annotation of the different behavioral channels takes a lot effort, since e.g. annotators with different language skills are required. In addition, annotation schemes have to be carefully designed to ensure that on the one hand the large amount of data can be summarized in a descriptive manner, and on the other hand the desired aspects of behavior are covered in enough detail to be formalized in a computational model.

Extracting culture-related behaviors from such a corpus is a great challenge, since it needs to be assured that behavioral differences are aroused by culture and not by other human factors such as personality, gender or the circumstances of the corpus recordings.

1.3.3 Build computational Models of Culture-related Behavior

After extracting behaviors from literature and the corpus study, gained insights are formalized in computational models. Previous work on virtual character behavior faced challenges such as natural language generation or nonverbal behavior customization before and suggests convincing techniques from the research area of artificial intelligence as a solution. To integrate cultural background in behavior, similar challenges have to be faced; however, variations have to be created to simulate different cultural backgrounds. For the integration of culture, it is not sufficient to simply change the appearance of a character. Instead more subtle differences need to be investigated. Starting from the classical distinction between "what to say" and "how to say it" in natural language generation, we need to adapt not only the content of a character's utterances to a particular culture, but also their form. The same goes for a character's nonverbal behavior. For example, a character might vary the number and quality of gestures depending on its assumed cultural background.

When building a computational model from a video corpus, difficulties can arise since the corpus is recorded under certain circumstances. Observed behavior, thus, is not necessarily transferable to other situations for a general application that reflects prototypical behavior for a certain cultural background. Therefore, computational models need to be concrete enough to grasp culture-specific differences in behavior, but at the same time be general enough to match different situations or contexts. Besides integrating concrete culture-related aspects of behavior, consistency between the different aspects needs to be assured to obtain natural behavior for a certain cultural background. In addition, characters need to be autonomous for a realistic simulation of conversational behavior and therefore, e.g. plan reasonable dialog acts.

Individuals belonging to the same culture do not all show exactly the same behavior. In a simulated system, this would be very unrealistic as well. Thus, a variability of behavior has to be provided for different characters without losing the common cultural background of their behavior.

1.3.4 Measure Impact on Human Observers

A key problem is to identify which of the implemented aspects of behavior have an impact on human observers and thus influence their perception, and which have not. To measure the impact of each aspect separately, they have to be evaluated in isolation. To isolate aspects is not trivial, since different aspects of behavior might correlate, e.g. the semantics of speech and speech accompanying gestures. To set up appropriate evaluation studies, these correlations have to be overcome.

1.4 Overview

This dissertation is structured as follows:

Chapter 1 - Introduction   This chapter introduces the aim of this dissertation and highlights its relevance. Further, the approach taken for the realization is summarized and the challenges that have to be faced are outlined.

Chapter 2 - Theoretical Background This chapter gives an overview of the theoretical background necessary for this dissertation. The first section investigates culture as it is described in the social sciences and social psychology. In particular, models that are suited for the integration into computational models are described in more detail. Culture can manifest itself on different levels of behavior. Thus, aspects of human behavior are addressed subsequently which are influenced by cultural background. The workflow of the dissertation is exemplified for the German and Japanese cultures. Therefore, cultural profiles are constructed for the two target cultures taking into account the models of culture described earlier in this chapter. Based on the profiles, expectations on behavioral differences are stated for the aforementioned aspects of behavior.

Chapter 3 - Related Work Related work in the area of virtual characters is reviewed in this chapter. Starting with the development from single agents to multi-agent systems, the newly raised topic of integrating culture is addressed. As a next step, an overview of systems and studies is presented that investigate the aspect of culture for virtual characters. Finally, we introduce approaches that successfully integrated the aspects of human behavior into virtual character behavior that are considered in this dissertation.

Chapter 4 - Empirical Background The empirical background of this dissertation is presented in this chapter. First, the methodology of annotating a multimodal corpus is introduced. Then, the acquisition of the corpus recorded in the German and Japanese cultures is described that serves as a basis for the empirical analysis. As a next step, we describe the annotation schemes that were designed for the analysis of culture-related behavioral aspects. Finally, results of the corpus analysis are presented that hold information about behavioral differences between prototypical German and prototypical Japanese behaviors as observed in the video corpus.

Chapter 5 - Conceptual Design and Technical Realization In this chapter, the technical realization of this dissertation is described. It starts from an overview of the procedure that was carried out in this dissertation which combines a theory-based and corpus-driven approach. Subsequently, the general approach taken for the implementation is described, pointing out the applicability of techniques from artificial intelligence for the approach. Concrete modeling of behaviors is then exemplified for the two cultures of Germany and Japan, taking into account our findings from literature as well as the corpus study. Finally, a demonstrator is introduced that generates example dialogs along with nonverbal behaviors for virtual characters in a virtual environment.

Chapter 6 - Evaluation of Behavioral Aspects   The chapter describes evaluation studies that were conducted to investigate whether human observers prefer agent behavior that was designed to reflect their own cultural background. For evaluation, the behavioral aspects were tested in isolation to find out which of the aspects have an impact on the judgment of human observers.

Chapter 7 - Contributions and Future Work   The last chapter of this dissertation summarizes the contributions of this approach to the research community and points out some future directions that are going to be investigated based on our results.

2 Theoretical Background

In this dissertation, culture-related differences in human behavior are formalized in a computational way to be simulated in a virtual agent application. As pointed out in our general approach (Section 1.2), as a first step, we address culture as it appears in the social sciences, in order to learn more about the notion of culture and, in particular, culture-related behavioral differences.

This chapter introduces the theoretical background of culture and human behavior as required for our purposes. In the first section of this chapter (Section 2.1), different definitions of culture are introduced to point out different approaches of investigating culture, e.g. on a national level or from an anthropological viewpoint.

Culture can manifest itself on different channels of behavior. Therefore, in Section 2.2, different aspects of human behavior are described that can, in principle, be influenced by people's cultural background and, thus, seem to be relevant to the simulation with virtual characters.

The workflow carried out in this dissertation is exemplified for the German and Japanese cultures. Therefore, in Section 2.3, profiles for these two cultures are presented based on the theories from the social sciences described earlier in this chapter. In addition, expectations for the two target cultures are stated for the aspects of human behavior that have been pointed out as being relevant before, based on reflections on the cultural profiles designed for this purpose.

Finally, this chapter is summarized in Section 2.4, including the assumptions on behavioral differences for the targeted cultures based on the findings from literature on culture and human behavior.

2.1 Culture

In this section, the theoretical background on culture is investigated. In the social sciences, there are very different approaches that explain the concept of culture. Culture can on the one hand be described as national cultures, distinguishing countries, and on the other hand, culture can correspond to groups such as ethical, regional or religious groups.

In general, many descriptions of culture are rather abstract and are, thus, not very helpful for building a computational model. Therefore, in this section, we concentrate on theories from the social sciences which explain culture along dimensional models or dichotomies that help understand culture in a more descriptive manner and therefore seem to be well suited for our purposes.

First, different levels of culture will be introduced that help understand to what extent culture influences human behavior at all. Subsequently, some dimensional models are described that categorize cultures along different attributes. In the last subsection, dichotomies of culture are presented as a more abstract and anthropological approach of distinguishing cultures.

2.1.1 Levels of Culture

In this subsection, theories will be introduced that use layers to describe the influence of culture on human behavior. These layers point out, among other things, that culture does not only determine behavioral differences on the surface but that it also works on cognitive level. Thus, when building a computational model, different approaches can be taken as well, such as building cognitive models of an agent's mind or modeling differences in behavior.

When investigating culture, the notion of levels can be used in different ways. On the one hand, culture can be seen as one layer within a model that influences human behavior along with other levels such as personality. On the other hand, culture can be divided into different levels itself, explaining how culture influences either internal values or external aspects such as behavior. With this subsection, it becomes clear that culture should only be seen as one factor that can be integrated into a virtual character's behavior among other things such as personality. However, culture constitutes an important factor in human behavior and should therefore be investigated. Another insight of this subsection is the fact that culture does not only influence human behavior that can be seen on the surface, but also determines people's mindsets and internal drives.

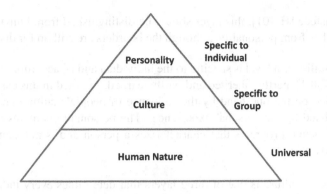

Figure 2.1: Hofstede's levels of uniqueness in a human's mental program [Hof01].

2.1.1.1 Culture as Part of a Mental Program

Human behavior depends on several personal factors such as gender, age, personality, emotional state or personal relationships. Culture as a social phenomenon influences a whole group of people. To what extent these personal and social factors determine an individual's behavior is hard to formalize. Hofstede [Hof01] refers to this as a mental program that individualizes every human and affects people's behavior. This so-called "software of the mind" can be categorized into three layers: human nature, culture and personality. These three layers are presented graphically in Figure 2.1 and are described as follows:

- **Human nature** represents the universal level of people's mental program and, thus, applies to every human individual. It contains basic physical and psychological functions and is inherited with people's genes. Thus, every human is able have emotions such as fear, joy, sadness, anger or love. Also abilities such as the facility to observe people's environments and talk to other humans are part of this level of the mental program.

- **Culture** is the middle layer of the mental program that determines human behavior. In contrast to the other layers, this layer is purely learned and not inherited. Culture is specific to the group and the environment, which ranges from the domestic circle, the neighborhood or workplace up to the living community of the country an individual lives in. Culture plays a crucial role in the perception and selection of behaviors, mainly without this being realized. Consequently, behavior is sometimes perceived as inappropriate without realizing that there is a cultural gap causing the problem. According to Hofstede [Hof01], this layer should be distinguished from human nature as well as from personality, although the boarders are still up for discussion.

- **Personality** as a level is specific to the individual and is, according to Hofstede [Hof01], partly inherited and partly learned. Learned in this case means modified on the one hand by the influence of people's culture and on the other hand by the personal experience. The personality contains a unique set of mental programs that characterizes a person and is not shared with anybody else.

In this model, culture is one of three layers that determines every individual's mental program. While human nature and personality are rather simple to understand, culture is hard to grasp. Although everybody intentionally knows what the term "culture" means, it is hard to describe what exactly culture is and how different cultures can be distinguished. Moreover, the influence culture has on people's values or thinking is difficult to formalize, as it is to explain what drives people to feel as a member of a certain culture. However, culture does influence human behavior and moreover, it influences on a subconscious level and is thus often not taken into account when critically reflecting on certain situations.

While the layers of human nature and personality have been investigated in virtual characters research a lot, e.g. Aylett and colleagues [ALD+05], Gratch and colleagues [GRA+02], or Rist and colleagues [RAB03a], the aspect of culture came into focus only recently (see Section 3.1 for an explanation). By adding culture to the behavioral models of virtual characters, a more complete simulation of a human's mental program as described by Hofstede [Hof01] can be reached.

2.1.1.2 Different Levels of Depth

In comparison to the theory described above, culture can not only be seen as one layer that influences human behavior, but can also be divided into several layers itself. Another model introduced by Hofstede and colleagues [HHM10] explains culture on several layers along the four terms symbols, heroes, rituals and values. Figure 2.2 shows these manifestations of culture at different levels of depth, with symbols as the most outer and thus most superficial level and values as the most inner and deepest level.

The layer of symbols covers words, gestures or pictures that have a particular meaning and are recognized by the members of a culture, such as clothes, jargon or

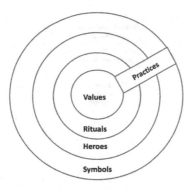

Figure 2.2: Hofstede's manifestations of culture at different levels of depth [HHM10].

hairstyles. According to Hofstede and colleagues [HHM10], new symbols are developed constantly while old ones disappear. Heroes are related to persons that are well known in a culture and serve as guidelines for behavior. Thereby, these heroes do not necessarily have to be living persons but can be imaginary such as Batman or Barbie. Rituals are collective activities that are considered essential within a culture, such as greeting or showing respect to others. In addition, rituals include discourse and thus the language that is used in certain interactions [HHM10].

As shown in Figure 2.2, the three layers described above are subsumed by the word practice, since they can be seen from the outside. According to Hofstede and colleagues [HHM10], the meaning, however, can not be seen from the outside and is dependent on the observer who judges only what can be seen.

The most inner layer in Figure 2.2 consists of values, which describe tendencies for members of a culture to prefer certain situations. According to Hofstede and colleagues [HHM10], values deal with parings such as good and evil, normal and abnormal, natural and unnatural.

2.1.1.3 Implicit and Explicit Levels

Another theory that describes levels of culture is introduced by Trompenaars and Hampden-Turner [THT97], who distinguish implicit and explicit levels (see Figure 2.3) that are ranging from very concrete to subconscious.

The most outer layer in Figure 2.3 constitutes the explicit layer holding things that can be observed in reality such as language, clothes, buildings or food. Ac-

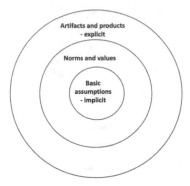

Figure 2.3: Implicit and explicit layers of culture [THT97].

cording to Trompenaars and Hampden-Turner [THT97], it is notable that the way this explicit layer of culture is judged, is rather dependent on the observer's cultural background.

The middle level consists of norms and values that are reflected by the explicit layer mentioned above. While norms are related to a group's sense of right and wrong, values are associated to the sense of good and bad [THT97]. Thus, norms determine how people think they should behave, and values determine the way people wish to behave.

The most inner layer of culture is determined by basic assumptions that have vanished from conscious questioning and have become self-evident. Trompenaars and Hampden-Turner [THT97] explain this phenomenon as a result of how people cope with their environment as a need for survival. How people cope with their daily problems has disappeared from their awareness and became absolute assumptions. These basic assumptions can be easily recognized by questioning them in a given culture, which will lead to confusion or even annoyance such as asking a US American or Dutch person why they think that all people are equal [THT97].

The middle layer of Trompenaars' and Hampden-Turner's model can be compared with Hofstede's most inner layer of culture (see previous subsection), since both focus on norms and values that determine people's thinking. Following the distinction between internal drives such as norms and observable differences such as outer appearance, when integrating culture into a virtual character system, different approaches can be taken as well such as building cognitive models of an agent's mind or modeling differences in behavior. For this dissertation, observable differences are modeled to point out differences in behavior using virtual char-

acters. Thus, the explicit level of culture is the most interesting one as it holds
information on outward differences.

2.1.2 Dimensional Models

Although culture is often described as an abstract concept that holds tendencies for
groups, there are approaches that define culture along different attributes. These
dimensional models constitute an excellent starting point for building behavior
models for virtual characters, since they describe culture in a very formal manner
that can be operationalized for computational models. In this subsection, different
dimensional models of culture are introduced.

2.1.2.1 Hofstede's Dimensional Model

The probably most well known example of defining culture along different dimensions was introduced by Hofstede and colleagues [Hof01] who investigated culture
on a national level. The theory is based on a broad empirical survey, covering more
than 70 countries. Primarily, only 40 countries were analyzed and extended to 50
countries and 3 regions later [Hof12]. Currently, a total of 74 countries are listed
[Hof12], whereas the scores on the dimensions are partly based on replications or
extensions of the original study. Originally, Hofstede and colleagues introduced
four dimensions to explain different cultures: power distance, individualism, masculinity and uncertainty avoidance. The fifth dimension, long term orientation,
was added afterwards in order to explain Asian cultures in a more appropriate
way, based on Confucian dynamism. So far, this dimension has been applied to 23
countries. Several years later, a sixth dimension, indulgence versus restraint, was
added to the model [HHM10] and applied to 93 countries and regions. Each of
the dimensions contains two extreme sides, and every culture is thus positioned in
a six-dimensional space represented by a value on each dimension. These scores
were originally supposed to lie between 0 and 100. But as more cultures were
added afterwards, some of the countries exceeded these borders, as they were more
extreme on a dimension than a country that was already rated on the most extreme
value.

At the current state of the art Hofstede's model holds the six cultural dimensions:
power distance, individualism, masculinity, uncertainty avoidance, long term orientation and indulgence. In the following, these dimensions will be further explained.

- The dimension of power distance describes the extent to which a different distribution of power is accepted by the less powerful members of a culture. Scoring high on this dimension indicates a high level of inequality of power and wealth within the society. A low score on the other hand supposes greater equality between social levels, including government, organizations and families.

- The individualism dimension describes the degree to which individuals are integrated into a group. On the individualist side, ties between individuals are loose, and everybody is expected to take care for him- or herself. On the collectivist side, people are integrated into strong, cohesive in-groups.

- The masculinity dimension describes the distribution of roles between the genders, which can be a crucial characteristic for a culture. The two extreme sides are masculine and feminine, whereas masculine values contain attributes such as being assertive or competitive while members of feminine cultures have moderate, caring values.

- The uncertainty avoidance dimension explains a society's tolerance for uncertainty and ambiguity. The extent to which a member of the culture feels uncomfortable or comfortable in an unknown situation is the key-factor of this dimension. Uncertainty avoiding cultures try to minimize the possibility of such situations and stick to laws and rules. Members are emotional and motivated by an inner nervous energy, whereas uncertainty accepting cultures are more tolerant to different opinions and do not express strong emotions.

- The fifth dimension, long term orientation, was included several years later to better explain Asian cultures better. One of the extreme sides, long term orientation, is associated with thrift and perseverance, whereas the opposite side, short term orientation, shows respect for tradition, fulfilling of social obligations and protecting one's face.

- The last dimension, indulgence, describes the subjective well-being that members of a culture experience. Cultures that score high on this dimension have a high percentage of people that consider themselves as very happy and as having a high level of control over their lives. Restrained societies controversially are more pessimistic with thrift being important instead of leisure.

As mentioned above, each culture that is categorized in this model is represented by values on each dimension [Hof12]. The scores of a culture on each of the dimensions have an impact on one another. Besides publishing the scores on each dimension, Hofstede and colleagues give explanations on how the individual scores influence the behavior of their members [Hof12].

Using Hofstede's dimensional model that investigates different cultures on a national level, seems to be a good basis for the integration of culture into the behavioral models of virtual characters, since it defines a complete model of culture along different attributes and can, thus, be integrated in a computational model.

2.1.2.2 Value-Oriented Model

Another approach that distinguishes cultures along different dimensions was introduced by Kluckhohn and Strodtbeck [KS61]. In comparison to Hofstede's theory described above, the authors do not focus on nationalities but describe different so-called value orientations in order to explain culture. According to the Kluckhohn and Strodtbeck, culture consists of explicit and implicit patterns that are transmitted by symbols and constitute the distinctive achievements of different groups. These value orientations cover the following:

- The essential *nature of people* varies from evil to good and explains to which extent people are considered as being trustworthy and good or bad and whether they need to be controlled or not.

- The *relationship to nature* describes what members of a culture think is the appropriate relationship towards the environment. The relationship can range from being determined by nature through external forces and genetics to the thinking that humans dominate nature.

- The *relationship to other people* describes how people prefer relationships and social organizations to be. This is explained in shades that reach from hierarchical (power is distributed unequally) to individual (equal rights for everybody).

- The *modality of human activity* is a value orientation that ranges from the simple concept of being to the concept that efforts will be rewarded and therefore people should work hard.

- The *temporal focus* of human activity describes how people think about time. The orientation can either be in the past, implying one should learn from history, in the present (living for today) or in the future, which results in planning and saving for the future.

With the dimensions, some of the concepts explained by other theories are picked up. Although this theory presents a classification of values in a dimensional manner, the impact on human behavior is described rather vaguely and thus hard to be measured in computational terms. In addition, the model covers aspects of culture rather than building a complete model. For these reasons, we consider Hofstede's model (see previous paragraph) as being better suited for our purposes.

2.1.2.3 Problem-Oriented Model

Trompenaars and Hampden-Turner [THT97] investigate culture according to the solutions people choose to deal with problems. Therefore, the authors distinguish three different categories of possible problems: (1) the relationship to other people, (2) the notion of time (3) and the relationship to the environment. Cultures differs in how their members are solving problems in the different categories.

The first category (relationships) includes different perceptions of following rules or friendship obligations and the understanding of oneself as an individual or as part of a group. In addition, this category determines to what extent it is acceptable to express emotions in different cultures and to what degree a person is involved in a business relationship. The importance of achievement in terms of what an individual has accomplished in comparison to the status he or she had been ascribed by birth, as well as gender or age are also part of this category.

Regarding communication, this category is of special interest, since assumptions about prototypical behavior are made. According to Trompenaars and Hampden-Turner [THT97], communication is the exchange of information, while information is the carrier of meaning, which in turn is culture-dependent. Regarding verbal communication, cultures are divided into Western, Latin and Oriental cultures. While Northern America, for example, is considered a Western culture, the Arab world counts as an Oriental culture, whereas in the Latin group, we find countries such as Mexico for example. Western cultures are described as verbal cultures where members get nervous and uneasy when there are long pauses. Interrupting the conversation partner is considered as impolite. Thus, turn taking is managed in such a way that one starts talking after the interlocutor has stopped. Latin cultures are described as being even more verbal and where interruptions are being regarded as showing interest in the conversation. In Oriental cultures, silence is a crucial part of communication and can be considered a sign of respect. Pauses are used to process information or assure that the conversation partner gives away the speaking floor.

The second category (attitude towards time) describes the culturally dependent view that people have of time.

On the one hand, this category describes differences in the importance of past, presence and future in different cultures. Trompenaars and Hampden-Turner refer to the "American dream" being the "French nightmare" [THT97], since there are vast differences in the perception of time in these two cultures. While in the American culture the present performance counts and people tend to have comprehensive plans for the future, in the French culture, people have a strong sense for the past and thus focus less on the presence and the future.

On the other hand, this category describes culture-related differences in the perception of the passage of time. While in some cultures the passing of time is perceived in a straight line as a sequence of separate events, in other cultures time is seen as a moving circle, holding possibilities for the past, present and future at a time [THT97].

In the third category (attitude towards the environment), the way a society looks at the world is investigated. In some cultures the truth, motivation and values that affect peoples' lives can be found within a person, while in other cultures the world is seen as more powerful than people and thus needs to be feared. Trompenaars and Hampden-Turner [THT97] explain this phenomenon with the following example: In Japan masks are worn over the nose and mouth when someone has a cold in order to not infect other people. In England, vice versa, these masks are worn by people when doing sports in order to not being polluted by the environment.

As for the value-oriented model described in the previous paragraph, the problem-oriented model covers aspects of culture rather than building a complete model. Thus, Hofstede's dimensional model still seems to be better suited to serve as a basis for a computational model. However, some of the categories of this model hold valuable information on behavioral differences. In particular, the different usage of silence in speech, for example, can be utilized to enhance culture-related behavior models of virtual characters.

2.1.3 Dichotomies

Another group of theories distinguishes cultural groups along antonyms. The phenomenon of culture can be seen as a concept, where dichotomies are defined and differences in behaviors are explained accordingly. Although these theories take a more anthropological approach, and are therefore more abstract than e.g. dimensional models, they also seem to be very well suited for our purposes since concrete distinctions regarding cultures are stated.

Culture-related dichotomies provide two distinctive versions of cultural background in a converse manner. Most dichotomies focus on one aspect of culture such as different perception of time, while they describe prototypical behavior for the groups that are being distinguished. These opposite descriptions of behavior can be used for the implementation of diverse versions of a computational model. In the following, some dichotomies are introduced that distinguish cultural groups.

2.1.3.1 High- and Low-Contact Cultures

Hall [Hal66] distinguishes so called *high-* and *low-contact* cultures. This concept is mainly related to space and territory. In some cultures it is, for example, common to claim one's personal space by placing a towel on a chair or a book on a desk. Regarding human communicative behavior, behavioral differences in proxemics and haptics can be observed.

Hall [Hal66] investigates the acceptable distances between communication partners as one determinant of proxemic behavior. He defines four different distance zones that surround an individual and are reserved for different people and interactions. The "intimate distance zone" is reserved for very close relationships, such as lovers, parents or close friends. The "personal distance zone" is reserved for focused and private interactions. According to [Pea93], this is the common distance that people stand away from each other at cocktail parties, office parties, social functions and friendly gatherings. The "social distance zone" is a common distance for people that we do not know very well, such as the postman, a local shopkeeper or a plumber. The "public distance zone" is considered a comfortable distance when addressing a large group of people. The proportions of these zones vary highly by culture. According to Ting-Toomey [TT99], the average conversational distance for Northern Americans with European background is approximately 20 inches, while it is between 14 - 15 inches for some Latin American groups and only 9 - 10 inches for Saudi-Arabs.

Pease [Pea93] describes several situations that lead to misunderstandings between members of different cultures due to different perceptions of spatial behavior. In an example, he reports on a conference in the US, where a Japanese attendee talked to an American participant, both showing different interpersonal distance behavior. In order to adjust to their culturally comfortable distance to each other, the American was moving backward from the Japanese, while the Japanese moved towards the American. On a video played at high speed, this gave the impression that both were dancing, with the Japanese leading. Not surprisingly, the American conference attendee might have perceived the Japanese participant as being pushy or overfamiliar, while the American might be considered as being cold or reserved.

Regarding haptics, Hall [Hal66] states that people from high-contact cultures tend to have higher tactile (touch) and olfactory (smell) needs than members of low-contact cultures who, vice versa, have more visual needs. In [TT99], Ting-Toomey summarizes work that categorizes national cultures regarding contact. High-contact cultures are, for example, the French, Italians, Latin Americans, Arabs and Africans, while U.S. Americans, Canadians, Northern Europeans and Australians are considered moderate-contact cultures and East Asians, such as Japanese or Koreans, are low-contact cultures. In Arab countries, for example, it is a common habit between two males to embrace or kiss for greeting or to link arms in a friendly way. Here again, different ideas of appropriate touching can lead to negative perceptions of the observer who might judge the behavior as being insincere or cold versus aggressive or belligerent.

Following Hall's categorization into *high-* and *low-contact* cultures, Ting-Toomey [TT99] characterizes the varieties of these cultural groups in more detail. According to her, features of high-contact cultures include direct facing, frequent direct eye contact, close interaction and a rather loud voice, whereas features of low-contact cultures include indirect facing, wider interpersonal space, little or no touching, indirect glances and a soft or moderate voice.

The classification into high- and low-contact cultures is very valuable for the integration into computational models. In particular, descriptions of behavioral differences, such as interpersonal distance or frequency of eye contact, can be used to model the nonverbal behavior of culture-specific virtual characters.

2.1.3.2 High- and Low-Context Cultures

In [Hal66], Hall describes another dichotomy focusing on differences in verbal communication patterns and introduces *high-context* versus *low-context* communication.

In low-context communication, meaning is expressed through explicit utterances. The speaker is expected to construct clear messages that can be understood easily without the need to decode other aspects of behavior such as silence or tone of voice. In contrast, in high-context communication little information is explicitly encoded and the conversation relies mainly on physical context. Besides verbal utterances, meaning is transported through context or nonverbal clues. According to Ting-Toomey [TT99], interlocutors are expected to "read between the lines" in order to decode the whole meaning of a verbal message. Social roles or positions as well as nonverbal behaviors can contain additional meaning.

Cultures can be categorized in regards of high- and low-context communication according to the preferred verbal communication of their members. A line can be drawn between Eastern and Western cultures. While most Western cultures are low-context cultures, most Asian cultures are high-context cultures.

In [TT99], Ting-Toomey states some characteristics of typical high- and low-context communication. People that use low-context communication prefer direct verbal style, person- and speaker-oriented language, self-enhancement and talkativeness. Vice versa, individuals that are used to high-context communication prefer indirect verbal style, status- and listener-oriented language, self-effacement and silence in communication. In direct verbal communication, as preferred in the US American culture for example, it is common to speak one's mind and to get to the point. Ting-Toomey [TT99] states an example with two neighbors, one complaining directly that the other is singing to loud and thus falling asleep is not possible. In a culture that uses indirect verbal communication, such as Japan, in the same situation the neighbor that feels disturbed would compliment the talent of the neighbor and his big enthusiasm. The other neighbor would then interpret this as a raising conflict and apologize for the inconvenience. This could easily lead to a misunderstanding between two individuals from different cultures, as one could possibly not understand the hidden message and thus not react accordingly. The two cultures from the example above would also differ regarding their preference in person- versus status-oriented language usage as well as self-enhancement versus self-effacement [TT99]. While in the US American culture first-name basis and direct address is preferred (person-oriented), in the Japanese culture proper roles and words are used (status-oriented). In addition, praising one's own achievements (self-enhancement) is common in the US American culture while understatement (self-effacement) is considered polite in the Japanese culture.

In a similar manner, as described above for high- and low-contact cultures that are suitable for the implementation of nonverbal behavior models for virtual characters, the categorization into high- and low-context cultures seems very appropriate to serve as a basis for verbal behavior models, since clear descriptions of differences in communicative behavior are available for the two groups.

2.1.3.3 Monochronic and Polychronic Cultures

Based on Hall's findings [Hal83], Ting-Toomey [TT99] analyzed another dichotomy. The division into *monochronic* and *polychronic* cultures that describe different perceptions of temporal regulation. Members of different cultures differ regarding how they structure, interpret or understand time. According to Hall and Hall [HH87], cited in [TT99], in monochronic cultures, time is experienced in a linear way, which can be divided into segments. In these cultures, a schedule has a very high priority and people tend to concentrate at one thing at a time. In contrast, in polychronic cultures, time is perceived as a concurrent occurrence of many things at a time. In these cultures the involvement of people is considered important, while holding on to schedules does not have a high priority. Consequently, members of polychronic cultures tend to do several things at a time.

The division into monochronic and polychronic time cultures also affects the perception of being late. In [TT99], a working unit for a prototypical monochronic culture is described as being 5 minutes long. Thus, if members of this cultural group are late for five minutes (one time unit), they tend to mumble something about their lateness, while a 15-minute delay (three time units) requires an apology. Being late for 30 minutes is considered rude and a serious apology is expected along with a good reason for the lateness. In polychronic cultures, vice versa, a prototypical working unit is about 15 minutes long. Thus, being late for 30 minutes (only 2 time units) does not necessarily require an apology in these cultures. On the contrary, the one who is waiting is expected to understand the latenesses, especially if there are reasons for it, such as taking care of the family.

In [TT99], Ting-Toomey summarizes some characteristics for monochronic versus polychronic cultures. According to her, monochronic cultures rely on a clock time, where appointments count. Activities are segmented and and task-oriented, achievements and the future are focused. Contrary, polychronic cultures have a flexible sense of situational time. Activities are taken simultaneously and relationship-oriented. Experiences and the past or present are focused.

Although this dichotomy does not provide clear descriptions of verbal or nonverbal behavioral styles as the previous ones, it can still be useful to enhance culture-specific virtual character behavior. For example, the preference of either performing tasks in a sequential manner or at a time respectively, can be integrated into a computational model.

2.1.3.4 Synthetic Cultures

In [HPH02], Hofstede and Pedersen introduce so-called synthetic cultures that are based on Hofstede's dimensional model described in Subsection 2.1.2. For the notion of synthetic cultures five of the six dimensions are operationalized. The sixth dimension, indulgence, was added to the model afterwards and thus has not been considered for synthetic cultures yet.

As described earlier, the scores of a culture on the different dimensions have an impact on one another. In order to better explain each dimension and the influence they have on the behavior of members of a target culture, they are observed in isolation for the description of synthetic cultures. Synthetic cultures are thus an abstract concept that illustrates a group that finds itself on one of the extreme sides on one of the cultural dimensions. This extreme side of a dimension that the synthetic culture stands for, is therefore exaggerated.

Synthetic culture can thus be seen as dichotomies as well, since each dimension generates two cultures that find themselves on one of the extreme sides of the target dimension. These cultures can be seen as opposites of each other that feel and act very differently.

In [HPH02], Hofstede and Pedersen define a profile for each synthetic culture that contains the culture's values, core distinctions, key elements as well as words with a positive or negative connotation.

Taking into account the individualism dimension, for example, the two opposite cultures would be the individualistic and the collectivistic cultures. The extreme individualistic synthetic culture has the core value "individual freedom" and the core distinction is the distinction between "me and others". Key elements are statements such as "honest people speak their mind", "laws and rights are the same for all" or "everyone is supposed to have a personal opinion on any topic". These key-elements are golden rules for appropriate behavior in this synthetic culture and explain the way in which members of that culture are thinking. Positive and negative words are added to the description of each synthetic culture that help understand a culture in a descriptive way. Words with a positive connotation in the extreme individualistic culture are for example: self, friendship, do your own thing, self-respect, dignity, I, me, pleasure, adventure, guilt or privacy. Words with a negative connotation on the other hand are words such as: harmony, obligation, sacrifice, tradition, decency, honor, duty, loyalty or shame. For the extreme collectivistic synthetic culture, which is located on the opposite side of the same dimension, the connotations of these words are exactly the other way round.

Stereotypical behavior is defined for synthetic cultures as well [HPH02]. Extreme individualistic cultures, for example, are described as verbal, self-centered, defensive, tending to be loners and running from one appointment to the next.

As pointed out in Subsection 2.1.2, we consider Hofstede's dimensional model of culture [Hof01] as very well suited to provide a basis on which to build behavioral models, since it provides a complete model of culture along different dimensions that can be operationalized in a computational way. The notion of synthetic cultures that extends the dimensional model in a descriptive manner, can additionally be used to implement culture-related differences. In particular, synthetic cultures with their values and behaviors are a valuable tool in order to understand cultures that score differently on a dimension compared to one's own culture, due to their prototypical nature and concrete descriptions of behavior.

2.2 Aspects of Human Behavior

As pointed out earlier, culture can manifest itself on different levels of behavior, while different expressive channels can be influenced by culture. Therefore in this section, different aspects of human behavior are described that can, in principle, be influenced by people's cultural background and, thus, seem to be relevant for our purposes. In addition, possible classifications are introduced for these aspects that can help build computational models. Using virtual characters for the simulation of cultural background, different channels of behavior can be addressed. Verbal behavior can be simulated using text-to-speech systems, while nonverbal behaviors can be naturally demonstrated through the characters embodiment.

Language, as main medium of human communication, is the most obvious barrier of intercultural communication. Besides language itself, verbal behavior can vary vastly across cultures. Regarding the content of communication, the semantics of speech is an interesting aspect that is dependent on the cultural background of the interlocutors and therefore considered as one important point in modeling culture-related differences in behavior in this dissertation.

When people communicate, they do not need to think about the management of their conversation. Tasks such as turn taking or pauses in speech are solved automatically without the person being aware of it. So, for example, one communication partner starts talking when the other one stops. These so-called communication management behaviors are dependent on cultural background as well and, therefore, considered as another interesting aspect of human behavior for the implementation of a computational model.

While verbal behavior is very explicit, there are other aspects of behavior that are more subtle and are sometimes not even perceived as influencing people's perception of each other. Regarding nonverbal behavior, the choice of gestures can vary as well as the style of performance. An interesting aspect of culture-specific behavior is the expressivity of nonverbal behaviors. How we exhibit a gesture can sometimes be more crucial to the observer's perception than the gesture itself. Thus, nonverbal behavior and expressive behavior in particular are considered as further culture-dependent aspect of humans behavior.

For the reasons mentioned above, aspects of verbal behavior, communication management behaviors as well as nonverbal behaviors are investigated as relevant aspects of human behavior that are dependent on culture in this dissertation. In this section, verbal behavior in the domain of small talk is described, as it is approached in the social sciences. Then, regulators are introduced that typically control the flow of a conversation and that are considered culture-specific behaviors. In the last subsection of this section, a classification of gesture types as well as expressivity parameters that explain differences in the performance of nonverbal behaviors are further described.

2.2.1 Verbal Behavior

Regarding verbal behaviors, culture can determine the content of a conversation on different levels. On the one hand, there are differences in what people say and on the other hand, there are variations in how people say things. For the choice of "what-to-say" different topics could be appropriate in certain contexts in some cultures while they are not appropriate in other cultures. Variations in "how-to-say" certain things can be found in e.g. different politeness strategies.

Since speech is a very wide research field, for this dissertation, we concentrate on the domain of small talk conversations for demonstration purposes. Small talk is particularly interesting from a culture-specific perspective, since conversations in this domain can differ vastly across cultures. For example, a topic could be considered as being appropriate in one culture, while it is considered inappropriate in another. We also chose this domain, since meeting someone for the first time is the standard first chapter of most language learning books and a very fundamental interaction in everyday communications that occurs in every culture as well as in cross-cultural encounters. In addition, this domain seems to be very well suited, since it is limited enough to be investigated in computational models, but not too limited to exemplify differences in culture-related behavior.

In order to formalize small talk in first-time meetings in a way that allows the integration of different cultural backgrounds into a computational model, we first need to understand and characterize small talk itself. Therefore, we describe small talk as it is defined in the social sciences and introduce prototypical sequences and topics for small talk conversations.

Small talk is often thought of as a neutral, non-task-oriented conversation about safe topics, where no specific goals need to be achieved. But besides being a simple chat, small talk can serve different purposes, such as establishing social relations, getting acquainted with a conversation partner or avoiding undesirable silence.

According to Kendon [Ken91], first-time meetings also play an important role for managing personal relations by signaling for instance social status, degree of familiarity or degree of liking. Argyl [Arg75], for example, describes first-time meetings as a ritual that follows predefined scripts. In a similar manner, Ting-Toomey [THT97] refers to first-time meetings as a ceremonies with a specific chain of actions.

Although rules for small talk seem to be loose, there are certain structures that explain the flow of an average small talk conversation. In [Sch88], Schneider describes a sequence that exemplifies the prototypical structure of small talk. This sequence of utterances is characterized as follows:

1. Question

2. Answer

3. Reverse question / understanding / acknowledgment / evaluation

4. Zero or more idle-moves

Step three and four can be performed several times. According to Schneider [Sch88], this sequence is prototypically used to discuss a topic within a small talk conversation and can be restarted for every other topic. Of course, this is only one sequence that describes the flow of discussing a topic and not necessarily every small talk conversation has to follow this line. However, it can help formalize the prototypical flow of a small talk conversation for a computational model.

Besides defining a prototypical sequence within a small talk conversation, possible topics need to be constrained. Obviously, not every topic is appropriate in an everyday small talk conservation. So-called *unsafe topics* such as death, serious illness, religion or sex are avoided. According to Kellermann and Palomares [KP04a], the choice of topics in everyday conversation depends on the personal relation between the interlocutors. Consequently, topics that are likely to be discussed in a casual small talk situation are predictable.

In [Sch88], Schneider categorizes topics that, in principle, might occur in small talk conversations into three groups, while the choice of topics depends on the social context:

1. The **immediate situation** holds topics that are elements of the so-called *frame* of the situation. In order to explain the idea of a frame, the author of [Sch88] uses a small talk situation that takes place at a party. Possible topics within a party frame could be the atmosphere, drinks, music, participants or food.

2. The **external situation** or "supersituation" describes all topics that hold the larger context of the immediate situation. This category is the least limited of the three. Topics within this category could be the latest news, politics, sports, movies or celebrities.

3. For the **communication situation** interlocutors are seen as a subset of the immediate situation. Thus, topics focus on the conversation partners e.g. their hobbies, family or career.

According to Schneider [Sch88], a typical small talk conversation begins with the interlocutors' immediate situation (e.g. the location where the conversation takes place or the weather). Successively, topics can either shift to the external situation (e.g. economy or news) or to the communication situation (e.g. hobbies or career). Whether the conversation addresses topics of the second or the third category described above is dependent on the social surrounding. While shifting to the external situation is more common in a social context, such as a party situation, shifting to the communication situation is typical for a conversation between strangers that want to avoid silence. As a result, topic selection in small talk depends on the conversation partners, their personal relation and social context.

However, Schneider [Sch88] only considers Western cultures in his studies and does not have a look at different topic selections in different cultures. Thus, they do not necessarily need to hold true for other cultural groups as well. According to Isbister and colleagues [ININ00], the categorization into safe and unsafe topics varies with cultural background. Consequently, a topic (such as talking about family members) can be considered as safe in one culture and as unsafe in another. If the distinction into safe and unsafe topics varies with culture, we expect that the overall choice of topic categories is also dependent on culture.

2.2.2 Communication Management

Another interesting aspect of human conversational behavior that is considered culture-depended are so-called communication management behaviors. Interrupting the conversation partner, for example, is perceived differently across cultures. While it is judged positively, as an increased interest in the conversation or the interlocutor in some cultures, such as France or Hungary, it is perceived as impolite in other cultures such as Germany or Japan. Thus, in a conversation where members of different cultural groups communicate, one interlocutor might feel offended because of being interrupted several times, while the other might have the impression that the conversation partner is not interested because of not being interrupted.

These communication management behaviors can be defined using so-called regulators. According to Ting-Toomey [TT99], regulators are consisting of *vocalics*, *kinesics* and *oculesics*:

- Vocalics: This category includes verbal feedback signals, e.g. expressions such as "uh-huh" in the English language. Other features of vocalics are the usage of silence in speech or interruptions of the communication partner's speech. Depending on how and how often these behaviors are used, a different rhythm of speech evolves.

- Kinesics: Kinesics include bodily nonverbal behaviors that are used to manage communication such as gestures or body postures.

- Oculesics: This category includes nonverbal behaviors that are conducted with the head or the eyes. Communication can, for example, be managed by gazing at the conversation partner or turning the head away.

According to Ting-Toomey [TT99], the aforementioned regulators are considered culture-specific behaviors, that *"act as the nonverbal traffic signs to control the flow of and pauses of conversations"*. In addition, regulators are learned at a very young age and are, thus, used at a very low level of awareness. Ting-Toomey

[TT99] also states that the discriminative use of regulators often causes intercultural distress and misunderstandings. However, people from contrastive cultures may not be able to name the reason for their frustration, since regulators are used subconsciously.

For this dissertation, verbal regulators are of special interest for integration into culture-related small talk dialogs, in particular concerning the usage of pauses in speech and overlapping speech. According to Ting Toomey [TT99], the beliefs expressed in talk and silence are highly dependent on culture. Verbal feedback is given in every culture, but the meaning can vary with the communicative function expressed by it. Besides the function of verbal feedback, its frequency and positioning within the conversation can vary across cultures.

2.2.3 Nonverbal and Expressive Behavior

Regarding nonverbal behavior, the questions asked for verbal behavior "what to say" and "how to say it" can arise as well. While some gestures are common in one culture, they do not necessarily transport the same meaning in another culture. An example includes the American OK-gesture (bringing the thumb and the index finger together to form a circle). While it means "OK" in the American culture, it is considered an insult in Italy and is interpreted as meaning "money" in the Japanese culture.

Besides different gesture choice, the performance of a gesture can also vary across cultures. Gesturing a lot and expressively is considered as being engaged in the conversations in Arab countries or Italy. However, it is considered inappropriate in other cultures such as Japan or Sweden. Regarding culture, how we exhibit a gesture can sometimes be more crucial to the observer's perception than the gesture itself.

Therefore, in this subsection, gestures are classified according to their types as well as to differences in their performance.

The most well known categorization of gestures has been done by McNeill [McN92]. Gesture types are described by the following classification:

- Deictic: Deictic gestures are pointing or indicative gestures. They can be either concrete (e.g. pointing at something) or abstract (e.g. pointing to the left and the right to express a contrast).

- Beat: Beat gestures are rhythmic gestures that are often repeated and follow speech prosody.

- Emblem: Emblems have a conventionalized meaning and do not necessarily need to be accompanied by speech. A nod for example is valued as yes in most cultures, or bringing the tips of thumb and first finger together while extending the other fingers is decoded as an "OK"-sign in Northern America as described above.

- Iconic: Iconic gestures explain the semantic content of speech. This is done in a concrete manner such as forming a round shape with the hands while talking about a ball.

- Metaphoric: Metaphoric gestures accompany the semantic content of the speech as well. In contrast to iconic gestures, they visualize abstract concepts by the use of metaphors. Forming a box with both hands, for example, could be used while referring to a previous conversation (visualizing the "conversation").

- Adaptor: Adaptors are hand movements towards other parts of the body. This is done, for example, to satisfy self or bodily needs or to manage emotions.

This categorization is not meant to be mutually exclusive. Consequently, a gesture may be attributed to more than one type. On their homepage [The12], the authors of the McNeill Lab state that "The notion of a type, therefore, should be considered as a continuum - with a given gesture having more or less iconicity, metaphoricity, etc.".

Besides the choice of the gesture itself, a gesture can differ significantly in its performance and vary vastly with cultural background. This can be described by the dynamic variation of a gesture.

Gallaher [Gal92] firstly investigated individual differences in nonverbal behavior and introduced so-called dimensions of style. The term 'style' is used intentionally to emphasize that also people that are less expressive have a unique nonverbal behavioral style. The four dimensions expressiveness, animation, expansiveness and coordination differences were identified. These dimensions prove to be consistent for individuals, stable over time, and stable across raters. These dimensions can be summarized as follows:

- Expressiveness: This factor describes how energetic a communicative act is. This could, for example, be measured by tone of voice.

- Animation: This dimension takes into account how engaged or lethargic e.g. a gesture is performed.

- Expansiveness: Expansiveness describes the liveliness of a nonverbal behavior by investigating the space that is taken for its performance. This could be measured by e.g. spatial extent of gestures, volume of voice or step length.

- Coordination: This factor observes the flow of movements. Nonverbal behaviors can be performed in a jerky of fluid manner, voice could, for example, be described as being calm.

The aforementioned dimensions of style were used for numerous studies that investigated nonverbal behavioral differences. To annotate gestures, Hartmann and colleagues [HMP06] describe six parameters that characterize a gesture's expressivity. The *spatial extent* describes the arm's extent toward the torso. The *speed* of the stroke phase of a gesture and the *power* of the arm before the stroke phase can vary as well. The *fluidity* describes the continuity between consecutive gestures, while the *repetivity* holds information about the repetition of the stroke. The last expressivity parameter, *overall activation*, counts the number of gestures that are performed. How gestures are executed, can depend on individual and social factors such as personality, emotional state or culture.

Another useful tool to annotate gestures is provided by McNeil [McN92], who introduces a temporal course of gestures. The dynamic of a gesture is annotated by the following phases:

- Preparation: In the preparation phase, the hands are brought into the gesture space.

- Hold: A hold might occur, when the gesture is meant to accompany the semantics of speech but is not aligned with the corresponding utterance yet.

- Stroke: The stroke phase carries the content of the gesture and can be categorized by the gesture types described earlier.

- Retraction: In the retraction phase, the hands are finally brought back into a resting position.

As stated earlier, nonverbal behavior is influenced by culture on several levels. First cultural background determines whether e.g. a gesture should be performed or not. Second, the choice of behavior, e.g. which gesture to choose, can be influenced by culture. Finally, the way the nonverbal behavior is conduced can vary with cultural background. For the integration of these differences into a computational model, the categorizations and dimensions introduced in this subsection constitute valuable tools, since they describe nonverbal behaviors along with their performance in a formal manner.

2.3 The German and Japanese Cultures

As pointed out in Section 1.2, the approach taken in this dissertation is exemplified for the German and Japanese cultures. Therefore in this section, cultural profiles for the target cultures are introduced based on the theories from the social sciences described in Section 2.1 of this chapter.

Based on these profiles, we subsequently state our expectations on behavioral differences on the aspects of human behavior that were pointed out as being relevant in Section 2.2.

The two cultures of Germany and Japan seem to be very well suited for our purposes, since Asian and Western cultures differ vastly in their cultural background and a clear line can be drawn for most theories.

In principle, there are cultures that might be even more distinctive than Germany and Japan, e.g. China would differ more from Germany regarding individualism since Japan is quite individualistic for an Asian culture. However, due to cooperation with our Japanese partners in the Cube-G project [RAN+07], a video corpus is available for the German and Japanese cultures, and we consider the two target cultures to be sufficiently distinctive.

2.3.1 Cultural Profiles

In Section 2.1, different theories were introduced that describe culture, e.g. by introducing cultural dimensions. In this subsection, the German and Japanese cultures are classified based on these theories.

In Subsection 2.1.2, dimensional models were introduced that describe culture along different dimensions or attributes.

Hofstede's model classifies national cultures using six dimensions. The scores of Germany and Japan on these six dimensions are summarized in table 2.1 along with the world's average [HHM10]. The positioning on these dimensions influences the behavior and thinking of the members of the target culture. These scores for Germany, Japan as well as the world average are graphically presented in Figure 2.4.

The Power Distance dimension (PDI) describes the extent to which a different distribution of power is accepted by the less powerful members of a culture. Regarding this dimension, Germany scores rather low, compared to the world average and Japan. Thus, people in Germany should hold the point of view that people are equal and everybody could in principle do what they like. In Japan, vice versa,

Culture / Dimension	Germany	World's Average	Japan
PDI	35	55	54
IDV	67	64	46
MAS	66	48	95
UAI	65	61	92
LTO	31	41	80
IVR	40	n.a.	42

Table 2.1: Scores on Hofstede's dimensional model for the German and Japanese cultures as well as the world's average [HHM10].

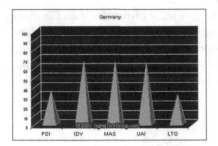
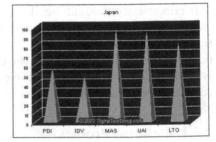

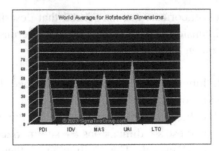

Figure 2.4: Scores on Hofstede's dimensions for Germany (upper left) and Japan (upper right) compared with the world's average (lower) (from [Hof12]; used with permission).

inequalities are more expected and desired and privileges for certain people are popular.

The Individualism dimension (IDV) describes the degree to which individuals are integrated into a group. The two cultures of Germany and Japan differ vastly along this dimension. While Germany scores higher than the world average, Japan scores lower. We can thus expect Germans to be a lot more individualistic, meaning that they would rather be convinced that everybody should be able do what they wanted to do than Japanese people, for whom the outcome for the group as a whole is much more important.

The gender or masculinity dimension (MAS) describes the distribution of roles between the genders and how masculine values are perceived. Both cultures score high on this dimension, with Japan holding the highest value in Hofstede's initial study ranking 50 countries [Hof03]. We can thus expect a gap between men's and women's values in both countries, since in masculine countries women are somewhat assertive, but not as much as the men. In addition, in both countries status symbols as well as material success and progress are considered important, yet to a much higher degree in Japan.

In the uncertainty avoidance dimension (UAI), the tolerance for uncertainty and ambiguity is defined. It indicates to what extent the members of a culture feel either comfortable or uncomfortable in unstructured or unknown situations. Again, both cultures score higher on this dimension than the world's average. Thus, members of both countries should feel comfortable in structured situations and hold on to rules. People tend to feel stress or anxiety and try to avoid unfamiliar risks. It is notable that Japan scores very high on this dimension compared to the word average and Germany. As mentioned earlier, the long term orientation dimension (LTO) has been added afterwards, in order to explain differences between Asian and Western cultures. In line with this, Germany scores low on this dimension, while Japan scores high. Values for long term orientation are, for example, thrift and perseverance which should be important in Germany. Examples for values for the short term orientation are respect for tradition, fulfilling social obligations and saving one's face, which are of great importance in Japan.

On the sixth dimension, indulgence versus restraint (IVR), which describes the degree to which members of a culture feel about their personal well-being, Germany and Japan score very similar. In total, 93 countries were ranked on this dimension, with values lying between 0 and 100. Within that ranking Germany and Japan find themselves on ranks 51 and 52. We can thus not expect vast differences related to this dimension. Members of the German and Japanese cultures are thus neither overly happy about their overall situation nor assumed to have a very negative attitude.

Figure 2.5 graphically compares the scores for the two cultures of Germany and Japan for the first five dimensions. By trend, both cultures score high on the masculinity and uncertainty avoidance dimensions, which suggests that they share

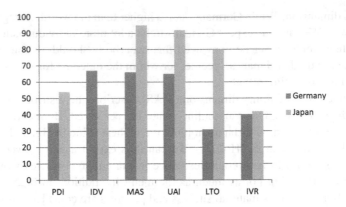

Figure 2.5: Scores on Hofstede's dimensions for Germany and Japan.

similar values in that sense. Still, the figure reveals that, although Germany scores rather high on these dimensions, there is still a great difference between Germany and Japan, since Japan scores even higher.

The greatest difference is observable in the long term orientation dimension, which is prototypical comparing an Asian and a Western culture. In a similar manner, the difference on the individualism dimension can be seen as prototypical for an Asian and a Western culture, although Japan scores rather high on this dimension compared to other Asian countries.

As another dimensional model, Trompenaars and Hampden-Turner's problem-oriented model was introduced. One category of the model takes into account a culture's "attitude towards time". Besides the different perception of time (which will be elaborated on later), differences in the importance of past, presence and future give additional information about the notions of time across cultures.

Trompenaars and Hampden-Turner measure time in different cultures using a so-called "circle-test" [THT97]. For the tests, members of different cultures were asked to draw circles representing past, present and future, while size and arrangement of the circles were observed. Circles can either be integrated, overlapping, touching-but-not-overlapping or are not related to another at all.

Figure 2.6 shows prototypical drawings for Germany and Japan. According to [THT97], for most Germans the past is interrelated to the present, and the present is also interrelated to the future. In contrast, in the Japanese version, all three circles are interrelated. Interestingly, half of the Japanese participants drew three concentric circles.

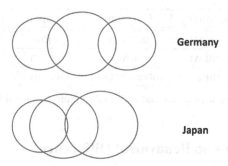

Figure 2.6: Past, present and future in Germany and Japan [THT97].

In Subsection 2.1.3, different dichotomies were introduced that differentiate cultures in two different groups. Investigating Germany and Japan, the two cultures are categorized very differently. Different categorizations along these dichotomies are summarized in Table 2.2.

Considering the distinction into high- and low-contact cultures, Germany belongs to the medium-contact group while Japan belongs to the low-contact group [TT99]. Touching the conversation partner and standing close in conversations should thus not be very common in both cultures but have a much higher acceptance in Germany than in Japan.

Having a look at verbal behavior and the distinction into high- and low-context cultures, Germany and Japan score very differently, too. In [TT99], Germany is mentioned as one of the most extreme low-context cultures, while Japan, in contrast, is named to be on the extreme high-context side. Conversations in the German culture should, thus, be very direct and explicit while in Japanese conversations the context has a much bigger emphasis and additional meaning is transported through other channels than just the semantics of speech, such as nonverbal behavior or silence.

The differentiation into monochronic and polychronic cultures, which is closely related to the different perception of time pointed out in Trompenaars and Hampden-Turner's model [THT97], can be carried out very easily for the German and Japanese cultures. According to [HH87], Germany is a classical example of a monochronic culture. Asian cultures and with it Japan, vice versa, belong to the polychronic group. In Germany, clock time should thus have a much higher importance and tasks are rather solved one after another. In Japan, the notion of time should be structured in a rather relational way and people are involved in several tasks at a time.

Dichotomy	Germany	Japan
contact	mediate	low
context	low	high
time	monochronic	polychronic

Table 2.2: Categorization of Germany and Japan taking into account different dichotomies.

2.3.2 Expectations on Behavioral Differences

In the previous subsection, cultural profiles for the German and Japanese cultures were introduced. Based on these profiles, in this subsection, we state our expectations on behavioral differences for the two cultures on the aspects of human behavior that were pointed out as being relevant in Section 2.2.

2.3.2.1 Differences in Small Talk

Regarding verbal behavior, in this dissertation the domain of small talk is investigated. In Subsection 2.2.1 we introduced a categorization of possible topics occurring in small talk as well as prototypical conversational sequences. In summary, a typical small talk conversation begins with the immediate situation and shifts to either the external situation or to the communication situation afterwards, which is dependent on social surrounding. While shifting to social topics is more common in a social context, such as a party situation, shifting to private topics is typical for a conversation between strangers who want to avoid silence. However, Schneider [Sch88] only considered Western cultures in his studies and did not have a look at different topic selections in different cultures. Thus, observations do not necessarily hold true for other cultural groups as well.

As mentioned earlier in this chapter, the categorization into safe and unsafe topics varies with cultural background [ININ00]. Consequently, a topic (such as talking about family members) can be considered as safe in one culture and as unsafe in another. If the differentiation into safe and unsafe topics varies with culture, we expect that the overall choice of topic categories is also dependent on culture.

In Section 2.3.1, Germany was categorized as a low-context culture, while Japan was categorized as a hight-context culture. Ting-Toomey [TT99] describes people belonging to high-context cultures as having a lower "public self" than people belonging to low-context cultures. A typical behavioral pattern for members of high-context cultures is not to reveal too much information during a first-time meeting. Bringing together small talk as a typical conversation for a first-time meeting and Schneider's categorization of topics [Sch88], we expect topics covering the communication situation to be more common in the German culture than in the Japanese culture.

Another dichotomy described in Section 2.3.1 is the division into monochronic and polychronic cultures. While Germany counts as a monochronic culture, Japan is a polychronic culture. One behavioral pattern described for monochronic cultures is that members tend to do one thing at a time, while members of the polychronic group prototypically tend to do several things at a time. Generalizing these behavioral patterns, monochronic cultures tend to finish one thing before starting another, while it is more common in polychronic cultures to switch back and forth between tasks. Regarding verbal behavior in the domain of small talk, topics are more likely to be discussed after one another in monochronic cultures and, thus, in a more sequential manner than in polychronic cultures, where we anticipate switching back and forth between topics.

According to [THT97], members of Western cultures are described to get nervous when there are long pauses in communication. In contrast, in Asian cultures, silence is considered as a sign of respect. In addition, we described Germany as an individualistic culture and Japan as a collectivistic culture. According to [HPH02], silence may occur in conversations without creating tension in collectivistic cultures, which does not hold true for individualistic cultures.

These two descriptions about cultures suggest that silence in communication is tried to be avoided in German conversations, while it should be likely to occur in Japanese conversations. But then, is does not appear very likely that small talk conversations in the Japanese culture shift to topics covering the communication situation in order to avoid silence, as described for Western small talk conversations by Schneider [Sch88], which is in line with observations made by Ting-Toomey [TT99].

In sum, the choice of topics as well as their sequence within a dialog should vary across the two cultures of Germany and Japan. Inspired by different definitions of culture and corresponding stereotypical behavior found in literature, we extracted the following expectations about culture-specific differences in small talk behavior distinguishing prototypical German and Japanese conversational behavior:

1. Less topics covering the communication situation should occur in Japanese small talk conversations than in German ones.

2. Topics are discussed in a more sequential manner in German small talk conversations than in Japanese ones.

2.3.2.2 Differences in Communication Management

In Subsection 2.2.2 regulators were introduced that are commonly used to manage the flow of a conversation. In this dissertation, vocalics as a subcategory of regulators are taken into account. These verbal regulators, referred to as communication management behaviors, are further investigated. In particular, the usage of silence in speech as well as overlapping speech are considered.

Following Hall's categorization of cultures [Hal59] into high- and low-context communication cultures, Ting Toomey [TT99] observes that conversation in high-context communication cultures relies mainly on physical context. Meaning can be transported through nonverbal cues, such as pauses, silence or prosody. In contrast, low-context communication cultures tend to explicitly code information. Clear descriptions and a high degree of specificity are used commonly in these cultures. As we stated in Section 2.3.1, Germany is one of the most extreme low-context cultures, while Japan finds itself on the extreme high-context side. Thus, communication management behaviors should occur more frequently in Japanese conversations than in German ones.

Regarding pauses in speech, Hofstede's dimensional model [HHM10] gives some interesting insights. As described in Section 2.3.1, Japan is a collectivistic culture along the individualism dimension. In these cultures, silence may occur in conversations without creating tension. In addition, pauses can be a crucial feature of conversations in collectivistic cultures. These observations do not hold true for individualistic cultures such as Germany. As a consequence, it should be more likely in the German culture that silence creates tension and, thus, pauses in speech are tried to be avoided. In Japanese conversations, vice versa, pauses can be considered a feature of the conversation and should thus occur more frequently.

Strengthening our expectations about the usage of silence in speech, Ting Toomey [TT99] states that the beliefs expressed in talk and silence are culture-dependent and that silence serves as a critical communication device in Japanese communication patterns. Pauses reflect the thoughts of the speaker and can contain strong contextual meaning. While in Western cultures, silence might be interpreted as failure to communicate, in Asian cultures it is used as a means of conversation.

In principle, verbal feedback is given in every culture but the meaning can vary with the communicative function expressed by the feedback. In Japanese conversations, communication partners explicitly communicate that they are listening by using the utterance "hai hai", while the literal translation "yes yes" would communicate more than that [TT99]. Overlapping speech is often considered as impolite in the sense of breaking in on the other person's speech. However, feedback utterances are often performed without trying to get the turn while the other one is still speaking. As we stated above, understanding signals are very common in Japanese conversation patterns. Thus, we expect a high degree of overlapping speech caused by verbal feedback in Japanese conversations that should be short but frequent.

This idea is strengthened by another dimension in Hofstede's model. High-power distance cultures are described as soft-spoken and polite, while interpersonal synchrony is much more important than in low-power distance cultures, whose members tend to talk freely in any social context [TT99]. One possibility to achieve interpersonal synchrony in a conversation is to give feedback. This feedback often occurs during the discourse of the interlocutor, which should occur more often in the Japanese culture due to their higher value on the power distance dimension and higher need for interpersonal synchrony.

Similar findings are described by Trompenaars and Hampden-Turner [THT97]. Western cultures are described as verbal and members are said to get nervous when there are long pauses. In addition, interruptions are considered as impolite. According to [THT97], communication in Western cultures is managed as follows: interlocutors start talking after the other conversation partner has stopped. In Western cultures, silence might be interpreted as failure to communicate and is thus tried to be avoided. Controversially, in Asian cultures, silence is an important feature and can be considered a sign of respect and is used to process information or to assure that the conversation partner intends to hand over the floor.

Summarizing our culture-specific expectations on communication management behavior drawn from literature for the German and Japanese cultures, we state the following expectations:

1. More pauses in speech are occurring in Japanese conversations compared to German ones.

2. Overlapping speech occurs more often in Japanese conversations due to more frequent feedback behavior.

2.3.2.3 Differences in Nonverbal Behavior

As pointed out in Subsection 2.2.3, nonverbal behaviors can vary across cultures on different levels. In that manner, not only the choice of gestures depends on cultural background but also its expressivity. Therefore, McNeill's gesture types [McN92] as well as parameters that describe a gesture's dynamic variation were introduced.

Regarding the German and Japanese cultures, nonverbal behavior should differ in both, selection of behavior as well as performance. In Subsection 2.3.1, we categorized Germany as one of the most extreme low-context cultures, while Japan is on the extreme high-context side [TT99]. As described earlier, in high-context communication little is encoded explicitly and the conversation mainly relies on physical context. Messages and symbols might seem relatively simple but contain a deep meaning. In contrast, low-context communication explicitly codes information. Thus, symbols and messages are direct and to the point. We therefore expect a more frequent use of direct gestures (deictic and iconic gestures regarding McNeill's classification) in German conversations than in Japanese ones. Vice versa, we expect more metaphoric gestures in Japanese conversations than in German ones.

Regarding a gesture's dynamic, it is sometimes more crucial to the observer how a gesture is exhibited than the gesture itself. The individualism dimension in Hofstede's model is related to the expression of emotions and the acceptable emotional display in a culture [HHM10]. In individualistic cultures such as Germany it is more acceptable to publicly show emotions than it is in collectivistic cultures such as Japan [Ekm92]. This also suggests that nonverbal behavior is expressed more emotionally in German conversations than in Japanese ones. Differences in the dynamic variation of a gesture can be described according to the expressivity parameters [Pel05]. We expect that displaying emotions more obviously should affect the expressivity in a way that parameters such as speed, power or spatial extent are increased.

In sum, we expect the following differences in nonverbal behavior for the German and Japanese cultures:

1. More direct gestures occur in German conversations than in Japanese ones, where gestures are more implicit.

2. Gestures should be more expressive in German conversations compared to Japanese ones.

2.4 Summary

In this chapter, the theoretical background for this dissertation is introduced. First culture is described as it occurs in the social sciences. As a next step, aspects of human behavior are identified that are influenced by cultural background. Since in this dissertation, the integration of culture-specific behavior is exemplified for the German and Japanese cultures, as a last step, profiles for these two cultures are defined and expectations about behavioral differences are stated.

As a starting point, different notions of culture were introduced. Some theories explain culture on different levels that influence the mindset and behavior of the members of a culture. Thereby implicit and explicit layers can be distinguished, explicit layers consist of things that can be observed in reality and implicit layers contain internal values and basic assumptions. For this dissertation, the explicit layer is of special interest, since this layer holds observable differences in verbal and nonverbal behavior that can be simulated using virtual characters. To describe culture in a way that enables the integration into a computational model, different dimensional models and dichotomies were summarized that help understand culture in a descriptive manner and therefore seem to be well suited for our purposes.

Subsequently, different aspects of behavior were introduced in this chapter that are influenced by cultural background and seem to be relevant for our purposes. Aspects of verbal as well as nonverbal behavior need to be taken into account, since through their embodiment, virtual characters are able to express themselves verbally and nonverbally. Regarding verbal behavior, we focus on the domain of small talk, since it is a prototypical conversation for a first-time encounter in inner-cultural as well as cross-cultural conversations. Within small talk conversations, the choice of topics as well as the flow of the conversation should vary with cultural background. To control the flow of a conversation, verbal regulators can be used that are influenced by cultural background as well. In this dissertation, the usage of pauses in speech and overlapping speech is investigated. Regarding nonverbal behavior, the selection and performance of nonverbal behaviors should differ across cultures.

The cultural theories introduced earlier are then used to categorize the German and Japanese cultures. Table 2.3 summarizes these differences. On a regional basis, Germany counts as a Western culture, while Japan is considered an Asian culture. As pointed out in Subsection 2.1.2, the most relevant dimensional model for our purposes are Hofstede's dimensions [Hof01], since they provide a complete

classification	Germany	Japan
regional	Western	Asian
contact dichotomy	mediate-contact	low-contact
context dichotomy	low-context	high-context
time dichotomy	monochronic	polychronic
power distance	low-power distance	high-power distance
individualism	individualistic	collectivistic
masculinity	masculine	masculine
uncertainty avoidance	avoiding	avoiding
long term orientation	long term	short term

Table 2.3: Summary of cultural profiles for the German and Japanese cultures.

model and explain prototypical behavior norms. Labels presenting the positioning of Germany and Japan on these dimensions, compared to a mediate score, can be found in Table 2.3. Regarding the dichotomies introduced in Subsection 2.1.3 that distinguish cultural groups and provide prototypical behavior for the groups, Germany and Japan can be categorized very differently. While Germany is a mediate-contact, low-context and monochronic culture, Japan is low-contact, high-context and polychronic.

Based on the cultural profiles, we state our expectations of behavioral differences on the aspects of human behavior that were pointed out as being relevant before. These expectations are summarized in Table 2.4. Regarding small talk behavior, we expect members of the German culture to talk more about private topics, while this should be avoided in Japanese conversations since people in Japan have a lower so-called public-self. In addition, due to the fact that Germany is considered a monochronic culture where members tend to do one thing at a time, topics are likely to be discussed in a sequential manner. In Japanese conversations, vice versa, switching back and forth between topics should be more common due to their polychronic cultural background. To manage communication, individualistic and low-context cultures such as Germany are assumed to avoid silence in speech, while it is used explicitly as a means of communication in collectivistic and high-context cultures such as Japan. As it is commonly used in feedback behavior, overlapping speech should also appear more frequently in Japanese conversations since understanding signals are a common behavior pattern in Japanese communication. Regarding nonverbal behavior, the differentiation into high- and low-context cul-

behavioral aspect	Germany	Japan
topic selection	more private	less private
flow of conversation	sequential	alternating
pauses	avoided	consciously used
overlaps	uncommon	common during feedback
gesture types	more direct gestures	more metaphoric gestures
nonverbal expressivity	more expressive	less expressive

Table 2.4: Summary of behavioral expectations for the German and Japanese cultures.

tures suggests that there should be more direct gestures in German conversations than in Japanese ones. In addition, in individualistic cultures it is much more common to publicly express emotions. We thus expect nonverbal behavior to be more expressive in German than in Japanese conversational behavior.

3 Related Work

In this chapter, related work in the domain of virtual agents is presented. Cassell defined the term embodied conversational agents as computer-generated characters that are able to demonstrate some of the properties that humans use in face-to-face conversations, such as producing and responding to verbal and nonverbal communication [CSPC00].

Over the years, virtual agent applications developed from single agent systems that presented information to interactive multiagent systems. Since culture is a social phenomena that describes a group of people who share a common value system, the integration of culture was feasible only when multiagent systems were available. At earlier points in time, personal backgrounds such as emotional state or personality were investigated. The approaches taken in these systems can give useful insights and can, at least partly, be reimplemented for the integration of culture. In the first section of this chapter, the development of virtual agent systems is described along with representative applications exemplifying the different stages.

In the recent years, the phenomena of culture came into focus. In Section 3.2, an overview of related work on virtual characters and culture is presented. With it, we focus on a categorization of related work along aspects such as aim, target group or simulated behavior. The technical background required to integrate culture into the behavioral models of virtual characters is presented in Chapters 4 and 5.

In Section 2.2 of the previous chapter, aspects of human behavior were introduced that are influenced by cultural background and seem to be relevant for the integration of culture into the behavior models of virtual characters. These behavioral aspects have been investigated for virtual characters before, however, without

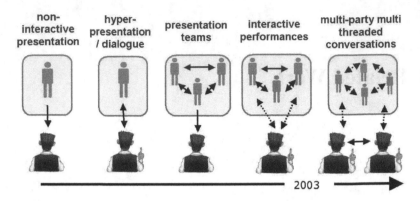

Figure 3.1: Development of virtual character systems (from [RAB+03b]; Used with permission. Copyright remains with the author.).

integrating cultural background. Therefore, Section 3.3 describes virtual character systems that successfully integrated the behavioral aspects considered in this dissertation.

3.1 From Single Agents to Multiagent Systems

Virtual character systems evolved over time from single agent systems to interactive multiagent systems. This trend was pointed out by Rist and colleagues [RAB+03b] who investigated agent-agent as well as agent-human interaction. The tendency is graphically presented in Figure 3.1, showing the development from virtual agents that simply present information, over agent teams that use the advantage of presenting in a dialog-style, to multiagent systems that are able to communicate with human users. Within systems allowing user-interaction, there are several possible developments: multiuser or multiagent applications, which both need to be reactive.

In the following, applications are introduced that are representative for the different stages of virtual character systems.

In their early years, virtual agents were mainly utilized to present information in a human-like manner. Through their embodiment they were able to inform users in a natural way, using verbal and nonverbal behaviors. As presenter agents they

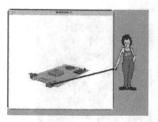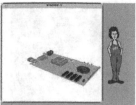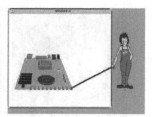

Figure 3.2: The presenter agent PPP Persona provides speech and pointing gestures (from [ARM99]; Used with permission. Copyright remains with the author.).

were not reactive, neither to the user nor to other computer-controlled agents. An example includes work conducted by André and colleagues [ARM99] who introduce a framework for the development of presentation agents which can be utilized for a broad range of applications. Depending on the agent's presentation goals and external parameters, such as information about the user's knowledge, a presentation script is generated. The agent PPP Persona acts similar to a TV host who presents information to the human user. Figure 3.2 shows the presenter agent that explains the elements of a technical device through speech and pointing gestures.

As a next step, virtual agents became interactive in such a way that they either react to the user or other virtual agents. An example for a character that interacts with a human user is given by Rist and colleagues [RAB+03b], where an interactive presenter agent reacts to the user's questions. Since natural speech interaction is problematic for technical reasons, the communication in their approach is reduced to chat-functionality. Thus, the user types questions in order to communicate with the agent. The reactive agent answers according to the user's input, using natural speech as well as nonverbal behaviors such as gestures and facial expressions.

Another example of an interactive virtual character was presented by Pelachaud and colleagues [PCdC+02]. In an early version, their agent Greta is a talking head that is able to converse with a human user by using synchronized verbal and nonverbal behaviors. As pointed out earlier, at this state of virtual character systems, personal factors were integrated into virtual character behavior for the first time. To this end, the Greta agent is provided with a personality, a social role and the ability to simulate human emotions by displaying different facial expressions. In Figure 3.3, the virtual character Greta displays different facial expressions for the emotions surprise and sadness. Additional expressions can be achieved by combining

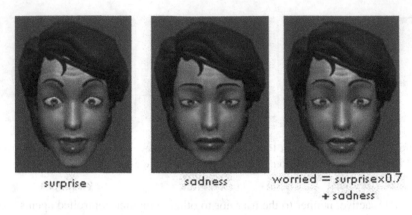

surprise   sadness   worried = surprisex0.7
                                                       + sadness

Figure 3.3: Different facial expressions shown by the virtual character Greta (from [PCdC$^+$02]; Used with permission. Copyright remains with the author.).

existing emotional expressions, e.g. worried by mixing surprise and sadness. As a further enhancement, interaction with the user is not limited to chat-functionality any more. In this application, the user interacts using natural speech.

An example of a full body virtual character includes the REA agent introduced by Cassell and colleagues [CBB$^+$99]. The virtual character acts in the role of a real estate agent and is shown on a life-size screen. The REA agent is capable of both, multimodal input understanding and output generation. On the user's side, natural speech as well as nonverbal interaction is recognized as input. Therefore, the user is recorded via microphones and cameras (see Figure 3.4). For multimodal output, the agent uses natural speech, gestures and body postures. In that vein, a natural multimodal conversation evolves.

Besides interacting with a human user, virtual agents might also interact with other agents. Realizing such multiagent systems, a whole team of agents can present information to users in an interesting way. In that manner, rhetorical tricks such as contrasting pros and cons or repeating the most important information can be realized. André and colleagues [ARvM$^+$00], for example, introduced such a system. A team of virtual agents is located in a car-selling application, where they interact with each other in the style of a role-play. Presentations are generated, depending on predefined attributes, such as the agents' personalities, roles or attitudes towards the product. As stated above, personal factors such as personality were first integrated into the behavior models of virtual characters to increase their

Figure 3.4: User interaction with the life-sized character REA (from [Bic03]; Used with permission. Copyright remains with the author.).

believability and achieve more interesting presentations. However, their successful approach of parameterizing personality to generate different dialog styles can be reproduced to simulate different cultural backgrounds as well.

Bringing together the two types of interaction, either with the user or with other virtual characters, interactive performances integrating the user and several agents were a next step. The presentation team described above [ARvM+00] was enhanced in such an interactive way. Rist and colleagues [RAB+03b] present the car-selling scenario described above with a human user interacting with the group of virtual agents. In the scenario, it is up to the user how active he or she is. Thus, the story cannot be planned in advance. To integrate the user into the virtual scenario, he or she is represented through an avatar. For interaction, a text-field is provided. A screenshot of the interactive car-selling scenario can be seen in Figure 3.5.

Another group of researchers focuses on storytelling and aims at integrating the user into an interactive story with virtual characters. An example includes the application Facade, described by Mateas and Stern [MS02]. The story of a married couple is narrated and a conflict occurs in the story line sooner or later. The user (in the role of a friend of the couple) finds the couple going into raptures about their lives and weaving around the fact that their marriage is falling apart. A screenshot of the system can be seen in Figure 3.6. The story is based on the play "Who's Afraid of Virginia Woolf?", which was chosen because the storyline can be bro-

Figure 3.5: Example of an interactive multiagent system with the user represented through an avatar (from [RAB+03b]; Used with permission. Copyright remains with the author.).

Figure 3.6: Interactive virtual characters in a story-telling application (from [Pro11]; Used with permission. Copyright remains with the author.).

ken apart into story beats that can be resequenced. The characters' activities are represented as goals that are supplied with one or more behaviors to accomplish it. The behavior selection process is influenced by the user's input and thus, each experiences a different story depending on his or her own interactions. For inter-action with the virtual characters, typed text input was chosen. On the output side, the characters use natural voices, facial expressions and gestures.

Another example that integrates the user into an interactive digital story is pre-sented by Pizzi and colleagues [PCLC07]. For their interactive digital drama, the French novel Madame Bovary by Gustave Flaubert constitutes the baseline. The user takes part in the role of the character Rodolphe who tries to encourage Emma (the main character) to cheat on her husband. Through interaction, the user is able to influence the characters' feelings which in turn affects their behavior. In this vein, the user can experience different outcomes of the story depending on his or her interactions. The characters' behavior is based on a multi-threaded planner. Thus, the system is highly reactive as the planner controls each character indepen-dently. For interaction natural language is processed. In another version of the system, emotional speech is used for interaction. Therefore, the user's voice is in-terpreted according to its emotion, which influences the characters' future actions [CPC+09]. Figure 3.7 shows the virtual character Emma reacting to the user's in-put. Using interactive stories that integrate the user into a virtual scenario, seems to be very well suited for the integration of cultural background as well. In that man-ner, a human user could, for example, explore a different culture and get to know behavioral differences. By using emotional speech input as described above, the language barrier between different cultural backgrounds could be overcome.

So far, systems were presented that allow communication for a single user with either one or several virtual agents. Interacting in a virtual world with several hu-man users is exemplified by Isbister and colleagues [ININ00]. In their multiuser application, a so-called helper-agent virtually joins two users of a chat room in case their conversation seems to stagnate. By introducing typical small talk topics, the agent can actively help create interesting and ongoing conversations between human interlocutors.

Another example of a virtual character that interacts with several users is given by Rehm and colleagues [RW05]. In their work, the authors describe a multi-player dice game, in which a virtual agent interacts with two human users. In their experimental setting, the agent takes part in the game as an active partner controlled by an emotional model. The multi-user game allows user-agent inter-action as well as user-user interaction. Figure 3.8 shows the experimental setting. The virtual character interacts using speech as well as nonverbal behaviors such as gestures, facial expressions and body posture.

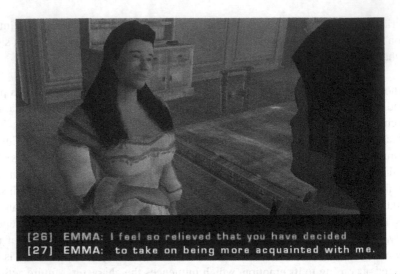

[26] EMMA: I feel so relieved that you have decided
[27] EMMA: to take on being more acquainted with me.

Figure 3.7: Interactive drama based on the emotional input of the user (from [CPC$^+$09]; Used with permission. Copyright remains with the author.).

Figure 3.8: Interactive virtual character communicating with two human users (from [RW05]; Used with permission. Copyright remains with the author.).

By observing the development of virtual character applications over time, it becomes clear that the integration of cultural background became an issue only at a later point in time, where multiple agents acted as a group. At earlier stages, personal factors that distinguish individuals such as personality were investigated. However, the approaches taken in these systems are valuable tools for the integration of cultural background since they can be reproduced to parameterize culture as well. In addition, interactive environments as described in the domain of interactive storytelling can serve as a basis for the integration of a human user into a virtual environment to explore a different culture.

This is in line with Hofstede's description of a human's mental program introduced in Subsection 2.1.1. The three levels of the mental program (human nature, culture and personality) strongly affect human behavior, and were therefore integrated to computational models for virtual characters as well.

- Human nature: Through the virtual agents' embodiment, human nature is simulated by expressing believable behavior. Virtual agent systems meet people's physical nature in ever more sophisticated ways using natural speech and nonverbal behaviors such as gestures or body postures. Basic psychological functions have been integrated into virtual agent systems as well. The ability to express emotions and act accordingly is, for example, described by Aylett and colleagues [ALD+05] or Gratch and colleagues [GRA+02].

- Personality: Personality is the level that is specific to the individual. Integrating models of personality to virtual character systems was a plausible aim, taking into account that most interactions with virtual agents took place in dyadic conversations and thus a personal layer was considered. Enhancing the behavior of virtual humans with a personality component has been a vast research field in recent years. Examples can be found in work by Rist and colleagues [RAB03a] or Kang and colleagues [KGWW08].

- Culture: In contrast to personality, culture is specific to the group and the environment, which ranges from the domestic circle, the neighborhood or workplace up to the living community of the country an individual lives in. Culture plays a crucial role in the perception and selection of behaviors, mainly without this being realized. Recently, the integration of cultural-specific behaviors into virtual agent systems has gathered momentum (see Aylett and colleagues [APV+09] or Jan and colleagues [JHM+07].

3.2 Culture in Virtual Agent Systems

The integration of culture is rather new in the domain of virtual agents, for the reasons described in the previous section. In this section, we present an overview of existing applications that investigate culture for virtual characters. Therefore, in the following subsection, we introduce a schema to categorize systems according to aspects such as aim, target group or simulated behavior.

Subsequently, the approaches are described in more detail focusing on the categorization. The technical background required for the integration of culture into the behavior of virtual characters is addressed later in this dissertation. In our categorization schema, we differentiate between systems that focus on education or training, and on research studies. While some systems aim to create cultural awareness in general, other systems train concrete cultural skills. Studies investigate how simulated behavioral differences are perceived by human observers, pointing out the importance of the integration of culture-related differences to virtual character systems.

3.2.1 Overview

In this subsection, we present a schema to categorize approaches that investigate culture for virtual characters. In Table 3.1 related work on agent culture is organized in alphabetical order. A more detailed description of the different approaches, focusing on their categorization, is provided in the subsequent subsections, while technical requirements are addressed later in this dissertation.

One way to distinguish existing work is to investigate the purpose of the approach. Thereby, it can be differentiated whether the approaches address education, training or studies. Related work will be structured accordingly in the following subsections.

System	purpose	simulated culture	behavioral aspect	target group	inter-action
ATL	training	Iraq, US	predefined roles	soldiers	role-play
BiLAT	training	Iraq	interaction rules/ negotiation	soldiers	menu
eCute	education	synthetic cultures	virtual drama	children	menu, full body
goEnglish	training	US	language, everyday life	immigrants	speech, menu
Iacobelli & Cassell	study	ethnicity	verbal, nonverbal	children	WoZ
Interactive Phrasebook	study	Middle East, US	politeness strategies		menu
Jan & colleagues	study	Arabia, US	proxemics, gaze, turn taking	English, Arabic, Mexican	no
Koda & colleagues	study	Hungary, Japan	facial expressions	Hungary, Japan	no
Mascarenhas & colleagues	study	synthetic cultures	rituals		no
ORIENT	education	synthetic cultures	symbols, rituals	children	mobile devices
SecondChina	education/ preparation	China	cultural activities	travelers	mouse, text
TLTS	training	Iraqi, Dari, Pashto, French	language, gesture selection	soldiers	speech, menu
VECTOR	training	Arabia	communication skills	soldiers	menu
Yin & colleagues	study	American, Latino	appearance, language, arguments	fluent in English & Spanish	no

Table 3.1: Overview of related work on agent culture.

This categorization is also supported by Hofstede [Hof91] who explains the acquisition of intercultural communication abilities in three steps:

- **Awareness:** The first step of gaining intercultural competence is being aware of culture-related differences in behavior. The most noticeable part of this step is not only to know about differences, but also to accept the fact that there is no better or worse way of interacting, but simply a different one. Consequently, individuals need to learn that one's own behavior routines are not superior to others.

- **Knowledge:** Gaining knowledge about culture-related differences in behavior is the next step. This implies learning about the target culture's symbols and rituals. This does not necessarily include that one shares the values of a culture, but at least has an idea on where these values differ from one's own values.

- **Skills:** Hofstede states that the steps of Awareness and Knowledge are sufficient to avoid the most obvious misunderstandings in cross-cultural communication. The third step of gaining skills in intercultural communication, however, needs more practice. This includes recognizing the symbols and heroes of the other culture and practicing their rituals.

Educational approaches want to help understand the first step of creating cultural awareness described above. These approaches aim at intercultural understanding by pointing out that behavior is sometimes just different from one's own but not necessarily wrong. Systems such as ORIENT introduced by Aylett and colleagues [APV+09] therefore use fantasy cultures that interact according to their own rules.

The majority of existing approaches focuses on training culture-specific competencies and therefore aim at fulfilling the second and third step described above, gaining knowledge and skills. Most of the approaches were conducted in the US for military purposes. Examples include the Tactical Language Training System (TLTS) described by Johnson and colleagues [JMV04] that aims at training skills in foreign languages, such as Iraqi.

Another group of related work concentrates on research studies that provide a deeper insight in how a certain behavior is perceived by human observers. An example is described by Koda and colleagues [KRA08] who investigate the different perception of facial expressions on avatars across cultures. This category is not a part of Hofstede's steps since they do not focus on acquiring intercultural communication skills, but want to help understand how virtual characters simulating different cultural backgrounds are actually perceived.

Another aspect that distinguishes the different approaches is the way culture is investigated. While some approaches want to realistically simulate existing national cultures, others use fantasy cultures to avoid stereotyping. Interestingly, most approaches that aim at education, and with it try to create cultural awareness in general, use abstract cultures, e.g. the above mentioned ORIENT system. Vice versa, systems that want to teach inter-cultural skills, typically use a national cultural background that the learner is being trained for, see, for example, the TLTS mentioned above. Regarding research studies, no clear line can be drawn since both, national and synthetic cultures, are feasible.

How cultural differences are simulated varies across the approaches as well. Thereby, the way culture manifests itself can be displayed very differently, e.g. by performing different rituals, speaking different languages or using different gestures or facial expressions. Again a line can be drawn between educational systems and training systems. While most educational systems focus on different activities across groups, training systems take into account more concrete behavioral differences. Research studies investigated very different approaches of displaying culture.

The group addressed by the various systems seems to depend on the purpose of a system as well. Educational systems are mainly used in applications made for children who shall discover a different culture and learn that different behavior does not need to be wrong. In contrast, training systems are vastly used for military purposes, to provide soldiers with cultural skills to be able to effectively communicate with members of the culture they are sent to. Research studies tend to test their systems with members of the cultural background that is simulated.

Interactivity is another aspect that varies across the different approaches. Interactive systems vary from simply using menu-based interaction, to natural speech or full body interaction. In general, education and training systems are interactive, since the user is in the role of a learner who experiences or practices behaviors in a target culture. Vice versa, most research studies are not interactive, since they focus on how virtual characters are perceived by human observers.

We consider the work described in this dissertation as belonging to the third group (research studies), since our aim is to formalize culture-related differences in behavior in a computational way to be simulated in a virtual agent application to investigate how human observers of the simulated cultural backgrounds perceive the behaviors. In comparison to studies introduced in the field so far, our approach

Figure 3.9: Group of users interacting with the ORIENT system.

is based on theory as well as a corpus study to formalize differences, and evaluated in the observed cultures afterwards. Thus, the workflow of our approach outlined in section 1.2 is carried out entirely investigating cultural background.

3.2.2 Education in Cultural Awareness

As introduced above, educational approaches aim at creating cultural awareness by simulating culture-specific rituals or activities. Therefore, a user typically enters a virtual world in which he or she interacts which virtual characters of a different culture in a story-like fashion. This is similar to interactive storytelling approaches described in Section 3.1.

A representative approach is presented by Aylett and colleagues [APV+09] who introduced the ORIENT application that uses virtual agents to develop intercultural empathy. In the system, fantasy cultures are presented that are designed based on Hofstede's dimensional model of culture [Hof01]. Virtual characters have their own symbols, rituals and cultural background. The underlying agent architecture is based on FAtiMA [DP05] that makes use of emotions to influence the agents' behavior, based on the OCC appraisal theory [OCC88]. To simulate culture, the ar-

Figure 3.10: Meeting a virtual guide (left) and watching a virtual musician (right) in SecondChina (from [HFF+08]; Used with permission. Copyright remains with the author.).

chitecture was extended to allow adaptation of the agents in such a way that actions are interpreted and selected dependent on culture. Thus, on the one hand, incoming events are perceived in a culture-specific way (which updates the emotional state of an agent) and on the other hand, the triggered reaction is performed according to cultural background. To achieve cultural awareness on the user's side, a group of users interacts as a team with a group of virtual agents. For interaction, several input devices are provided such as a dance mat for navigation, mobile phones and objects that use RFID technology. Figure 3.9 shows a group of users interacting with the ORIENT system, using the different input devices.

Following up on the ORIENT application described above, the eCute project aims at creating a virtual learning environment that teaches cultural awareness, understanding and sensitivity [eCu12]. For the project, two different scenarios shall be created in order to teach learners of different age groups (late primary children and young adults). The virtual characters' cultures are based on Hofstede's synthetic cultures [HPH02] to exemplify prototypical culture-related differences in behavior. The eCute project will focus on culture-specific expressive emotional behavior and is thus based on theories derived from the social psychology, emotion research and intercultural communication. Besides observing the behavior of different cultures, the user will be able to interact with the virtual characters using intuitive input devices.

A different approach is presented by Henderson and colleagues [HFF+08]. In comparison to the systems described above, no abstract cultures are used for illustration. Instead, the authors want to give the user the chance to understand how to participate in an existing culture. Therefore, an island called SecondChina was created within the online platform SecondLife [Lin12], where the user can interact in a virtual world resembling China. In that manner, the user can explore the culture and certain behaviors of their members and prepare him- or herself without commitment before going there in real life. For the process of understanding, two components are provided: web-based text information, and interaction with virtual characters in SecondChina. These components can be accessed in random order and are designed to support each other. In the virtual environment, the user can either follow a virtual guide (see Figure 3.10 left) or explore the virtual world on his or her own. Exploration includes observing culturally important actions such as watching a group of characters doing taichi in the park or listening to a musician playing the *erhu* in a teahouse (see Figure 3.10 right).

As pointed out earlier, the approach described in this dissertation does not aim at education and, thus, differs from the approaches described in this subsection. Instead of creating cultural awareness in general, we focus on creating culture-specific behavior exemplifying prototypical differences in aspects of communicative behavior for the German and Japanese cultures.

3.2.3 Training in Cultural Competencies

The majority of applications in the field of integrating culture into virtual character systems aims at training culture-specific competencies. Thereby, approaches simulate national cultures and teach concrete behaviors such as negotiation styles.

An early approach of teaching intercultural competencies was done in 2005, in the Adaptive Thinking and Leadership System (ATL) [RDMH05]. In a virtual environment, teamwork, intercultural communication and adaptive thinking is taught to human users. In the multi-player scenario each user is assigned to one of the following roles: an US soldier, an Iraqi citizen or an invisible evaluator. Cultural knowledge is given to the players in advance, while users are told to interact appropriately for their assigned role. In an evaluation study using self-reports, the authors found out that participants thought they learned about their own strengths and weaknesses.

The probably most well known system that aims at training culture using virtual agents is the Tactical Language Training System (TLTS), described by Johnson and colleagues [JMV04]. The main goal of TLTS is to teach soldiers functional skills in foreign languages and cultures. So far, four versions of TLTS have been implemented: Iraqi, Dari, Pashto, and French [JV08]. The focus of the system lies

Figure 3.11: Screenshot of the TLTS, where the user avatar greets a person from a different culture (from [JMV04]; Used with permission. Copyright remains with the author.).

on verbal communication. Learners have to learn a foreign language in order to complete the tasks provided by the system. To accomplish the tasks, the player has to speak with the virtual characters using a microphone, which in return respond in their culture-related way. The TLTS contains a virtual village with virtual characters that have a different cultural background. To gain communicative skills, the learner should develop rapport with the people living in the virtual world and learn how to communicate appropriately. The tasks the user has to solve contain everyday activities, such as asking for directions or ordering food as well as to negotiate effectively with members of the foreign culture. The user is represented through an avatar in the virtual scenario for which the learner can speak and choose gestures. Figure 3.11 shows a screenshot of the TLTS in an Iraqi environment.

Vice versa, Johnson introduces the goEnglish system [Joh10] that was developed to teach the English language as well as the American culture to immigrants who have basic knowledge about the English language but limited knowledge and practice of conversational skills. A set of lessons is provided that focus on the language and culture of everyday life in the United States. The situations have been derived from interviews of immigrants to the United States who report about situations that they found surprising.

Figure 3.12: Screenshots of the BiLAT environment during a negotiation (left) and the reflective tutoring system (right) (from [KHD⁺09]; Image of BiLAT used with permission from the University of Southern California, Institute for Creative Technologies. Copyright 2007 University of Southern California, Institute for Creative Technologies.).

Kim and colleagues [KHD⁺09] introduce another system that focuses on gaining intercultural skills in order to communicate with the Iraqi culture. In comparison to the TLTS described above, the BiLAT system does not focus on the Arabic language but teaches negotiation skills to soldiers. In the system, communication with the virtual characters is realized by menu-based interaction. Before training with BiLAT, a one hour video is shown to the learner and several small tasks have to be solved after watching it. In order to interact successfully in a negotiation, the user has to adapt to some Iraqi interaction rules and has to use an integrative negotiation style.

Figure 3.12 left shows a screenshot of the BiLAT environment during a negotiation. In the virtual meeting, a so-called "trust meter" is constantly updated that monitors the progress of the negotiation and shows the user which actions increase or decrease the trust level. The notion of culture is integrated into the BiLAT system in several ways. On the one hand, the virtual characters have knowledge about a prototypical Iraqi business meeting and follow their etiquette. On the other hand, the user's interactions as well as the virtual agents' reactions contain cultural elements, which in turn affect parameters such as trust. In addition to the virtual training scenario, the BiLAT system provides an after-action review (AAR) for each meeting that helps the user understand the underlying cultural considerations behind the actions and reactions that took place during the training session (see Figure 3.12 right).

Similar to the TLTS and the BiLAT system, the Virtual Environment Cultural Training for Operational Readiness (VECTOR) system aims at teaching intercultural competencies in the Arab culture in a military domain [BDS+05]. In the virtual environment, users can navigate through the scenario freely and interact with virtual characters, using menu-based action selection. The main goal of the system is to teach face-to-face intercultural communication skills. A possible training task is e.g. to stop a bomber from attacking a target. In comparison to the training systems described above, VECTOR provides an authoring tool, which was designed to allow non-computer experts to create additional cultural contexts. The authoring tool is based on an instructional design process model that allows the specification of learning objectives as well as the creation of scenario segments.

Focusing on politeness strategies, Wu and colleagues introduced an intelligent tutoring system that teaches intercultural competencies [WM10]. The authors state that different politeness strategies have been proven to affect the user's perception of interactive systems and that differences in the usage and perception of politeness strategies can be dependent on cultural background. In that manner, the aspects of etiquette in different cultures are integrated to an Interactive Phrasebook. In the Interactive Phrasebook, the culture of a virtual agent can be customized, which affects the agent's perception of the user's utterances. The authors focus on Middle Eastern cultures and the US American culture. In the interaction, the user can communicate with the virtual agent by selecting phrases and/or gestures. The etiquette engine subsequently calculates the appropriateness of the selected action (i.e. based on the social relationship between the interlocutors), and categorizes the action into polite, nominal, or rude. In a review mode, the user can actively reflect on previous dialogs and learn about eventually unexpected reactions taken by the character considering the reasons that aroused the action.

In comparison to the systems described in this subsection, the focus of the work described in this dissertation is different from training inter-cultural competencies. However, it is similar to the approaches described here, regarding the focus on existing national cultures and concrete aspects of behavior. A major difference is that in our approach, we do not train behavior for one target culture, but point out differences in behavior between two cultures. Therefore, prototypical behaviors for the German and Japanese cultures are simulated and shown to human observers who judge the perception of these behaviors.

3.2.4 Research Studies

In the group of related work described in this subsection, the focus lies on investigating how the simulated cultural background of virtual characters is actually perceived by human observers. Therefore, different aspects of behavior were integrated and analyzed in various approaches.

An approach that takes into account the impact of the virtual agent's culture-specific visual appearance was done by Koda and colleagues [KRA08] who investigated whether emotions are judged the same way across different cultures. Images showing different faces for virtual characters as well as their emotional expressivity were designed for that purpose in different cultures. Their results show that participants from different cultures perceive agents differently and that there is an in-group advantage for the correct interpretation of emotional displays. For example, a facial expression created by a Japanese designer is rather recognized by a Japanese participant than by an observer from a different cultural background.

In a later approach, Koda and colleagues [KRNT10] had a closer look at different regions of the face and conducted a cross-cultural study in Hungary and Japan in order to test the impact of facial regions as cues to recognize the emotions of virtual agents. In their results, the authors report that Japanese participants found facial cues in the eye region more important than Hungarian participants, who, by contrast, concentrated more on facial cues in the mouth region. Figure 3.13 shows the cartoonish character used for their study, showing six different combined facial expressions on different regions of the face.

An approach that investigates behavioral differences has been taken by Mascarenhas and colleagues [MDA+09]. In their work, the authors focus on the use of rituals to generate culture-specific behavior for virtual agents. A ritual is described as a symbolic social activity that is carried out in a predetermined fashion. Therefore, special goals and plans are defined within the system architecture. For the simulation, two groups of agents were created that only differ in their rituals. To integrate the concept of culture, Hofstede's dimensions [Hof01] were taken as a basis, and synthetic cultures were created that showed typical behavior for their positioning on the target cultural dimension. Figure 3.14 shows their characters in a dinner scenario. Characters in the left picture rush to the table, representing a low power culture, while characters in the right picture are waiting for the elder to sit first, as they are representing a high power culture. In an evaluation study, human observers were asked to categorize the cultures by using sets of adjectives, and whether they observed differences across the cultures. Their results indicate

Figure 3.13: Virtual character displaying facial expressions on different regions of the face: happy eyes and neutral mouth (top left), happy eyes and sad mouth (top middle), neutral eyes and happy mouth (top right), neutral eyes and sad mouth (lower left), sad eyes and happy mouth (lower middle) and sad eyes and neutral mouth (lower right). (from [KRNT10]; Used with permission. Copyright remains with the author.).

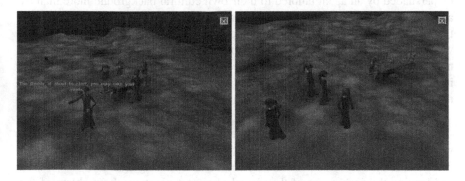

Figure 3.14: Group of virtual characters interacting in different culture-specific rituals (from [MDA⁺09]; Used with permission. Copyright remains with the author.).

that participants significantly observed differences in the cultures and were able to relate these differences to the phenomena of culture.

An evaluation study that investigates existing cultures was done by Yin and colleagues [YBC10]. For their study, two different virtual characters were designed, one representing a member of the Anglo-American culture and one resembling a member of the Latin-American culture. The appearance of the dwelling in the background as well as the music playing was adapted to match the cultural background of the agents. Both agents were bilingual, using English and Spanish text-to-speech engines. In addition, in their conversations with the user, the agents used different ways of argumentation. While the Anglo-American agent focused on the interlocutor's well-being, the Latin agent showed interest in the participant's family and friends. For their evaluation study, participants that were fluent in English and Spanish and who were a member of one of the cultural backgrounds studied and who had lived for at least two months in a county of the other cultural background, were invited. Their results indicate that the Latin agent was perceived as significantly more Latin than the Anglo-American agent, while the Anglo-American agent was perceived as slightly more American than the Latin agent. In addition, agents that spoke English were rated as significantly more American, while Spanish-speaking agents were rated as significantly more Latin. Interestingly, participants stated that the agent's language influenced their perception of the agent more than their cultural background. In addition to directly asking about the cultural background of the character, the agents' credibility and trustworthiness were investigated. Results indicate that participants tend to trust and be persuaded by an agent tailored to their own cultural background more than by an agent from a different cultural background. In their discussion, the authors state that in their evaluation it is not clear which of the aspects (appearance, language, way of argumentation, etc.) influenced the participants' judgment and which did not. We take this as an advice and therefore want to focus on one aspect at a time in the evaluation part of this dissertation. With it, we aim to investigate which of the aspects we take into account have an impact on human observers.

Another approach investigating different ethnicities in the American culture, was presented by Iacobelli and Cassell [IC07]. In their approach, the authors focus on different verbal and nonverbal behaviors. By changing the behaviors only and leaving the appearance of the virtual character constant, the problem of the aforementioned evaluation study is avoided. Using a virtual peer and kids of different ethnic backgrounds, the authors tested the perception of the ethnic identity of the virtual characters on human observers. Their evaluation indicates that the kids were able to relate the virtual agents correctly, and that they engaged with the virtual peers in a promising way for educational applications.

Jan and colleagues [JHM+07] take into account differences in nonverbal behavior for national cultures using a group of virtual agents. In particular, gaze, proxemics and turn-taking behaviors are investigated. Figure 3.15 shows two groups of

Figure 3.15: Virtual characters showing culture-specific proximity behavior (from [JHM⁺07]; Used with permission. Copyright remains with the author.).

characters that show different proximity behavior, representing the two cultures of Arabia and the US. In their evaluation study, the groups showing culture-specific nonverbal behaviors were shown to human observers. Their results reveal that participants perceived differences between behaviors that are in line with their own cultural background, and behaviors from different cultural backgrounds.

Interestingly, in their work [JHM⁺07], Jan and colleagues point out that a multimodal corpus would be very helpful to get a deeper insight into differences in nonverbal behaviors. Their work is very much in line with our approach, since we focus on several aspects of human behavior across two national cultures as well. In line with their suggestions, we think a video corpus recorded in the two observed cultures is a helpful tool. Therefore, we present an approach that exemplifies behavioral differences across the German and Japanese cultures taking into account suggestions from literature as well as findings from a corpus study. Regarding cultural background, we are presenting the first approach that carries out the whole workflow described in Section 1.2.

3.3 Integration of Behavioral Aspects

In the previous subsection, related work on integrating cultural background into the behavior of virtual agents has been introduced. As stated earlier, our approach aims at integrating several aspects of verbal as well as nonverbal behavior exemplified for the German and Japanese cultural backgrounds.

In Section 2.2, we introduced aspects of human behavior that are influenced by cultural background and seem to be relevant to our purposes. These behavioral aspects have been investigated in the domain of virtual characters before. So far, most of these behavioral aspects have been considered per se or in correlation with personal factors, such as personality or personal relationships, however, without relating these behaviors to different cultural backgrounds. In this subsection, we introduce related work that is representative for the aspects of behavior we are considering for our purpose, to gain a better understanding of how these aspects can be integrated into the behavior models of virtual characters.

3.3.1 Small Talk

As introduced in Section 2.2.1, we focus on small talk as a domain for verbal behavior since it is of a prototypical nature for first-time encounters and exists in every culture.

In addition to being a pastime or being used to avoid unpleasant silence, small talk can be used to build trust and rapport between human communication part-ners. According to Reeves and Nass [RN96], users establish social relations to computer-based systems, too. In that manner, developing virtual agents that have the ability to use small talk can help influence social relations towards them posi-tively, too.

Cassell and colleagues [CBB+99], for example, describe the virtual agent REA that interacts with a user in the domain of real estate sales (see also Section 3.1, where this system served as an example for an interactive virtual character). In [BC99], Bickmore and Cassell introduce an advanced version of the REA agent, where the social component is enhanced by the agent's capability to engage in small talk. Besides accomplishing specific tasks in the real estate domain, the agent is designed to use casual small talk to build trust and rapport with the user. According to the authors, in applications where the development of social relations is intended, small talk can be a crucial part of the system's social intelligence. For an evaluation study, two different conditions were scripted: task-oriented and so-cial, whereas the social script was identical to the task script except that it addi-tionally contained small talk. The authors state that the participants' opinions on the small talk condition ranged widely. Some of the users did not like the condi-tion, many others did who stated that the small talk was an important part of their expectations with regard to dealing with a real estate agent. Results also indicate that using small talk with virtual characters can lead to increased trust. Interest-ingly, this only holds true for participants that have an extroverted personality. This suggests that the perception of small talk does vary with the user's personal background. We thus think that the perception could vary with cultural background, too, and that integrating culture as a social factor in the generation of small talk can be a crucial aspect.

In addition to the REA agent, Bickmore [Bic03] describes an exercise adviser agent that promotes exercise among students in order to evaluate the effectiveness of relational agents in health behavior change. Therefore, the agent needs to be capable of building relationships with people to influence their exercise behavior. Small talk was integrated to the system as a tool to improve the naturalness of the virtual character. In an evaluation study, significantly more laughter was observed in conversations containing a lot of small talk, compared to dialogs where small talk was almost absent. These results suggest that the usage of small talk in communication with virtual characters can influence the user's perception positively.

Cavazza and colleagues [CdlCT10] describe a virtual agent that serves as a personal companion, whose primary purpose is to carry on a conversation with the user. In their demonstration, the user's day at work is discussed, while the virtual character responds by giving comfort, warnings or advice. Through this non-task-oriented conversation about an everyday life domain, a social relation between the user and the virtual character is established.

Another purpose of small talk in computer-based systems is described by Isbister and colleagues [ININ00] (see also Section 3.1, where this system served as an example for a multiuser system). A so-called Helper Agent, in the appearance of a dog and the role of a party host, virtually joins a group of users in a chat room. The virtual character interacts with the human interlocutors in case their conversation stagnates, by introducing prototypical small talk topics. That way, the agent can actively help create interesting and ongoing conversations between the conversation partners. Thereby, the agent distinguishes between safe and unsafe topics. The authors state that this division depends on culture. Thus, some topics are safe in one culture and unsafe in another. To avoid the problem of integrating different cultural backgrounds, however, in their application topics remain limited to those that are either safe or unsafe in all cultures (such as weather and music for safe topics, or religion and money for unsafe topics). In an online study, where students from America and Japan joined the chat room, the agent's ability to assist in intercultural conversations was evaluated. Results indicate that the agent made positive contributions to the participants' experience. In addition, it influenced the users' perceptions of each other and of each others' cultural background.

Regarding the integration of culture, we expect differences in the perception of small talk behavior, since, for example, there are differences in the categorization into safe and unsafe topics. If, for example, topics are integrated into an agent dialog that are safe in one culture but unsafe in another, the relation that should be established to a virtual character using small talk could be influenced in a negative way in the culture where the topic is considered a taboo. Thus, when simulating small talk for different cultural backgrounds, different models of prototypical behavior need to be created.

3.3.2 Communication Management

Another behavioral aspect that depends on cultural background and seems to be interesting for our purposes, as pointed out in Subsection 2.2.2, are communication management behaviors that handle the flow of a conversation and include e.g. the usage of silence in speech. Using communication management behaviors in virtual character systems has been vastly researched, while mechanisms of proper turn taking behavior pose a great challenge to computer-based dialog systems.

Jonsdottir and colleagues [JTN08], for example, describe an attempt of using machine learning to build an agent that learns turn taking during interaction and adjusts its behavior to its communication partner. Therefore, optimal pause durations are learned to minimize speech overlaps. As the authors state, the shortest duration of silence between turns is not always the most efficient technique. This suggests that adding intentional pauses to a virtual agent dialog can influence the user's perception positively.

Another approach of learning turn taking behaviors has been presented by Sato and colleagues [SHT⁺02]. The authors analyzed a corpus of conversations between human users and a spoken dialog system in order to train a decision tree. Unlike most existing approaches, the system's turn taking behavior is not only based on the perception of pauses in the user's utterances, but additionally includes other features such as recognition results or prosodic features, e.g. pitch. Evaluating their approach indicates that the learned decision tree outperforms the baseline strategy, which takes the speaking turn at every user pause.

Sidner and colleagues [SKLL04] describe a model of engagement for a conversational robot, based on an analysis of human-human conversations. Engagement is described as "the process by which two (or more) participants establish, maintain and end their perceived connection during interactions they jointly undertake". According to the authors, the appropriate use and correct interpretation of engagement signals are necessary prerequisites for the success of an interaction. In particular, in their system, pauses are used to recognize inattentiveness of the user, which encourages the robot to show engagement behaviors.

In a similar manner, the REA agent (see Section 3.1 and previous subsection) makes use of detected pauses in the user's speech. Cassell and colleagues [CNB⁺01] describe that short pauses are leading to feedback behaviors such as head nods, using para verbals (such as "Mmhmm") or short statements (such as "okay") as reaction to the pause in the user's speech and to encourage the user to go on.

Based on this work, Nakano and and colleagues [NRSC03] developed a grounding model for the kiosk agent Mack that provides route descriptions for a paper map. The agent uses verbal and nonverbal grounding acts to update the state of the dialog. The authors state that pauses in speech additionally have an influence on the choice of subsequent actions.

Traum and Heeman [TH96] also considered grounding behavior in dialogs. In their work, the authors had a closer look at the co-occurrence of turn-initial grounding acts and utterance unit signals, such as prosodic boundary tones and pauses. For their analysis, silence was categorized into two groups: short silence (less than half a second) and long silence (longer than half a second). Although their results suggest that grounding is highly correlated to boundary tones and less to pauses, the authors state that long pauses are positively related with the previous utterance being grounded, and that those pauses seem to be an indicator of utterance unit completion.

The impact of personal background of the interlocutors to the flow of a conversation was investigated by Cassell and colleagues [CNB⁺01] who analyzed behavioral differences in conversations between friends compared to conversations between strangers. Therefore, differences in features such as eye-gaze, head nods or interruptions were analyzed to build a computational model of the role of relationships in language use between humans and embodied conversational agents. Interestingly, the authors state that details, such as leaning in towards one another, laughing, telling jokes at one another's expense and interrupting each other, differ from culture to culture.

As described earlier, the usage of regulators that are used to control the flow of a conversation, such as pauses in speech are highly dependent on culture. Therefore, different models of communication management and feedback behavior need to be designed when simulating prototypical conversations for different cultural backgrounds.

3.3.3 Nonverbal and Expressive Behavior

Another aspect of human behavior that we introduced in Section 2.2.3 as being dependent on cultural background and relevant to our purposes, is nonverbal behavior and, in particular, the expressiveness of nonverbal behaviors. Through their embodiment, virtual characters are able to express themselves nonverbally in an expressive manner and thus nonverbal communication for virtual characters has been researched widely.

Several systems focused on the challenge of automatically adding appropriate nonverbal behavior to given verbal behavior. The probably most well known system, BEAT, was introduced by Cassell and colleagues [CVB01]. As input, it receives plain text and generates synchronized nonverbal behavior for a virtual character. The behavior is selected on the basis of linguistic and contextual analysis of the input text and predefined rules derived from research in human conversational behavior. In their work, the authors describe behavior selection according to so-called filter functions that regulate how often nonverbal behavior is performed by a virtual agent. Such filters can reflect the personality, affective state or energy level of an agent. Similarly, these filters could be applied to cultural background as another aspect that affects the selection of nonverbal behaviors.

Many other system creators were inspired by their work. Breitfuss and colleagues [BPI09], for example, present an approach based on the BEAT system, where nonverbal behavior for a speaker and a listener agent is generated. Appropriate gaze and gestures are added to a given input text, which can be displayed in virtual worlds such as Second Life.

Another system inspired by BEAT was introduced by Lee and colleagues [LM06]. In comparison to the BEAT system, it generates BML scripts which constitute a standard input for a variety of virtual character systems and, thus, the nonverbal behavior generator aims to be a more general approach that can be reused in several applications. Nonverbal behavior is generated based on rules that were extracted from a set of video clips. The syntactic and semantic structure of the input text as well as the affective state of the virtual character are taken into account for the generation of nonverbal behavior. Therefore, speech-utterances have been labeled by the authors and their co-occurrences with nonverbal behaviors have been analyzed, focusing on head movements, facial expressions and body gestures. Different cultural backgrounds have not been considered in their system.

Besides the choice of gestures, the way a gesture is conducted can vary with cultural background. In Subsection 2.2.3, the expressivity dimensions have been introduced that describe a dynamical variation of nonverbal behaviors according to a set of parameters. These parameters have already been successfully integrated into the nonverbal behavior model of a virtual character by Lamolle and colleagues [LMP+05]. The virtual character Greta [Pel05] is designed to display verbal and nonverbal behaviors dependent on personal and social background as well as according to a set of dynamic variables such as believes, goals and emotions.

The virtual character's expressive behavior has been developed on the basis of an annotated corpus, taking into account emotions, context and multimodal behaviors. To point out differences in expressive behavior, variations of the agent are deducted from a default agent by a behavioral profile. The profile specifies an agent's expressivity and predispositions, describing which modalities are preferably used. Depending on the predispositions, an agent could, for example, be more expressive than the default agent regarding the face, but less expressive regarding gestures and body postures. Taking into account the expressivity dimensions, the intensity, velocity, duration or delay of the chosen signal can be varied for the corresponding modality. An agent could, for example, perform fluid movements with gestures close to the body, while another could show jerky movements that are conducted with a wider spatial extent.

We are very much inspired by the systems described above and want to build on their ideas in order to create different nonverbal behaviors simulating different cultural backgrounds for virtual characters.

3.4 Summary

In this chapter, related work has been introduced. When integrating culture-specific aspects of behavior into the behavioral models of virtual characters, several types of related work can be considered, such as virtual character systems in general, the integration of culture or the integration of the targeted behavioral aspects.

This chapter starts off with an outline of the development of virtual character systems over time. Thereby, a trend can be observed from non-interactive single agent systems to interactive multiagent systems. For demonstration purposes, we introduced selected systems that are representative for certain stages of virtual character systems.

In Chapter 2, culture has been introduced as a social phenomenon that is specific to a group rather than to an individual. Thus, when observing the development of virtual character applications over time, it becomes clear that the integration of cultural background came into focus only recently, when multiple agents acted as a group. At earlier points in time, personal backgrounds such as emotional state or personality were investigated. However, the approaches taken give useful insights and can, at least partly, be reproduced for the integration of culture.

As a next step, systems were presented that investigate culture for virtual characters. Therefore, we introduced a schema to categorize systems according to aspects such as aim, target group or simulated behavior. Subsequently, the approaches were described in more detail focusing on the categorization, while the technical background required for the integration of culture into the behavior of virtual characters is addressed later in this dissertation.

Distinguishing the approaches according to their purpose seems very well suited to structure related work in this area. Thus, the subsequent subsections summarize the approaches with regard to their purpose: education, training and research studies.

The first category, educational approaches, aim at creating cultural awareness. They usually take a more general approach of integrating culture, e.g. by simulating culture-specific activities for abstract cultures. Educational approaches often want to help children understand that different behavior is not necessarily wrong and therefore let them enter a virtual world in which a different culture can be explored in a story-like fashion.

The second category aims at training cultural competencies. Approaches are therefore more concrete and usually focus on existing national cultures and specific tasks that have to be solved in the target culture. Most approaches in this category find themselves in a military domain to provide soldiers with cultural skills to be able to effectively communicate with members of the culture they are sent to. For this purpose, users are integrated into interactive scenes where behavioral aspects such as language skills or negotiation strategies are trained.

The third category of related work focuses on research studies in order to gain a deeper insight in how culture-specific virtual characters are perceived by human observers. Thereby, approaches can differ immensely. Examples include synthetic cultures as well as national cultures, and the simulated cultural background can manifest itself either in concrete aspects of behavior or in behavioral routines.

After summarizing approaches that integrate culture to virtual character systems, we introduce approaches that successfully integrate the aspects of human behavior that we pointed out as being relevant to our purposes. As described in Section 2.2, we want to focus on the domain of small talk behavior and add culture-specific communication management behaviors as well as nonverbal behaviors. Related work in this section is thus structured accordingly. Small talk is often integrated into virtual characters' conversational behavior in order to positively influence the relationship that a user develops towards it. However, since small talk behavior depends on cultural background, different models need to be created to, e.g. avoid topics that are taboo in a certain culture. In a similar manner, communication is managed differently across cultures. Therefore models of e.g. feedback behavior should vary for different cultural backgrounds. Integrating nonverbal behaviors has been a wide research field so far. Since culture on the one hand influences the selection of nonverbal behavior and, on the other hand, their performance, representative approaches are introduced that focus on the generation of nonverbal behaviors or differences in expressive behavior.

Although the approaches described in the last section did not integrate cultural background, they give useful hints on how relevant aspects of behavior can, in general, be integrated into the behavioral models of virtual characters.

4 Empirical Background

Behavioral differences described in literature are helpful to understand different behavior and are a good guideline for the behavior of virtual characters. For the implementation of computational models, however, they are sometimes too abstract and do not provide enough data to design the differences. A multimodal corpus recorded in different cultural backgrounds that holds information on the observed aspect of behavior is a helpful tool. By analyzing such a corpus, deeper insight into the target behavior is obtained.

This approach has been applied for the creation of virtual character behavior for other human factors [KNKA07] [MAD⁺05]. However, cultural background has not been investigated for computational models so far. The methodology of analyzing a video corpus in order to build behavioral models for virtual characters is described in Section 4.1. The approach seems to be very well suited for the integration of cultural backgrounds as well. Thus, it is further taken as a guideline for our purpose of simulating cultural differences for virtual characters.

Recording such a video corpus is a time and resources consuming task, since a large amount of data is needed from at least two different cultures. This dissertation was developed within the Cube-G project [Aug09] that recorded such a corpus in the German and Japanese cultures. In Section 4.2 the acquisition of the corpus is described with the different scenarios that were recorded.

Culture-related behaviors were analyzed, taking into account the behavioral tendencies found in literature and described in Chapter 2. The annotation of the corpus is introduced in Section 4.3. Therefore, the tool used for this step is described as well as the annotation schemes that were designed to investigate verbal as well as nonverbal behavior. Subsequently, the analysis of the annotated video data is presented in Section 4.4. Finally this chapter is summarized in Section 4.5.

4.1 Method of Utilizing a Multimodal Corpus

In this section, the methodology of annotating and analyzing a video corpus that serves as a basis for the behavior of virtual characters is introduced. By analyzing a video corpus that holds information on the target behavior, deeper insight as well as a statistical description can be obtained. This approach has been taken to successfully explore human factors that influence behavior [KNKA07] [MAD⁺05]. For the integration of cultural aspects, this approach seems to be very well suited as well; nevertheless, it has not been used so far. Thus, in this section, the method of annotating a multimodal corpus in order to build a virtual character's behavior is introduced for approaches that investigate other aspects that influence human behavior.

A well-known system that is based on a video corpus is presented by Kipp and colleagues [KNKA07] who aim at achieving more natural behavior for virtual characters. Based on a multimodal annotated corpus, the system generates nonverbal behavior in the style of a particular speaker for any given input text. The authors exemplified their approach for two human speakers, Jay Leno (JL) and Marcel Reich-Ranicki (MR), two famous TV talk-show hosts with active nonverbal behavior. For their approach of generating individualized gestural behavior two steps need to be taken: (1) a preprocessing phase (offline) and (2) a runtime system (online).

During the preprocessing phase, the gestures within the video corpus are annotated using their own coding scheme, provided in [KNA07]. This rather time-consuming step has to be taken for every human speaker who is to be remodeled. As a result of this preprocessing phase, a gestural profile is produced for the particular speaker and an animation lexicon is updated.

In the runtime system, conversational gestures are produced resembling a given human speaker by using the gestural profile created in the offline phase. During this phase, the system creates a gesture script from the gesture profile and the animation lexicon and passes it to an animation engine. The process of the two phases, as presented in [KNKA07], is graphically shown in Figure 4.1 (preprocessing) and Figure 4.2 (runtime).

This process is able to generate unique gestures which can be used to simulate individualized virtual agents. As mentioned above, in [KNKA07] this has been

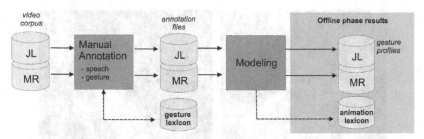

Figure 4.1: The offline phase is conducted for every human speaker in Kipp and colleagues' approach (from [KNKA07]; Used with permission. Copyright remains with the author.).

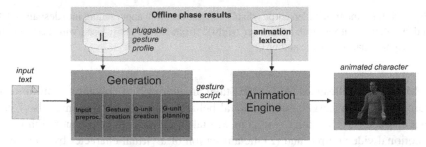

Figure 4.2: Online phase that produces individualized behavior resembling the target speaker (from [KNKA07]; Used with permission. Copyright remains with the author.).

exemplified for two human speakers. In an evaluation study, the authors showed that human observers were able to correctly assign the virtual character's behavior to the speaker taken as a basis.

In the approach by Kipp and colleagues [KNKA07], the models of particular speakers are computed automatically from the data, which constitutes the state of the art. This approach would, in principle, be applicable for the integration of cultural background as well. However, since our focus in not to model aspects of behavior for one particular speaker but to prototypically simulate different cultural backgrounds, taking the same approach would present a great challenge to the learning process due to the large amount of data needed to model culture. In the approach taken by Kipp and colleagues [KNKA07], 9 minutes of video data were analyzed for both speakers, while for modeling culture, several individuals are needed from each culture to e.g. regulate the influence of gender or personality. For that reason, in this dissertation models are based on the statistical analysis described later in this chapter.

Figure 4.3: Frame from video corpus displaying the emotion anger fading into despair (left), and simulation with a virtual character (right), (from [MAD+05]; Used with permission. Copyright remains with the author.).

Martin and colleagues [MAD+05] take an approach of annotating multimodal corpora for the integration of emotional behavior into the behavior models of virtual characters. Therefore, two steps are taken as well: (1) the annotation of an emotional video corpus and (2) the animation of a virtual character by copy synthesis.

Based on annotated video recordings of human speakers, the authors manually define markups augmented by expressivity parameters which are then forwarded to an animation engine to generate individual behaviors. For annotation, the authors used the Anvil tool [Kip01] and coded information on several levels: regarding the whole video (global level), related to emotional segments (local level) and a time-based annotation of multimodal behaviors.

The speech transcribed for the recorded person is used as a starting point and enriched with tags that drive the animation of the agent, derived from the analysis of the annotated video. Figure 4.3 left shows a frame for the video corpus where a women talks about a recent trial in which her father was kept in jail. Figure 4.3 right shows the corresponding virtual character, displaying the emotion anger, which later fades into despair. From the global level of annotation, a behavioral profile is defined for a virtual character. Thus, virtual agents with different behavioral profiles might display different behaviors on the same input file where emotions are specified.

This approach seems to be very well suited for the integration of cultural background as well, since e.g. a given conversation could be performed very differently by members of different cultural backgrounds. However, for the integration of culture, a large data set is required to capture prototypical behaviors that differ with cultural background.

Using a video corpus as a basis, it can be modeled what is visible in human behavior, while it does not explain why a certain signal is expressed. This approach, thus, aims at modeling the external layer of culture (see Section 2.1.1) that explains what is visible on the surface and does not consider implicit layers of culture that constitute what drives people internally to behave in a certain manner.

The advantage of using a video corpus was also pointed out by Jan and colleagues [JHM⁺07] who state that a multimodal corpus would be very helpful to model convincing cultural background for virtual characters in their future work. In a later approach, Harrera and colleagues [HNJT11] introduce such a corpus that investigates different cultures in dyadic conversations versus four-person conversations. Their results suggest that aspects such as proxemics or gaze behavior vary with group size and culture, but not necessarily in the same manner as suggested by literature. This outcome demonstrates the suitability of analyzing a corpus instead of purely relying on literature. In comparison to the work described in this dissertation, the findings of the above-mentioned corpus study have not been integrated into a virtual setting yet.

Their conclusions are in line with Allwood and colleagues [AAL11] who claim that more studies and reviews of the claims that have been made in literature are needed, as well as direct analysis of recorded communicative interaction within the framework of different social activities. In addition, Allwood and colleagues [AAL11] discuss some challenges that need to be faced when building conversational virtual agents, e.g. whether agents of different cultural backgrounds should strive for an even distribution of the observed aspect, or whether they should try to adapt to the style of the user.

4.2 Corpus Acquisition

To ground our expectations on culture-related behavioral differences into empirical data, we analyzed a video corpus recorded in the German and Japanese cultures. The corpus was recorded within the Cube-G project (CUlture-adaptive BEhavior Generation for interactions with embodied conversational agents) [RAN⁺07], which constitutes the frame of this dissertation. The project investigates whether and how the nonverbal behavior of agents can be generated from a parameterized

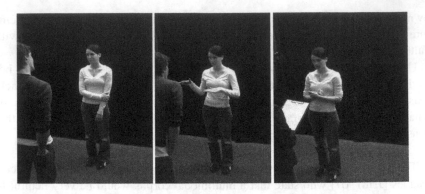

Figure 4.4: Screenshots from the video corpus recorded in Germany in three prototypical scenarios.

Figure 4.5: Screenshots from the videos corpus recorded in Japan in three prototypical scenarios.

computational model, which should be employed in edutainment applications to increase cultural awareness and to train behavioral routines. To this end, a corpus was recorded in Augsburg, Germany and in Kyoto, Japan at the universities of two of the project partners.

Recording such a cross-cultural corpus is a time and resource consuming task as outlined by Rehm and colleagues [RAB+09a]. First of all, a huge amount of data is required to explain culture-related differences in behavior. Therefore, at least two cultures are needed in which to record the corpus. Even when focusing on one culture only, observed behavior can be influenced by the context in which the recordings are taken. A cross-cultural study is even more challenging since the cultural aspects need to be singled out from amongst other factors such as context of the recordings or personality of the participant. In addition, it needs to be assured that the participants in the different cultures are facing the same conditions. Therefore, the setup of the recordings needs to be well chosen and reproducible elsewhere, while clear scripts need to be constructed and reasonable advice given. Also technical limitations, such as choice of camera or size of recording area, need to be specified in advance. In addition, the scenario recorded in the corpus needs to be able to grasp cultural differences in behavior, but at the same time needs to be kept general, such that it can be reproduced in all recorded cultures. When designing such a study, developers should also be careful to leave their own cultural background behind, as fas as possible, and to avoid making culture-related design heuristics an issue. The Cube-G corpus provides a good solution to these challenges, as it is recorded in a standardized manner and provides a rich set of data for the German and Japanese cultures.

For the video corpus, more than 20 participants were recorded in each culture, each running through three scenarios. Each scenario was recorded with one student interaction partner and one professional actor. The participants did not know that they were interacting with actors. In this vein, we were able to ensure high control over the recordings. On the one hand, we could assure that participants did not know each other in advance. On the other hand, we were able to assure that all scenarios lasted for around the same time. Actors were told to be as passive as possible and to allow the participant to lead the conversation. Only if communication seemed to stagnate, actors should get more active. In that manner, we could assure that as many topics or ideas as possible were brought up by the participants and not by the actors. To allow all gender combinations, we hired four actors: one female and one male actor from each target culture. It should be noted that dyads were held in each person's mother tongue and thus Japanese students interacted with Japanese actors and German students with German actors.

For the acquisition of the corpus, three prototypical social interaction scenarios were videotaped:

- First-time meeting: The interaction partners get acquainted with one another in order to better be able to solve a task together later. This scenario is a variation of the standard first chapter of every language textbook.

- Negotiation: In this prototypical interactive situation, the participants have to negotiate with one another to reach a state which is satisfactory for both sides.

- Status differences: The participant has to explain the outcome of the previous negotiation to someone with a higher social status.

These scenarios have been chosen for two reasons. First, they represent standard situations that occur in every culture and might easily happen in cross-cultural encounters, too. Moreover, different verbal and nonverbal behaviors can be expected for these scenarios recorded in different cultures.

Participants were told that they took part in a study by a well-known consulting company for the automobile industry which takes place at the same time in different countries. To attract their interest in the study, a monetary reward was granted depending on the outcome of the negotiation.

Each of the participants was told that they would have to solve a task with another student and therefore the two of them had to get acquainted with one another. While having a small talk conversation to get to know each other, the video taping had already started to record the first scenario. The same two interlocutors participated in the second scenario, a negotiation. For the third scenario, the student interacted with the second actor who played the role of our business partner who claimed to be interested in the results of the recordings. For the approach described in this dissertation, the first scenario was taken into account due to its prototypical nature.

To control gender effects, a male and a female actor were employed for each role, who had to interact with the same number of male and female participants. For the acquisition of the corpus, at least ten male and ten female students were recorded. The actual number of participants differed between Germany and Japan. 21 students (11 male, 10 female) participated in the German data collection and 26 students (13 male, 13 female) in the Japanese collection. For each participant, around 25 minutes of video material was collected, around 5 minutes in the first time meeting, around 10-15 minutes in the negotiation and around 5 minutes in the status difference scenario. Figure 4.4 and Figure 4.5 show examples from the video corpus in all three scenarios recorded in the two cultures of Germany and Japan.

To ensure equal conditions on both sides, the same design was used in Germany as well as in Japan. To this end, a recording booth (around 3 x 3 meters) was created that featured two video cameras and a microphone. Each of the video cameras recorded one of the interlocutors (student and actor), while the microphone was installed between them at the side of the booth. Further information on the setting of the video recordings can be found in [RAB+09b].

4.3 Annotation

For the approach taken in this dissertation, the behavioral tendencies drawn from literature are grounded into empirical data in order to gain a deeper insight into behavioral differences. To this end, the video corpus described above was annotated regarding the aspects of behavior that seem to be promising to show culture-related differences according to our findings from literature (see Section 2.2). Aspects of behavior were taken into account on different levels: (1) verbal behavior, (2) communication management and (3) nonverbal behavior.

Annotating multimodal behavior is challenging, since the aspects of behavior need to be broken down into variables and structured in a way that culture-related differences within as well as across the aspects of behavior can be analyzed. Therefore, suitable annotation schemes were designed for both, verbal and nonverbal behavior, that can be aligned to investigate correlations between the aspects. These annotation schemes are described in more detail in the subsequent subsections.

Following the approaches described in Section 4.1, we use the Anvil tool [Kip01] for annotation. Using the tool, events that occur in the video can be transcribed on parallel tracks that run along a time line. Elements that are positioned on each track are, thus, aligned in a timely manner.

Annotations were conducted by student workers of Augsburg University and Seikei University. Annotation of speech transliteration and translation had to be done in the country where the respective videos had been recorded for language reasons. Nonverbal behavior was less critical in this regard and was annotated in both in Germany and in Japan. Figure 4.6 shows an example annotation containing an example video from the German part of our video corpus. In the figure, an annotation element holding a deictic gesture is highlighted. Every element is defined as an interval between a start- and an end-time. In the Anvil tool, the information that is held by each element is a complex object with attributes and values rather than a simple label. In that manner, a gesture, for example, can be annotated according to its type and expressivity, while the expressivity can be annotated along several dimensions such as speed and spatial extent, holding different values for each attribute. In addition, relations between the tracks can be defined. Thus, e.g. the start- and end-time for a gesture has to be set only once for both tracks, type and expressivity.

The tool is particularly well suited for our purposes since the tracks, including the attributes and values for the elements, can be specified by the user of the tool

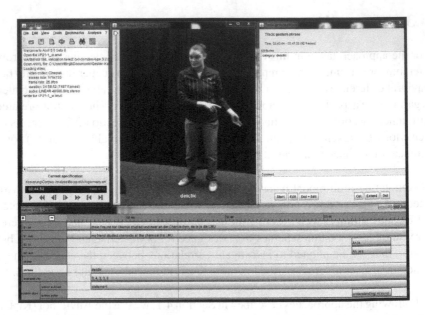

Figure 4.6: Screenshot of an annotation in the Anvil tool [Kip01] including a video of a participant and the corresponding time line of annotated actions.

independently, and is thus not bound to a specific theory. This so-called coding scheme can be dynamically expanded with additional tracks to e.g. add more behavioral aspects. In addition, timely correlations between different channels of behavior can be observed and analyzed. In the following subsections, the coding schemes employed in this dissertation, including aspects of verbal and nonverbal behavior, are being introduced.

4.3.1 Verbal Aspects

For the annotation of verbal behavior, coders with different language skills are needed since the video corpus was recorded in the participants' mother tongues. In that manner, half of the dialogs were held in German, while the other half was held in Japanese. In order to make annotations available for analysis without the need to be able to speak one of the languages, speech was transcribed and translated into English.

Since the German and the Japanese languages differ vastly, e.g. in their characters, grammar and word order, we decided to annotate speech at sentence level. In

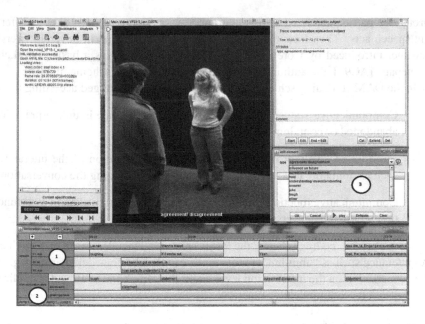

Figure 4.7: Annotated speech of a German participant performing an agreement / disagreement action.

that manner, a clear translation for the whole sentence can be given, which would not be possible by annotating and translating word by word.

Therefore, in our verbal coding scheme the first four tracks hold the content of speech during the dialogs in the interlocutors' native language as well as in English for both, the participant and the actor. Thereby, the translation track is related to the native language track, since start- and end-points of each sentence on the time line are equal. Figure 4.7 shows an example annotation with annotated verbal aspects. As mentioned above, the first four tracks hold the semantics of the speech, indicated by number ① in Figure 4.7, in the following order: (1) Participant's native speech, (2) English translation of participants's speech, (3) actor's native speech and (4) English translation of actors' speech.

In addition to transliteration and translation, the communication style of the participant was annotated. Therefore, a group of tracks was created, holding the participant's actions, the actor's actions as well as the phase of the conversation holding the current topic (see Figure 4.7, number ②). In the first two tracks of the group, the participant's and actor's utterances were annotated according to different speech acts. Therefore, the DAMSL (Dialog Act Markup in Several Layers) scheme, introduced by Core and Allen [CA97], was taken as a basis. On their homepage [AC97], the authors explain the structure of their scheme in detail.

In the DAMSL coding scheme, each spoken utterance is tagged according to its

- Communicative status: indicating whether an utterance is uninterpretable, abandoned or containing self-talk

- Information level: providing an abstract characterization of the utterance, such as doing the task, talking about the task or managing the conversation.

- Communicative function: categorizing the utterances according to their function within the conversation.

In the DAMSL coding schema, the levels are not independent from one another. An utterance such as "uhm-hm", for example, can thus be considered as managing the conversation on the information level and at the same time as an understanding utterance in its communicative function.

The communicative function is the most interesting dimension to analyze differences in dialog behavior across cultures, as it labels utterances with their communicative meaning. This dimension can be further divided into the "Forward Looking Function" and the "Backward Looking Function"; the former explains how the current utterance constraints future beliefs and actions of the participant, such as making commitments for the future, while the latter holds information on how the current utterance relates to the previous discourse, such as answering a question or acknowledging a previous action.

For our purpose, the DAMSL annotation scheme as provided in [CA97] is too complex. In our annotation, we focused on the following subset of utterances:

- Forward Looking Function
    - Statement: The speaker makes a claim about the world.
    - Info request: The utterance is a question or another form of information request.
    - Influence on future: The speaker wants to influence either the listener's or his/herself's future actions.

- Backward Looking Function
  - Agreement: The utterance indicates the speaker's point of view concerning a previous action (positive or negative).
  - Hold: The speaker performs an action that leaves the decision open and evokes further discussion.
  - Understanding: Actions that make sure that interlocutors are understanding / not understanding each other, without stating a point of view.
  - Answer: Answer to a previous information request (please note that an answer is always a statement too).

In Figure 4.7, the annotation of an agreement/disagreement is exemplified including the set of utterances used in this dissertation (indicated by number ③).

As stated in Subsection 2.3.2, we expect culture-related differences in the choice of topics during small talk conversations in our video corpus. Thus, in the last track of our verbal coding scheme, the current topic of the conversation is annotated. Therefore, initially a set of topics was provided to the annotators that were likely to occur during the conversations. During the process of annotation, this set was constantly expanded to match the topics that actually occurred in the corpus.

Please see Appendix A.1 for the coding scheme of verbal aspects as it was used in this dissertation.

4.3.2 Nonverbal Aspects

This dissertation was developed within the Cube-G project [RNA+09] that investigates culture-related differences in nonverbal behavior. For annotation, we focus on hand gestures and body postures. The first four tracks of our verbal coding scheme (transliteration and translation of participant and actor) were reused to be able to better relate speech to nonverbal behaviors. For reasons of a clear arrangement on a computer screen, other aspects of verbal behavior were excluded from the annotation scheme of nonverbal behavior. However, the two schemes can easily be combined afterwards for further analysis. Please see Appendix A.2 for the coding scheme of nonverbal behaviors.

Figure 4.8 shows an example annotation of nonverbal behaviors from our video corpus. For the annotation of gestures, a group was created that contains the gesture's type and expressivity (indicated by number ①).

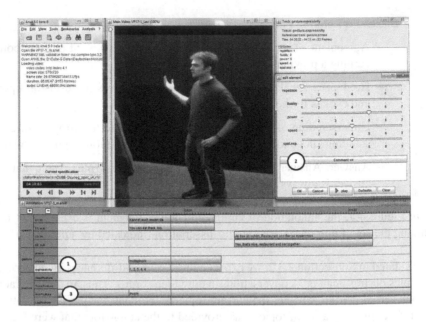

Figure 4.8: Annotated nonverbal behavior of a German participant performing a gesture with moderate expressivity.

The gesture type was annotated taking into account McNeill's classification [McN92] who introduces five different gesture types (see Subsection 2.2.3 for more details). To this end, each gesture was assigned to one of the following types: deictic, emblem, iconic, metaphoric and adaptor. Usually these categories are not meant to be mutually exclusive, thus, for our annotation, only the main type of gesture was taken into account. McNeill's categorization of gestures has already been used successfully in the domain of virtual characters, e.g. by Krenn and Pirker [KP04b].

A gesture's dynamic variation was annotated according to the expressivity parameters introduced in Section 2.2.3. Thus, the five parameters repetition, fluidity, power, speed and spatial extent were taken into account. In Figure 4.8, the annotation of a metaphoric gesture is highlighted, including the interface for the annotation of its expressivity (indicated by number ②). Each parameter was annotated using a seven-point scale, with one holding a small value and seven a large value for the parameter. The only exception includes the parameter repetition, where the value denotes the exact number of repetitions of the stroke of a gesture. In order to explain differences in the gestural expressivity in a more descriptive manner to our annotators, example videos were recorded and provided.

For the annotation of different postures, Bull's posture coding scheme [Bul87] was employed. The full coding scheme includes several parts of the body that can be used for the description of postures, such as head, arms, trunk or legs. For this dissertation, arm postures were taken into account (see Figure 4.8, number ③). 32 different arm positions were included to the coding scheme, such as PHEw - put hands on elbow, PHWr - put hands on wrist, JHs - join hands or PHB - put hands back. Please see Appendix A.3 for a full list of arm postures as used in our annotation scheme.

4.4 Analysis

The annotated corpus was analyzed comparing the two cultures, in order to get a deeper insight into culture-related differences in behavior in a statistical manner. The first scenario of the Cube-G corpus recorded the participants while getting acquainted with one another (first-time meeting). For our analysis, we focused on this scenario, since we were mainly interested in small talk conversations.

4.4.1 Verbal Aspects

For the analysis of verbal behavior, 21 German and 11 Japanese videos were annotated. Thus, all German first-time meetings were taken into account for our analysis as well as half of the Japanese conversations (annotation was not completed for the Japanese corpus), see also [ENL+11].

From our literature research, we expect that the choice of topics as well as their sequence within the dialogs should vary across the cultures. In particular, we extracted the following tendencies about culture-specific differences in small talk behavior comparing the German and Japanese cultures. On the one hand, less personal topics should occur in Japanese small talk conversations than in German ones, and on the other hand, topics are likely to be discussed in a more sequential manner in German small talk conversations than in Japanese ones.

Following Schneider [Sch88], we categorized topics occurring in the conversations into immediate, external and communication situation (see Subsection 2.2.1 for further information on the categorization). Considering our experimental setting at a university campus with students as participants, we chose to classify topics as follows:

- **Immediate situation**: Participants talk about the experimental setting, the task itself or about reasons, why they are participating in the study.

- **External situation**: The students talk about their studies, the university in general (as a supersituation for recordings at a university), friends or other people they know, or about public topics such as music or movies.

- **Communication situation**: Interlocutors focus on personal topics concerning themselves, such as their places of origin, hobbies, going out at night, personal habits or even their health.

For our analysis, we built lists of frequency data, holding the occurrences of topic categories during the conversations, and compared the two cultures or the frequencies of topic categories within each culture respectively. Please see Appendix B.1 for the complete data, containing the topic frequencies, mean values and standard derivations, observed in the small talk conversations from our video corpus.

Analyzing the distribution of topics across the cultures, we observed topics covering the immediate and external situation more often in the Japanese conversations than in the German ones, while topics covering the communication situation occurred more often in the German conversations. Comparing the choice of topic categories across Germany and Japan, we used the independent two-tailed t-test. We found significant differences for all three topic categories ($t(30) = -2.61$, $p = .014$, $r = .43$ for the immediate situation; $t(30) = -2.20$, $p = .036$, $r = .37$ for the external situation, and $t(30) = 2.201$, $p = .035$, $r = .37$ for the communication situation).

The prototypical distribution is graphically shown in Figure 4.9, using the average percentage of occurrence. This is in line with literature, since in the Japanese culture little personal information is provided during first-time meetings. In addition to our expectation (more personal topics in the German conversations), we found that topics covering the immediate situation and external situation are more common in Japanese conversations, and we gained a deeper insight in how topics are prototypically distributed in our corpus for the two cultures.

As a next step, we investigated the two cultures separately by applying the dependent two-tailed t-test.

Figure 4.9: Average distribution of topic categories during small talk conversations recorded in Germany and Japan.

In the German data, we found significant differences between the usage of topics covering the external and communication situation compared to the immediate situation (t(20) = -5.67, p < .001, r = .79 for immediate vs. external situation, and t(20) = -3.49, p = .002, r = .62 for immediate vs. communication situation). Observing the frequency data, the external and communication situation occurred equally often in the German conversations, while participants talked less about the immediate situation.

In the Japanese conversations, we found significant differences between the usage of topics covering the immediate situation and communication situation compared to the external situation (t(10) = -5.76, p < .001, r = .88 for immediate vs. external situation, and t(10) = 3.44, p = .006, r = .73 for external vs. communication situation). According to our data, Japanese participants discussed the external situation more often than topics covering the immediate and communication situation.

From our second tendency extracted from literature, we expected topics to be discussed in a more sequential manner in Western small talk conversations compared to Asian ones. In our corpus, we therefore assume that topics are reintroduced and discussed several times in Japanese conversations, whereas this behavior should not occur very frequently in German dialogs.

For our analysis, we counted the amount of topics that arise in each small talk dialog as well as the shifts between topics. If, for example, a pair of communication partners talked about their studies first, then switched to talk about soccer and then talked about a movie they had seen in the cinema, this would mean that they discussed three topics (studies, soccer, movie) and had two topic shifts between them (studies - soccer, soccer - movie). In another conversation, interlocutors might also talk about their studies in the beginning, then switch to soccer and finally come back to talk about their studies again. In our analysis, this would compute to two topics (studies, soccer) and two topic shifts between them (studies - soccer, soccer - studies). In a conversation where studies are discussed and the conversation is concluded with soccer, this would add up to two topics (studies, soccer) and one shift (studies - soccer). Thus, the same number of topics does not necessarily mean the same number of topic shifts and vice versa. In that manner, we were able to compare conversations in terms of how many topics occurred in a conversation in relation to the sequence of their occurrence or reappearance respectively.

To exemplify how topics and topic shifts can be organized within a conversation, in the following example dialogs, dialogs are summarized as they occurred in the German and Japanese corpora. In the examples, *A* indicates the actor's speech, while *P* indicates the participant's speech.

Table 4.1 contains extractions of the conversation of participant number 18 of the German video corpus. In the conversation, 8 different topics were discussed, while 11 topic shifts occurred.

Topic	Content
reason	A: And ahm, well I am ahm actually ahm well, student in Munich, and, yes, Well, I have my girlfriend here in Augsburg, and I actually visited her, but somehow she had to work and then (...)
studies actor	P: And what do you study in Munich? A: Ahm theater history. P: In which semester? (...)
origin subject	A: And you? P: Originally I come from Lindau at Lake Constance. And I moved to Augsburg eight months ago (...)
studies subject	P: Ahm, do an apprenticeship here (...) and the apprenticeship is called management assistant in event organization (...)
future plans	P: Yes, then study somewhere, preferably in Austria. A: In Austria? Why in Austria? (...) P: 27 000 citizens, that's not a huge city. A: Yes, that's right (...)
going out	P: There's one club, but, every weekend going twice to that club. A: Nyes, it doesn't get you anywhere (...)
preferred places	P: And how do you like Munich? A: Super. P: Yes? A: I totally like it. P: Not too expensive and all? (...)

future plans	P: Right, what can you actually do after it? A: Oh well, all sorts of things. Well you can work at the theater directly (...) And well of course you can go to research and stay at the university or so, don't know. P: Hm
studies actor	P: How long does the study last? How many semesters do you have to ...? A: Well from now on ahm, I two. P: Two semesters? A: Yes, until Master's degree (...)
friends	P: What does your girlfriend do? Studying here, too? A: Ahm no, she does here, she she does her apprenticeship here (...) Else it'll get difficult, if she wants to stay here (...)
preferred places	A: Vienna or so would be great. P: Yes, Vienna is, my absolute dream is to study in Vienna (...)

Table 4.1: Example dialog from German video corpus.

In contrast, Table 4.2 holds extractions from participant number 21 of the Japanese corpus. In the conversation, only six topics were discussed, while 13 shifts between the topics occurred. Please note that the examples contain the original translations and may thus not be grammatically correct.

Topic	Content
studies actor	P: What do you do? A: Well, I'm studying Science since 4 years. (...)
studies subject	P: I study Psychology in the faculty of Education, and...then (...)
studies actor	P: I'm not sure at all what are studied in your faculty (laughing). A: Aha(laughing). Well, I'm studying on the laser, of Physics. P: Oh-oh-oh, I have no idea. (...)
studies subject	A: What do you study there? P: I... study... about ???... of the clinical... Psychology. A: Un-huh, does Psychology belong to your faculty, right? (...)
studies actor	P: I cannot imagine about your faculty, from my little knowledge. A: Well, everyone is ordinary in the faculty. (...) I have an examination in this September, so I'm studying for it (...)
studies subject	P: Actually also I'll take an exam. or the master course in ??? next year..., er. A: Ah, I see. P: For it I need to prepare. (...)

studies actor	A: In my, in my faculty many people want to go to the master course, too, so there are many choices where they go (unlike to your faculty). P: Oh; A: thus generally it's not so competitive as your case. (...) I'm not good at it in the faculty.
reason	P: Ah, why do you participate in this experiment. A: Well, I have a friend in the course of Informationology, and he said to me that there will be the experiment like this and asked me to go together (...)
task	P: Well, what will be happen? A: I think so. Camera. P: It's like a TV program where such experiments are done... (laughing) (...)
reason	A: And how did you know this one? P: Ah-ah-ah, during the class the teacher nofitied us of it. (...)
task	A: ??? is this therefore an experiment about Psychology? (...) P: by the way someone talked in German, and... A: Er, I don't understand it. (...)
language skills	A: I don't even speak English. P: But in the first year. A: Ah, I've learned French a bit. P: Ah French. (...)
hobbies	P: Eh, what is your hobby? (laughing) A: Eh, well, I don't have anything I call as hobby. P: I see. A: Reading books or so. (...)

Table 4.2: Example dialog from Japanese video corpus.

In a preliminary analysis that was conducted at an earlier point in time (see [ERA11]) with the first eight videos from our video corpus, results regarding topic shifts were promising, although not statistically significant. Our analysis revealed that in both cultures the exact same number of topics was discussed. Thus, in the four German videos we found 26 topics as we did in the four Japanese videos. Regarding shifts between topics, we found 38 topic shifts in German conversations and 46 topic shifts in Japanese conversations (all videos were approximately 5 minutes long). Analyzing the more complete data set, as used for the verbal analysis during this dissertation, results are less promising. However, the tendency is still in line with our expectation, assuming that there should be more frequent topic shifts in the Japanese data set. Please see Appendix B.2 for the list of frequency data from the German and Japanese video corpus. Although results are not statistically significant, the data gives some insight into how many topics and topic shifts should be integrated into our computational model.

In our annotation, dialog utterances were coded according to a subset of the DAMSL scheme [CA97]. Please see Appendix B.3 for the list of frequency data containing the occurrences of DAMSL dialog utterances in our German and Japanese data sets along with mean values and standard derivations. Please note that the speech act "influence on future" is not further considered in our analysis, since it rarely occurred in our video corpus.

Comparing the two cultures, we found significant differences using the independent two-tailed t-test in the usage of questions ($t(30) = -2.50$, $p = .018$, $r = .42$) and answers ($t(30) = 2.32$, $p = .027$, $r = .39$). While Japanese participants asked more questions, German participants gave more answers. This could be influenced by the high- and low-context nature of the two cultures. According to Brett [Bre00], low-context cultures tend to use many question-answer pairs, whereas high-context cultures develop information from the context. Although German participants did not use more questions, there seems to be a culture-related difference in how information is exchanged.

Other interesting tendencies can be found in the occurrences of "understanding" and "agreement" utterances. While an agreement utterance indicates the speaker's point of view, an understanding utterance signals understanding without stating a point of view. Although not statistically significant, a trend can be observed in our corpus suggesting that German participants use more agreement utterances than Japanese participants ($t(30) = 1.51$, $p = .142$, $r = .27$), while Japanese participants use more understanding utterances than German participants ($t(30) = -1.65$, $p = .109$, $r = .29$). This is in line with expectations about the two cultures: giving verbal feedback without stating a personal opinion is assumed to be very common in the Japanese culture, while stating an opinion is more common in Western cultures. In particular, Ting-Toomey describes that in Japanese conversations, partners explicitly communicate that they are listening by using the utterance "hai hai", while the literal translation "yes yes" would communicate additional meaning [TT99] (see Section 2.3.2).

Hold utterances occurred more often in the Japanese conversations than in the German ones ($t(30) = -1.99$, $p = .055$, $r = .34$ using the independent two-tailed t-test). This is not surprising, since leaving decisions open is a typical behavioral pattern for members of the Japanese culture.

4.4.2 Communication Management

For the analysis of differences in communication management across Germany and Japan, we calculated the number of pauses in speech as well as overlapping speech. These behavioral aspects were not annotated explicitly in the video corpus, but calculated from the annotation of the participants' speech transliterations. Thus, we were able to analyze the same subset of videos that was analyzed regarding verbal behavior, described in the previous subsection. In that manner, the whole German video set (21 videos) and the first 11 videos from the Japanese video set were taken into account.

For the analysis of pauses in speech, we considered as a pause the parts of the conversation where none of the conversation partners spoke and took into account pauses that lasted for more than one second and two seconds respectively. In that manner, we sorted out very brief pauses that are used for breathing, for example. Please note that pauses over 2 seconds are also included in those that last for more than 1 second. Regarding overlapping speech, we considered time spans where both conversation partners spoke at the same time. Thus, pragmatics, such as using overlaps for feedback behavior, have not been taken into account yet. In order to distinguish between overlapping speech that lasts for only a very short period of time and longer overlaps, we calculated the occurrences of overlaps that last for more than half a second and less than half a second respectively. Please see Appendix B.4 for the list of frequency data from our corpus analysis, containing the communication management behaviors pauses and overlapping speech along with mean values and standard derivations.

As described in Section 2.3.2, we expect more pauses in speech in the Japanese conversations than in the German ones. Comparing the two cultures, we found more pauses in speech in the Japanese conversations. Comparing the number of pauses in speech across the two cultures, using the independent two-tailed t-test, we achieved significance for both, pauses that last for more than 1 second ($t(30)$, $p < .001$, $r = .92$) and pauses that last for more than 2 seconds ($t(30) =$, $p < .001$, $r = .85$).

In the German videos, we found on average 6.24 pauses that lasted for more than one second, and 0.52 pauses on average that lasted for more than 2 seconds. In the Japanese videos, we observed 28 pauses on average that lasted over 1 second, and 9.18 pauses that lasted for more than 2 seconds. Figure 4.10 shows the distribution of short (more than 1 second) and long pauses (more than 2 seconds) that were found on average per minute in each video.

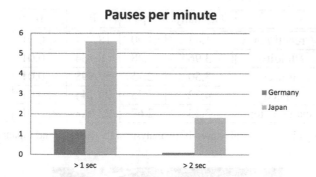

Figure 4.10: Average distribution of pauses per minute in conversations recorded in Germany and Japan.

Regarding overlapping speech, results are less obvious. In a preliminary analysis, that was conducted at an earlier point in time (see [ERA09]), after annotating the first eight German and the first eight Japanese videos from our video corpus, we found significant differences between the cultures using the independent t-test. In particular, we observed more overlaps in the Japanese conversations compared to the German ones (t(14) = -1.85, p = .043, r = .44). On average we observed 6.4 overlaps per minute in German conversations, whereas in Japanese dialogs, on average we found 9.3 overlaps per minute.

Investigating the full data set as used in this dissertation, however, we did not achieve any significant results comparing the frequency of overlaps across the two cultures. We think this might be due to the reason that in both cultures breaking in on each other's speech is considered impolite. Thus, for the analysis of communication management behavior, the semantics of speech should be taken into account as well, distinguishing overlaps that are used for turn taking in comparison to feedback behavior. In that manner, a qualitative analysis of speech should be more suited for our purpose than a simple quantitative comparison of the amount of overlaps (as investigated in the previous subsection, where speech utterances such as understanding or agreement were analyzed).

4.4.3 Nonverbal Aspects

Within the Cube-G project [RNA+09], the nonverbal behavioral aspects gestures and postures were taken into account. For the analysis of nonverbal behavior, the whole video corpus was analyzed, since transliteration and translation of the

	Germany	Japan	F	p
repetition	1.43	1.90	18.264	< 0.01
fluidity	3.96	3.48	68.434	< 0.01
power	3.50	2.75	57.998	< 0.01
speed	4.32	3.33	99.144	< 0.01
spatial extent	3.23	2.67	22.688	< 0.01

Table 4.3: Results of gestural expressivity analysis in the German and Japanese data.

Figure 4.11: Gestures with different levels of expressivity performed by a German participant (left) and a Japanese participant (right).

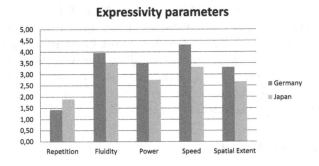

Figure 4.12: Average ratings of gestural expressivity parameters in the German and Japanese corpus.

Japanese language were not needed in this case, which constituted the major difficulty in the case of verbal behavior.

As described in Subsection 4.3.2, gestures were annotated according to their classification into McNeill's categories [McN92] and expressivity parameters [Pel05]. Regarding gesture types, our analysis revealed that the overall number of gestures per minute is comparable in both cultures. For the frequencies of McNeill's gesture types, no statistically significant differences were found in the data. However, when classifying gestures into gestures that carry meaning and adaptors, significant differences were achieved. Our analysis revealed that the Japanese video data contained significantly more adaptors than the German one. This differentiation was suggested by the video material because we observed self-touching hand movements more frequently in the Japanese corpus.

Expressivity parameters were coded on a seven-point scale. Comparing the two cultures, we found significant differences for all parameters using ANOVA. Results of this analysis are presented in Table 4.3. As expected, gestures were performed more expressively by German participants than by Japanese ones. In particular, gestures were performed faster and more powerfully in the German videos than in the Japanese ones. In addition, German participants used wider space for their gestures compared to Japanese participants who used less space. Gestures were also performed more fluently in the German conversations, but the stroke of a gesture was repeated more in the Japanese conversations. Figure 4.11 exemplifies this phenomenon. The gesture performed by the German participant (left) was conducted powerfully and with a wide spatial extent, while the gesture performed by the Japanese participant (right) needs little space and is performed rather slowly. Figure 4.12 graphically shows the average ratings of the expressivity parameters in the two target cultures.

For the analysis of postures, the corpus was annotated according to Bull's coding scheme [Bul87], taking into account arm postures. As outlined by Rehm and colleagues [RNKWT12], putting hands into the pocket occurred most frequently in the German data (40.6%), followed by folding arms (18.9%), putting a hand on the elbow (13.9%), and putting hands behind the back (6.8%). In the Japanese data set, joining the hands occured most frequently (29.6%), followed by putting the hands to the face (20.9%), putting hands behind the back (14.8%) and putting a hand to the wrist (12.2%).

category	Germany	Japan
self-touch	PHIPt (put hands to pocket)	PHFe (put hand to face)
one-handed	PHEw (put hand to elbow)	PHWr (put hand to wrist)
two-handed	FAs (fold arms)	JHs (join hands)
hidden	PHB (put hands back)	

Table 4.4: Posture types frequently observed in the German and Japanese corpus.

Figure 4.13: Prototypical body postures identified from the corpus for a German cultural background.

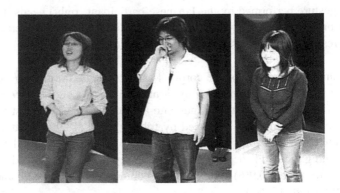

Figure 4.14: Prototypical body postures identified from the corpus for a Japanese cultural background.

Table 4.4 summarizes the arm postures frequently observed in our video corpus along with a possible categorization. Interestingly, for the first three categories, postures that regularly occurred in one culture barely occurred in the other culture. The only example constitutes putting the hands behind the back, which was observed in both cultures. However, it was not covered by the coding schema how the hands are put together behind the back, as provided for body postures that happen with the hands in front of the body.

Taking into account the data from Table 4.4, we consider the self-touching postures as well as one- or two-handed postures best suited to demonstrate culture-related differences. Figure 4.13 and 4.14 exemplify these prototypical body postures with German and Japanese participants form the video corpus.

4.4.4 Correlation of Verbal and Nonverbal Behavior

For the generation of culture-specific behaviors for virtual characters, the co-occurrence of verbal and nonverbal behavior is another interesting aspect. Thus, in this subsection we have a look at how gesture types accompanied dialog acts in our video corpus (see also [EDH+10]). Since we focus on communicative behaviors during dialogs in this dissertation, adaptors are not considered in the analysis, since they are not meant to support the semantics of speech. Emblems are not considered either, since we concentrate on gestures that are of a general nature and can be used in several different conversations. The reason for this exclusion was also that we did not find many emblems in our video corpus and can therefore not draw meaningful conclusions. This is in line with observations done by Martin and colleagues [MAD+05] who state that they found only few emblems in their video corpus.

For the analysis of verbal and corresponding nonverbal behavior, all 21 German videos were taken into account and a subset of 7 Japanese videos, where annotation was available for both, verbal and nonverbal behavior. Previously, behaviors were observed in isolation for dialog utterances (see Subsection 4.3.1) and gesture types (see Subsection 4.3.2).

To analyze the correlation of the behavioral aspects, lists of frequency data were built and the independent two-tailed t-test was applied to compare the cultures. During the dialog-utterances "hold" and "influence on future" rarely any gestures occurred and were thus not further investigated. Table 4.5 shows the probabilities that a gesture is performed during a given utterance.

gesture co-occurrence	Germany	Japan
info-request	**5%**	**11%**
answer	10%	10%
statement	24%	15%
agreement/ disagreement	2%	4%
understanding/ misunderstanding	0%	0%

Table 4.5: Average probabilities that a gesture occurs during a given utterance in German and Japanese conversations.

Germany	beat	deictic	iconic	metaphoric
info-request	0%	**67%**	**33%**	0%
answer	25%	25%	21%	29%
statement	27%	17%	27%	29%
agreement/disagreement	50%	50%	0%	0%
Japan	beat	deictic	iconic	metaphoric
info-request	0%	**75%**	0%	**25%**
answer	25%	12.5%	37.5%	25%
statement	16%	26%	35%	23%
agreement/disagreement	0%	100%	0%	0%

Table 4.6: Probabilities of gesture types occurring during a given utterance in the German and Japanese data sets.

The analysis of verbal behavior revealed that there are significant differences in the occurrence of info-requests in the Japanese videos compared to the German ones. Interestingly, observing the correlation of verbal and nonverbal behavior, this dialog utterance was the only one where we observed strong trends. In particular, we found more gestures in the Japanese conversation compared to the Germany ones ($t(26) = -1.86$, $p = .075$, $r = .34$).

After investigating the probabilities that a gesture occurs during a speech act, we further explored the type of gesture in correlation to dialog utterances. Table 4.6 shows the probabilities for a gesture type during an utterance, given that a gesture occurs. Again our analysis revealed meaningful results only for info-requests. We found significant differences in the usage of deictic (t(26) = -1.83, p = .079, r = .34) and metaphoric gestures (t(26) = -2.79, p = .010, r = .48) that occur during info-requests. According to our data, Japanese participants showed more deictic and metaphoric gestures during info-requests than German participants.

4.5 Summary

In this chapter, we applied the method of annotating and analyzing a multimodal corpus to extract statistical data and behavioral tendencies that can be used to build behavioral models for virtual characters. This method is very helpful, since theories described in literature are a good guideline that can inspire the simulation of behaviors but are mostly too abstract for the implementation of a computational model. The approach has successfully been used to individualize virtual character behavior (see Section 4.1) and seems to be very well suited for the integration of cultural background as well.

This dissertation was developed within the Cube-G project [Aug09] that recorded a video corpus in the German and Japanese cultures. For empirical verification, the corpus was analyzed regarding the aspects of behavior that were pointed out as being relevant for our purpose in Section 2.2. In particular, aspects within the following categories were investigated: (1) verbal behavior, (2) communication management and (3) nonverbal behavior.

For the annotation of verbal behavior, speech was transcribed and translated for both interlocutors. In addition, speech acts were labeled according to a subset of the DAMSL coding scheme [CA97], distinguishing dialog utterances such as question, answer or agreement. Regarding the content of the dialogs, topics that occurred during the conversation were annotated and classified into topics that cover the immediate, external or communication situation [Sch88]. Communication management behaviors, in particular the usage of pauses in speech and overlapping speech, were not annotated explicitly but computed from the annotated speech tracks.

For the annotation of nonverbal behaviors, gestures and postures were taken into account. Gesture types were labeled according to McNeill's gesture classification [McN92], distinguishing types such as deictic, beat or iconic gestures. In addition, gestures were annotated taking into account their dynamic variation. To this end, expressivity parameters [HMP06] such as speed, spatial extent or fluidity were coded. For the annotation of postures, Bull's coding scheme [Bul87] was employed investigating arm postures such as PHWr (put hands on wrist) or PHB (put hands back).

Analyzing verbal behavior across the two cultures, we found significant differences in the choice of topics that are discussed during the small talk conversations. In particular, we found that topics covering the immediate and external situation occurred more often in the Japanese conversations than in the German ones, while topics covering the communication situation occurred more often in the German conversations. This is in line with literature, where members of the Japanese culture are described as having a lower public self and tend to not reveal too much information during first-time meetings.

Comparing the occurrence of speech acts across the two cultures, significant differences were found in the usage of questions and answers. In addition, we found differences in the usage of agreement and understanding utterances by trend. While Japanese participants used more understanding utterances, German participants used more agreement utterances. This in in line with literature, since giving verbal listening feedback is a common behavioral pattern in the Japanese culture, while stating an opinion is more common in Western cultures.

For the analysis of communication management behaviors, pauses in speech as well as overlaps in speech were calculated. In that manner, either time spans where none of the interlocutors spoke or both talked at the same time were considered. In line with literature, we found significantly more pauses in speech in the Japanese conversations compared to the German ones.

Regarding overlapping speech, we did not achieve any significant results comparing the frequencies across the two cultures. Pragmatics, such as using overlaps for feedback behavior, were not taken into account in this analysis. However, the analysis of speech utterances in the analysis of verbal behavior suggests that culture-related differences can be found by investigating the quality of speech, instead of the pure quantity of overlaps.

Comparing gesture types across the two cultures, significantly more adaptors were found in the Japanese data set, distinguishing gestures that carry meaning and adaptors. Regarding gestural expressivity, we found significant differences for all parameters comparing the two cultures. Gestures were performed faster, more powerfully, with a wider space, more fluently, but with a lower rate of repeated strokes in the German videos than in the Japanese ones.

The analysis of postures gave interesting insights into posture types that commonly occur in the two cultures. Interestingly, postures that occurred regularly in one culture, rarely occurred in the other one.

Finally, the correlation of gestures and speech acts was investigated. Therefore, the occurrence of gestures during a given speech act, as well as the most probable gesture type during an utterance was analyzed.

In this chapter, findings from literature were grounded into empirical data. With it, additional insights were obtained that are useful for the integration into the behavioral models of virtual characters. The resulting statistical information, such as common topic distribution, prototypical gesture performance or choice of body posture, extend the descriptions from literature and can be used additionally for the integration into a computational model.

5 Conceptual Design and Technical Realization

In this dissertation, culture-related behaviors are integrated into the behavioral models of virtual characters. The conceptual design and technical realization carried out for this purpose are further described in this chapter.

Integrating culture into the behavioral models of virtual characters is a challenging task. Starting from the classical distinction between "what to say" and "how to say it" in natural language generation (see, for example, the survey given by Bateman and Zock [BZ03]), we need to adapt not only the content of a character's utterances to a particular culture, but also their form. For example, a character might choose different topics in small talk and use different communication management behaviors, e.g. to indicate politeness depending on the culture it represents. Plan-based approaches have been taken successfully to parametrize personality traits for virtual character dialogs by André and colleagues [AKG+00]. Following their approach, we use a plan-based system for the integration of different cultural backgrounds in small talk dialogs.

In a similar manner, a character's nonverbal behavior needs to be adapted to match different cultural backgrounds, although the impact on people's perception may be a lot more subtle. For example, a character might vary the number and quality of gestures depending on its assumed cultural background. For the modeling of culture-specific nonverbal behavior, a Bayesian network approach was chosen which is very well suited for this purpose as we have to deal with uncertain knowledge in this domain. This approach has already been taken successfully by Bergman and Kopp [BK09] for the generation of iconic gestures to express spatial information considering individual patterns of gesture formulation. We therefore consider this approach as equally well suited for the generation of nonverbal behaviors with different cultural patterns.

The aim of this dissertation is to model different culture-related aspects of behavior. Thus, instead of addressing which technique might be best suited for our aim, we follow approaches that already successfully implemented solutions to similar problems in an intuitive manner.

This chapter is structured as follows: In the first section, we present a detailed overview of the workflow that was carried out in the course of this dissertation. Subsequently, we introduce the general approach by describing the technical background utilized along with related work that successfully used the concepts to generate parametrized behavior for virtual characters. Then, the modeling of culture-related differences for several aspects of behavior is investigated for the German and Japanese cultures using the introduced concepts. Finally a demonstrator is presented that exemplifies culture-specific dialog behavior in a virtual environment.

5.1 Procedure

The approach taken in this dissertation combines the two approaches usually taken to integrate social aspects into the behavioral models of virtual characters: the bottom-up and top-down approaches.

For the top-down approach, definitions of culture and in particular, descriptions of culture-related differences in behavior are extracted from literature and integrated into the behavior of virtual characters. Thus, it is a model-driven approach where schemes which have already been established in the social sciences are transformed into a computational model that simulates stereotypical behavior. A system taking that approach and aiming at simulating national cultures is the Tactical Language Training System (TLTS), described by Johnson and colleagues [JMV04]. The focus of the system lies on gaining skills in verbal communication, while gestures can be performed by the avatar to support language (see Section 3.2 for a description of the system). A very different top-down approach, compared to TLTS, has been taken by Mascarenhas and colleagues [MDA+09]. Instead of simulating existing national cultures, fantasy cultures are presented that are designed using a dimensional model of culture as well as the concept of synthetic cultures (see Section 2). In their work, the authors focus on the use of rituals to generate cultural-specific behavior for virtual agents (see Section 3.2 for a description of their system).

In contrast, the bottom-up approach is data-driven. Therefore, a corpus of human behavior is recorded and analyzed. Statistical findings extracted from the corpus are then simulated with virtual characters. As stated in Chapter 4, this approach has been used successfully to integrate human factors but has not been applied to culture so far. The system presented by Kipp and colleagues [KNKA07], for example, aims at more natural behavior for virtual characters by generating nonverbal behavior in the style of a particular speaker based on a multimodal annotated corpora.

As stated above, the approach taken in this dissertation, combines the top-down and bottom-up approaches. Behavioral differences described in literature are helpful to understand culture-related differences and are a good guideline to model behavior. For the implementation of computational models, however, they are sometimes too abstract and do not provide enough data to design the differences. By analyzing a video corpus that holds information on the target behavior, a statistical description or the extracted tendencies are gained. Thus, in the combined approach, the social sciences teach us which behavioral aspects could be of interest when building a model that describes culture-specific behavior, while we learn from the empirical data how differences in these aspects manifest themselves in a concrete manner.

For the approach taken in this dissertation, the tasks of the workflow shown in Figure 5.1 were carried out and exemplified for the two cultures of Germany and Japan.

As a first step, research literature from the social sciences was reviewed regarding definitions of culture and stereotypical behavior. In addition, literature that addresses human behavior was reviewed to select a set of aspects to be further investigated for our purposes. Based on these findings, cultural profiles and expectations concerning behavioral differences were created for the two cultures of Germany and Japan (see Chapter 2).

Findings from the first step constitute the basis for our second step, the empirical corpus study, where expectations concerning behavior differences are grounded into empirical data. Therefore, a video corpus has been recorded in the two target cultures, annotated and analyzed taking into account the hypotheses that have been extracted from literature (see Chapter 4).

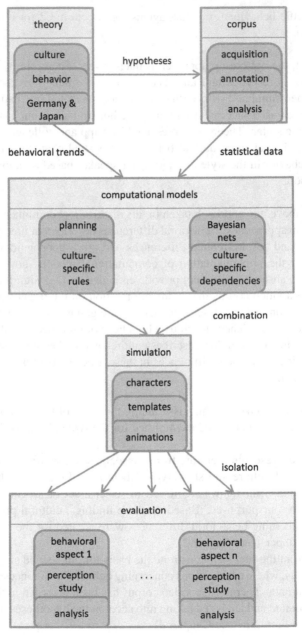

Figure 5.1: Approach of this dissertation, including the steps that were carried out.

Results from the literature study as well as the statistical data from the corpus analysis serve as an input to build computational models of culture-related behaviors. Therefore, appropriate AI techniques were selected and methods to select stereotypical behavior were modeled to exemplify differences for the German and Japanese cultures. Generated culture-specific behavior was then simulated in a demonstrator that holds culturally different virtual characters, as well as knowledge bases that hold appropriate verbal and nonverbal behaviors for the agents. The conceptual design and technical realization is presented in this chapter.

The last step carried out in this dissertation consists of an evaluation of the realized aspects of behavior. To verify which of the aspects have an impact on human observers, the aspects were evaluated in isolation. Thus, different studies were designed to satisfy the target aspect. For each aspect, we investigated whether human observers prefer agent behavior that was designed to resemble their own cultural background. Thus, different versions of the studies were realized for Germany and Japan (see Chapter 6).

Findings from the evaluation studies hold great potential to refine the behavioral models of culture-related behaviors, as suggested by Cassell [Cas07]. For this dissertation, however, the steps described above are executed only once. A refinement based on the results of the corpus analysis is nevertheless planned for our future work.

5.2 General Approach

There are several possible approaches to determine the behavior of virtual characters, such as plan-based approaches or the usage of finite state machines. Many topical discussions argue which of the approaches is best suited for the implementation of virtual character behavior and conversational behavior in particular. Since the aim of this dissertation is to model different culture-related aspects behavior for virtual characters, and not to identify the most appropriate approach for it (if that is possible after all), we do not provide a discussion on the suitability of the technical background that is used for our purpose. Instead, we follow approaches that already successfully implemented solutions to similar problems in an intuitive manner.

According to Rist and colleagues [RAB03a], AI-based approaches, and plan-based approaches in particular, are becoming more and more popular to control the behavior of synthetic characters. André and colleagues [AKG+00] introduce an early approach of a plan-based system that simulates differences in personality traits for virtual character dialogs. Inspired by their work, we use a plan-based approach, too, for the generation of culture-specific conversational behavior. Since language is the main channel in human communication, we consider it a good starting point for our behavior generation.

Regarding nonverbal behavior, Bayesian networks have been used successfully to implement individual patterns of gesture formulation, e.g. by Bergman and Kopp [BK09]. Taking a Bayesian network approach is very well suited for our purpose as well since we have to deal with uncertain knowledge in the domain of culture-related behavior.

In the following subsections, we introduce these two techniques along with related work that successfully used the concepts to generate parametrized behavior for virtual characters, while the transfer to modeling culture-related differences for the German and Japanese cultural backgrounds is introduced in the subsequent section.

5.2.1 Behavior Planning

An early approach that used planning to generate behavior for virtual characters was presented by André and colleagues [AKG+00]. In their work, the authors describe a virtual market place in which seller agents provide product information to potential buyer agents which use different strategies for selling or buying a car. The underlying platform provides several agent components, each containing a behavior planner that controls the performance in the interactive conversation in a highly dynamic way. The characters' behavior is determined by several attributes such as interests, attitudes or personality traits, which can be specified for each character individually. In their demonstrator, the agents' behaviors vary with their personal settings which e.g. results in focusing different features of the car or using different dialog acts. With their system, the authors successfully exemplified the integration of personal backgrounds into the behavior planning of virtual characters.

Parameterizing virtual character behavior for different personality traits is very much related to our aim of generating culture-related behaviors. In [AKG+00], André and colleagues dealt with similar problems as the ones that have to be solved for our purpose and provided solutions that can be transfered to the integration of cultural background in an intuitive manner. For these reasons, we follow up their approach and apply a plan-based approach for the generation of culture-related dialogs in this dissertation.

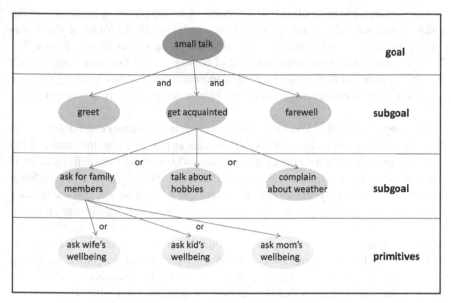

Figure 5.2: Example for plan decomposition in a dialog.

For planning, a complex goal is decomposed into smaller subgoals and finally into a stream of actions that can be performed to solve a given task. Classical planning problems include finding solutions to logistic problems or mathematical games using building blocks such as the towers of Hanoi. Using a planning system for the generation of speech is not an obvious solution at first sight. Regarding speech from a linguistic viewpoint, however, where speaking is considered as a way of acting, the correlation to planning problems becomes more clear. Therefore, speech is considered a concept where action strategies are applied and sequences are constructed. Therefore, we consider planning as well suited for the generation of dialog behavior for virtual characters.

In classical HTN (Hierarchical Task Network) planning, the planning system starts with an initial state-of-the-world and with the objective to create a plan to perform a set of tasks. Therefore, the concept of problem reduction is applied and the planner recursively decomposes tasks into subtasks. This reduction reaches an end, when a primitive task can be performed by the planning operators. For the decomposition of non-primitive tasks into subtasks, methods need to be provided that hold information on how to decompose a certain task into subtasks.

This concept can be applied to the domain of dialog planning by decomposing a dialog into subdialogs and speech acts respectively. To demonstrate this transfer, we present an abstraction of a possible dialog decomposition in Figure 5.2. In the example, the communicative goal of having a small talk conversation with someone can be fulfilled by performing a sequence of subgoals: greeting the conversation partner, getting acquainted with him or her, and finally saying goodbye.

The subgoal of getting acquainted with a conversation partner can further be fulfilled by conducting one of several subgoals such as talking about the family of the interlocutor of complaining about the weather. Which of the steps will be taken is determined by the methods of the planning domain. For example, a precondition for talking about family members of the interlocutor could be e.g. that the speaker is familiar with the interlocutor and knows about his or her family situation (see Figure 5.2). If the preconditions described above are not valid, the speaker needs to take another approach such as talking about his or her own interests. If the precondition is fulfilled, a primitive can be selected such as asking for the wellbeing of the interlocutor's wife. Again, a precondition for this primitive could be the fact that the speaker knows that the interlocutor actually has a wife. The primitive can then finally be executed by the target planning operator. The example demonstrated how, depending on character-specific attributes, the selection of planning steps to achieve a goal can be varied and with it the sequence and choice of actions performed.

As mentioned above, this approach has already been successfully applied for the generation of dialogs with personality as a parameter by André and colleagues [AKG+00]. In a similar manner, we aim at taking the approach to parametrize culture-specific behavior.

A later approach by Avradinis and Aylett [AA03] presents a system where the agents' behavior is driven by a planning system based on the agents' motivation and emotion. Unlike other approaches, in their system the characters' goals and motivations are not necessarily initial and can emerge or increase over time. Therefore, SHOP [NMAC+01], a forward chaining HTN planner, was adapted to integrate continuous operations and handle timing.

The SHOP planner has been chosen as a basis since it allows partial planning due to its hierarchical nature and has proven to be efficient. To match the needs of continuous planning, it has been combined with the MACTA-planner [AAG00], a non-hierarchical continuous agent-based planner, in order to produce a HTN-based, continuous generative planning system.

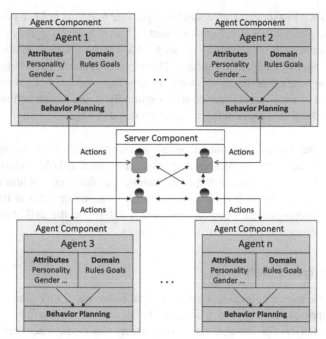

Figure 5.3: Overview of distributed system architecture for verbal behavior generation.

Similarly, for the implementation of our system, we use the JSHOP2 planner [Uni], a Java version of the Simple Hierarchical Ordered Planner SHOP [NCLMA99], and slightly adapted it for our needs. The planner meets our requirements in a very satisfying manner as it is completely domain-independent. In addition to classical HTN planners, the SHOP planner provides so-called function calls that allow an easy communication with external components such as virtual environments. In addition, the SHOP planner provides the use of axioms. These axioms are very well suited for our purposes since they can be used to e.g. model decisions such as distinguishing whether an action is considered appropriate in a culture or not.

The software was modified for our needs, since we wanted to create a distributed system to simulate autonomous virtual agents, each planning their own behavior, which are able to cope with several communication partners interacting on different threads at runtime. Figure 5.3 shows the architecture of this distributed version. An arbitrary number of agents can be logged in and communicate with each other via a server that administrates the agents. The system is thus realized in a server-client architecture. The server component holds common data such as the verbal knowledge base and is in charge of handling the communication between the agents by sending notifications of performed actions. Each of the clients contains their own instance of the hierarchical planner and thus holds its own domain knowledge, attributes and behavioral rules. In that manner, agents are realized in an autonomous way. Incoming messages have to be added dynamically to the knowledge base of an agent at runtime. Therefore, a dynamic knowledge base was added to the original planning software. During the process of behavior planning, the planners of each agent thus decide individually if and which action should be triggered, taking into account the updated knowledge base.

Initially, each behavior planner expects a *planning problem* containing the state-of-the-world and goals, as well as a *planning domain* that holds behavioral rules and executable actions. In our implementation, the planning problem defines the agents' profiles along with their attributes such as name or cultural background, while the planning domain contains rules that determine the dialog sequence as well as operators that represent dialog utterances.

5.2.2 Bayesian Networks

For the modeling of culture-specific nonverbal behavior, a Bayesian network approach is applied. This approach has already been taken successfully by Bergman and Kopp [BK09] for the generation of gestures taking into account individual patterns of gesture formulation. In particular, in their system iconic gestures are generated to express spatial information for landmark descriptions. Therefore, a corpus was recorded containing landmark descriptions of human participants. After annotating and analyzing the corpus for their purposes, a prototype that performs iconic gestures was developed with a virtual character.

For behavior generation, a Bayesian decision network was employed that considers both general behavior patterns as well as individual patterns of gesture formulation, since, according to the authors, the performance of gestures varies across speakers. We therefore consider this approach as equally well suited for the generation of nonverbal behaviors with different cultural patterns and aim at employing Bayesian networks to generate nonverbal behaviors for speakers of different cultural backgrounds.

Bayesian networks are described as a formalism to represent probabilistic causal interactions by Jensen [Jen01]. They are a probabilistic graphical model that represents variables and their conditional dependencies in a directed acyclic graph. A classical example of an Bayesian network is a model that represents the probabilistic relationships between diseases and symptoms. The network model can be used in both directions and can thus either calculate probabilities for a set of symptoms

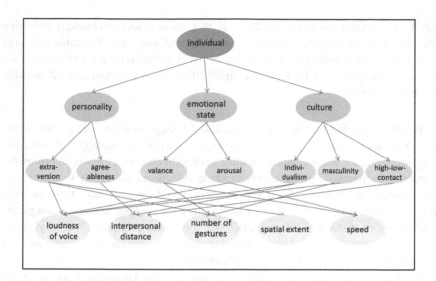

Figure 5.4: Bayesian network exemplifying the dependencies between personal and social factors and nonverbal behavior.

for a given disease, or compute the probabilities of the presence of various diseases for given symptoms.

In a similar manner, Bayesian networks can be employed to model the dependencies of the social background of a person and observed behavior in an intuitive way. To demonstrate this transfer, we present an abstraction of possible dependencies between human factors and nonverbal behavior in Figure 5.4. The model exemplifies how the influence of personality, emotional state or cultural background on nonverbal behavior could be modeled using a Bayesian network. The links in the network represent the coherence between causes and effects. In our example, a high degree in the extroversion dimension of the personality of a character could, for example, result in a louder voice, more frequent gesture use and more expressive behavior in terms of the speed of the gesture. Vice versa, from observed behavior, probable cultural background or emotional state can be calculated and allow a diagnostic inference on a given set of individuals.

As exemplified in Figure 5.4, different aspects can influence a person's nonverbal behavior. While some of these aspects have already been modeled using Bayesian networks such as emotions, e.g. by Ball [Bal02], or personal differences, e.g. by Bergmann and Kopp [BK09], the integration of cultural background using this approach has not been considered so far. In related work, Bayesian networks have been used in both directions, to either generate behavior for a virtual character (causal inference) [BK09], or to estimate the user's emotional state (diagnostic inference) [Bal02].

We think that for the integration of cultural background into the nonverbal behavior models of virtual characters, Bayesian networks are equally well suited as they are for other human factors. Culture-related behavior is a non-deterministic concept. Individuals belonging to the same culture do not all show exactly the same behavior. In a simulated system, this would be very unrealistic as well. Bayesian networks cope well with uncertainty by making assertions about the probability of different performances. To cope with this issue, we may represent the systems uncertain beliefs, for example, by a probability distribution over different levels of a particular aspect of behavior.

By using a Bayesian network approach, culture-related behavior can be modeled in a rather intuitive manner. Dimensional models as described in Subsection 2.1.2 seem especially well suited for this approach, since the dimensions can simply be represented by different nodes in the network. Mappings from dimensions to stereotypical behavior can be modeled by the transitions to different aspects of nonverbal behavior.

Tendencies described in literature and verified by our corpus can be further used to formulate the relations of cultural background and nonverbal behaviors.

5.3 Modeling Culture-related Differences

In the previous section, the technical background was introduced that is used in this dissertation for the integration of cultural background into the behavior models of virtual characters. Other human backgrounds such as personality have been considered before using these AI techniques.

In this section, the integration of culture into the verbal and nonverbal behavior models of virtual characters is exemplified for the German and Japanese cultures taking into account our findings from literature and the corpus study described in Chapters 2 and 4. As stated earlier, for the implementation of verbal behavior, a plan-based approach was chosen, while for nonverbal behavior a Bayesian network was employed.

5.3.1 Small Talk and Topic Selection

For the simulation of virtual character dialogs, the distributed planning system introduced in Subsection 5.2.1 is used. To generate small talk dialogs for different cultural backgrounds, the underlying planning component needs to be enculturated. Thus, our approach goes beyond traditional natural language generation by adding a cultural component. In this dissertation, culture-related differences in small talk are exemplified for the German and Japanese cultures. Therefore, behavioral tendencies extracted from literature and verified by our video corpus are implemented. In particular, we summarized the following tendencies:

- **Tendency 1**: In Japanese dialogs less personal topics occur than in German ones.

- **Tendency 2**: Topics are discussed in a more sequential manner in German dialogs compared to Japanese ones.

To integrate these tendencies into the behavioral models of virtual agents, culture-specific knowledge and rules are created that determine appropriate topics as well as the preferred sequential flow of conversation for each agent and culture.

For realization of the first tendency, topics were categorized according to our findings from the literature review and corpus study. In that manner, each topic was tagged to either cover the immediate situation, external situation, or communication situation (see Section 2.2.1).

In addition, in each agent's knowledge base a personal motivation is provided for each of the topics. This motivation represents the agent's internal drive to talk about the particular topic, e.g. because of an increased personal interest in the topic or a general desire to talk a lot.

To distinguish cultures, thresholds were added to the knowledge bases that arise from cultural background and topic category. These culture-specific thresholds are based on our observations from the corpus study that were in line with our initial expectations derived from literature (see Figure 4.9).

Please see Appendix C.1 for an initial knowledge base of a character, holding its personal background and interests, categorized topics and culture-specific thresholds exemplified for Germany and Japan.

Following the results from our corpus analysis, the German threshold for the immediate situation is rather high, compared to the other categories, since this category is the least common for prototypical German conversations. Thresholds for topics covering the external or communication situation are equally high, as observed in our corpus data.

For the Japanese culture, the threshold for topics covering the communication situation is highest, since it was least observed in our video data, followed by the immediate situation. Topics covering the external situation were observed frequently in the Japanese data, thus, the threshold is rather low.

Dependent on the values in the knowledge base, topics are selected differently. In particular, a higher personal motivation increases an agent's interest to talk about the particular topic, while a higher threshold means that the category of the topic is more difficult to be addressed.

For the process of topic selection, an atom was added to the behavioral rule set of each agent that determines whether a topic is appropriate to be introduced, based on the cultural background of the character (see Appendix C.1). Only if the topic is considered appropriate, it is going to be introduced by the target agent.

In the implementation, a topic is considered appropriate if the agent's personal motivation is higher than the culture-specific threshold for the category of the topic. In that manner, every topic might, in principle, be introduced by every agent, as it is possible to talk about every topic in both cultures. However, as a result from the rules of the planner, it is less likely that a topic is selected by an agent that is not common in its cultural background. In particular, only if the character's motivation for a certain topic is very high for any reason, it might address the topic although it is not common for the agent's simulated culture.

The example knowledge base from Appendix C.1 holds a character with a German cultural background and moderate motivations for one topic of each category. According to the rules of the planner, the agent would talk about movies (external situation) and its job (communication situation) during a first-time meeting but not about the weather (immediate situation).

By changing its cultural background to Japanese and leaving its personal motivations consistent, however, the agent would choose to talk about the weather (immediate situation) and movies (external situation). In that manner, the private topic is avoided for the simulated Japanese cultural background as it is considered inappropriate. Only if the agent's personal interest in that topic would be very high, the topic would nevertheless be introduced.

By using the findings from our corpus study for the design of culture-related thresholds, generated dialogs have a similar topic distribution as the small talk conversations recorded in the target cultures and thus resemble prototypical first-time meetings from the corpus. By changing the thresholds, however, other dialog situations could be simulated.

According to the second tendency described above, topics are discussed in a more sequential manner in German dialogs compared to Japanese ones, where switching back and forth between topics is more common.

For the implementation of the tendency, we took as a basis the prototypical small talk sequence described by Schneider [Sch88] (see Subsection 2.2.1). To this end, for each topic four dialog acts were created: (1) question, (2) answer, (3) reverse-question and (4) reverse-answer.

To determine the sequence of a conversation, another culture-specific threshold was added to the knowledge base of each character (see Appendix C.1). The threshold defines how difficult it is in a given culture to drop a topic and thus interrupt the sequence by introducing a different topic. To simulate the tendency, the threshold is set higher for the Japanese culture, compared to the German one. In that manner, according to the cultural thresholds, the sequence is rather followed by a simulated German cultural background, while it is more likely that the sequence is interrupted by a character with a simulated Japanese cultural background.

In particular, following the sequence means, in our implementation, to perform all four dialog acts for a given topic, while interrupting the sequence means to perform only the first two steps of the sequence and to introduce a different topic instead of asking a reverse-question. Therefore, another atom was added to the planning component of each character, determining whether a topic is completed sequentially or not.

According to the atom (see Appendix C.1), a topic is processed sequentially by an agent if its personal interest in the topic is higher than the culture-related threshold. Thus, an agent with a simulated German cultural background will stick to the prototypical sequence even if its personal motivation for the topic is rather low, while a character with a simulated Japanese cultural background interrupts the sequence more easily.

The German agent from the example knowledge base in Appendix C.1 keeps talking about the weather in case that topic was introduced by its interlocutor, since its personal motivation for the topic is higher than the threshold for the German culture. In that manner, it follows the sequence and asks a reverse question although its personal motivation for the topic is only on a medium level.

Changing the character's culture to Japanese and leaving its motivations constant, however, affects that choice. In this case, the agent interrupts the sequence, since a higher personal motivation for the target topic would be needed for a

Japanese character to follow it. Instead of asking a reverse question, the character introduces a different topic. Which topic the character chooses to introduce is, vice versa, dependent on the first tendency as described above.

In the current implementation, interrupted topics can be revisited at a later point in time by the agent that chose to introduce a different topic in the first place. In case no other topic is available that is wished to be introduced, the remaining two actions of the interrupted topic are performed. An autonomous resumption of a topic by the agent that introduced it initially is thus not addressed in this dissertation, but constitutes an interesting task for our future work.

So far only the small talk sequence introduced by Schneider [Sch88] was exemplified to simulate prototypical German or Japanese cultural backgrounds. However, other sequences can be addressed using the approach.

5.3.2 Nonverbal Behavior

Regarding the process of nonverbal behavior selection, culture can manifest itself at different levels of the generation process. Culture does not only determine what we communicate but also how we communicate it. In that manner, not only different nonverbal behaviors need to be designed for the virtual characters but also methods to perform nonverbal behaviors in a culture-specific manner. In our combined approach, taking into account theories from the social sciences as well as a video corpus recorded in Germany and Japan, on the one hand we identified aspects that can be used to perform nonverbal behaviors in a culture-specific way, and on the other hand extracted nonverbal behaviors from the video corpus that are prototypical for the two cultural backgrounds.

For the former, animations of a general nature were created which can be performed showing different levels of expressivity. For the latter, corpus-based animations were modeled to resemble gestures or body postures from the video corpus. The realization of these different approaches is described in the subsequent paragraphs.

5.3.2.1 Culture-Specific Adaptation

Gestures can be performed differently by members of different cultural backgrounds. How a gesture is performed is sometimes more crucial for the perception of the observer than the choice of gesture itself.

As described in Section 5.2.2, we employ a Bayesian network to calculate the level of expressivity for nonverbal behaviors for a given cultural background.

As a first step, a Bayesian network is exemplified for Hofstede's dimensional model (see Subsection 2.1.2). Dimensional models are very well suited for this purpose, since the dimensions can simply be represented by different nodes in the network. Using Hofstede's model, clear mappings are available from existing national cultures such as Germany and Japan to the cultural dimensions [HHM10], as well as descriptions of how these dimensions influence the behavior of the members of a culture [HPH02].

Regarding nonverbal behavior, we focus on interpersonal distance, loudness of voice and expressivity, since these aspects were of special interest for the Cube-G project [RAN$^+$07]. Differences in the dynamic variation of a gesture can be described along the expressivity parameters (see Subsection 2.2.3). For our approach, the parameters power, speed, spatial extent and overall activity are employed. However, these aspects serve as examples and other behaviors can be integrated using this approach as well.

Figure 5.5 shows our Bayesian network that describes the dependencies of cultural background and nonverbal behavior, using Hofstede's dimensional model [HHM10]. The network was implemented using the GeNie modeling environment [Dec07]. We modeled it top-down, from national cultures to the dimensions of culture, and from the dimensions to the aspects of nonverbal behaviors that are influenced.

For the first layer of the network, Hofstede's scores [HHM10] of the target cultures on each dimension are used. To determine the probabilities of the Bayesian network, the scores on the dimensions were classified into three discrete values (low, medium, high). For example, Japan scores very high on the masculinity dimension (with 95 out of 100). Thus, the probability for a high value on this dimension is very high in the network, too (0.95), while the probabilities for a medium or low score are low (0.04 for medium, and 0.01 for low).

For the second layer, synthetic cultures are used as a basis, since they help understand the correlation of the cultural dimensions to prototypical behavior, while behavioral tendencies are provided by Hofstede and colleagues [HPH02] for each dimension separately. In the following, the relations between the cultural dimensions and nonverbal behaviors extracted from [HPH02] are further described.

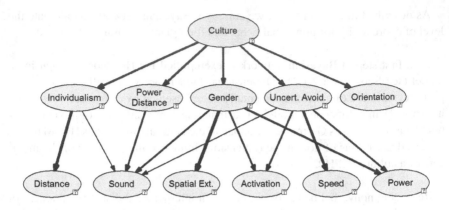

Figure 5.5: Bayesian network exemplifying the dependencies of cultural background and nonverbal behavior using Hofstede's model.

Individualistic cultures are described as being verbal and likely to stand out visually when in groups. Vice versa, collectivistic cultures can be very silent and are physically very close with in-groups. Taking these tendencies into account, we draw a connection between the individualism dimension and the nonverbal behavior clues distance and sound. Thus, with increasing individualism the physical distance between individuals and the loudness of the voice increase.

As the individualism dimension (IDV) is the only dimension that has a direct impact on the interpersonal distance between communication partners (see Figure 5.5), the dependencies in the Bayesian network are rather simple (see Table 5.1). As mentioned above, according to Hofstede's synthetic cultures, individualistic cultures tend to stand free in groups, whereas members of collectivistic cultures have a close physical distance, especially to in-groups. Thus, in our network, the distance increases with increasing individualism. With a low score on the individualistic dimension, the probability for low distance is high (0.8), for a medium distance much smaller (0.19) and for a high distance almost non existent (0.01). In a culture scoring medium on the individualistic dimension, the most probable distance is medium (0.6), whereas the probabilities for high or low distances are equally distributed (0.2). Vice versa, in individualistic cultures with a high score on the individualistic dimension, the most probable distance is high (0.8), followed by a medium distance (0.19), while the probability for a low distance is very low (0.01).

Distance / IDV	low	medium	high
low	0.8	0.2	0.01
medium	0.19	0.6	0.19
high	0.01	0.2	0.8

Table 5.1: Probabilities for interpersonal distance behaviors dependent on the individualism dimension of a culture.

Besides individualism, the power distance dimension has an impact on the loudness of the voice. High power distance cultures tend to speak much but in a low voice, whereas low power distance cultures are described as speaking louder. The probability for loud sound, thus, increases with decreasing power distance.

The masculinity dimension (labeled as gender in our network) affects several behavioral aspects. Masculine cultures are described as being verbal and rather loud, while feminine cultures are described as being soft spoken. Thus, in our network, with increasing masculinity the loudness of the voice is also rising. For this dimension, Hofstede also states that masculine cultures are active during conversations. Thus, the overall activation of nonverbal behaviors is increased with increasing masculinity, describing the probability that a lot of gestures are used. Another feature of masculine cultures is that they tend to use animated gestures. Thus, the expressivity parameter power is increased in our model with increasing masculinity, since the power feature describes how powerful a gesture is executed. The expressivity parameter spatial extent describes the amount of physical space in which a gesture takes place. To calculate the most probable expansion of a gesture, the masculinity dimension plays a crucial role as well. On the one hand, masculine cultures use animated gestures. On the other hand, feminine cultures do not need much space. Thus in our network, the probability for using little space when a culture is low in masculinity is influenced strongly, whereas probabilities are not as strongly affected for high masculinity.

The uncertainty avoidance dimension affects several aspects of behavior as well. Hofstede describes cultures that try to avoid uncertainty as being rather loud and cultures that are tolerant concerning uncertainty as being not so loud. Thus, in our network, the probability for loud voices increases with increasing uncertainty avoidance. Nonverbally, uncertainty avoiding cultures are described as being expressive and using many gestures. Thus, the probability for a high overall activation increases with increasing uncertainty avoidance. In addition, uncertainty tolerant cultures are described as not hectic, whereas uncertainty avoiding cultures are described as emotional. Consequently, in our network the expressivity parameters speed and power are increased with increasing uncertainty avoidance.

For the long term orientation dimension, no explicit tendencies in nonverbal behavior are described. Thus, this dimension is not considered in our model.

The impact each dimension exerts on each behavioral aspect is demonstrated by the arrow thickness in Figure 5.5. Considering the loudness of voice, for example, people belonging to masculine cultures are described as loud, whereas feminine cultures are described as never too loud [HPH02]. This results in a strong influence in the network as Hofstede uses the word "never". The uncertainty dimension also influences the sound feature. Hofstede describes cultures that try to avoid uncertainty as rather loud and cultures that are tolerant concerning uncertainty as not loud. Thus, in our network the probability for loud sound increases with increasing uncertainty avoidance but the influence of this cultural dimension is not too strong as Hofstede uses the word "rather" in this case.

The overall activity feature describes the frequency with which gestures are used in a conversation. This feature depends on the masculinity and uncertainty avoidance dimensions. For the masculinity dimension, Hofstede states that masculine cultures are active and use animated gestures. For the uncertainty avoidance dimension, he describes uncertainty avoiding cultures as expressive and using many gestures. Thus, the probability for many gestures increases with both, increasing masculinity and increasing uncertainty avoidance. For example, a low score in the masculinity dimension in combination with a low score in the uncertainty avoidance dimension leads to a high probability for low overall activity (0.98) and low probability for medium or high activity (0.01 each). In comparison, a low score on the masculinity dimension in combination with a medium score on the uncertainty avoidance dimension leads to almost equal distribution between low and medium activity with slightly more on the low activity side (low: 0.5; medium: 0.4; high: 0.1), since the influence of the masculinity dimension is stronger.

Figure 5.6 shows the probabilities for prototypical nonverbal behavior for an assumed German cultural background, as calculated by our Bayesian network. According to the model, the interpersonal distance should be rather high, the loudness of the voice should be located between medium and high as are the expressivity parameters. This prediction appears quite appropriate considering a German cultural background. Interpersonal distance should be rather high, especially compared to e.g. Asian and Mediterranean countries, where interpersonal distance is

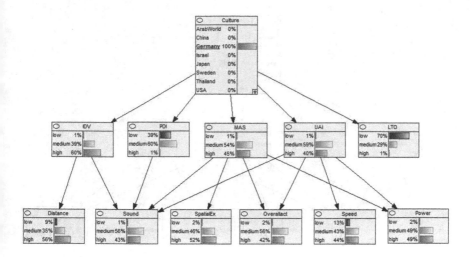

Figure 5.6: Results of the Bayesian network for an assumed German cultural background, based on Hofstede's dimensional model.

low. Loudness of voice and expressivity of nonverbal behavior is located between medium and high, which seems appropriate as well, since it should be higher than e.g. for most Asian or Northern European countries, but lower than for e.g. Arab or Mediterranean countries.

Running the Bayesian network with an assumed Japanese cultural background, results are less promising (see Figure 5.7). The calculated interpersonal distance is located on a medium score, which appears right, since distance should be very low with friends and family members, while it should be rather high for e.g work colleagues, especially in case they are of higher social status. Results for loudness of voice and expressivity of nonverbal behavior are somewhat surprising. Values are located medium or very high, which does not appear correct when imagining a prototypical Japanese conversation. This effect can be explained by the high score of the Japanese culture on the masculinity and uncertainty avoidance dimensions that are strongly related to the expressivity of nonverbal behaviors. Taking into account other countries that score high on these dimensions, such as Arab countries or Italy for example, this correlation appears more evident. Masculine attributes such as showing power through status symbols and uncertainty avoiding attributes such as following rules strictly are very present in the Japanese culture. Regarding nonverbal behavior, other factors such as saving one's face seem to be more dominant, since e.g. showing emotions in public is considered as loosing face.

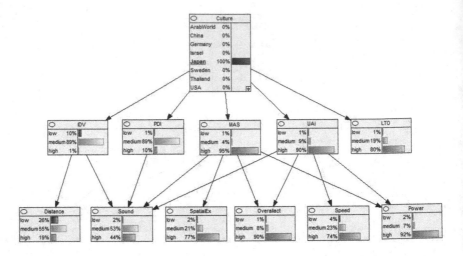

Figure 5.7: Results of the Bayesian network for an assumed Japanese cultural background, based on Hofstede's dimensional model.

The results of our Bayesian network reveal a weakness of a purely theory-driven approach. While the dimensions are a helpful tool to understand culture, they are not sufficient to generate appropriate behaviors for every country in a single model. This strengthens our idea to analyze a video corpus recorded in the target cultures to get a deeper insight into behavioral aspects. As the analysis of our video corpus revealed, the expressivity of gestures was significantly lower in the Japanese data set compared to the German one (see Subsection 4.4.3).

The purely theory-based approach described above was conducted at an early stage of this dissertation, where analyzed corpus data was not available yet. Learning a Bayesian network from the corpus data seems to be a promising next step for our future work. Comparing the resulting networks can give additional insights considering the applicability of the approaches. Still, the theory-based approach is suitable for other purposes. In that manner, abstract cultures could be simulated that exemplify, for example, prototypical masculine behavior. For the simulation of national cultures, vice versa, an approach using empirical data seems to be more promising.

An advantage of using Bayesian networks for culture-related nonverbal behaviors is that the networks are deterministic in both directions, and can thus be used

Figure 5.8: Beat gesture from the German video corpus (left) performed by a virtual character (right).

bottom-up as well. That way, it can be reflected on the most probable cultural background based on observed behavior. This has been exemplified by Rehm and colleagues [RBA08], where a user's behavior is tracked on the lowest layer of the network (nonverbal behavior) by using a Wii remote controller to estimate the most probable culture as a result. Therefore, the meaning of a gesture does not need to be understood by the system, but its expressivity can help interpret it in a culture-related manner. In addition, not all aspects of nonverbal behavior need to be recognized. This can be of particular importance for such a system, since the recognition of user behavior might be unstable and there might be no input available for all aspects at any time.

5.3.2.2 Corpus-Based Animations

The approach of using a Bayesian network to customize nonverbal behaviors is not well suited in any case. Emblems, for example, might loose their meaning when being performed in a different way. In a similar manner, members of different cultures might just use different gestures instead of exhibiting the same gesture in a different style. For these reasons, this dissertation considers concrete animations for different cultural backgrounds as well.

Figure 5.9: Metaphoric gesture from the Japanese video corpus (left) performed by a virtual character (right).

A crucial problem of designing culture-related animations for virtual characters is that the animators themselves are influenced by their own cultural background, since they are the ones who judge the naturalness of the animated behavior. A German pointing gesture, for example, is usually executed using the index finger for pointing, while in a typical Japanese pointing gesture the whole flattened hand is used. If the programmer is, for example, a member of a Western culture, the character will be animated in such a way as well. Observed by a user from a different cultural background, e.g. a member of an Asian culture, this behavior could be judged as being impolite. To avoid this problem, we used our video corpus as a basis. In that manner, short video clips were extracted from the corpus holding stereotypical nonverbal behaviors. These clips were given to designers who were asked to exactly rebuilt what is shown in the video.

In our corpus analysis, gesture types were distinguished according to McNeill's gesture classification [McN92] (see Chapter 2.2.3 for more details). Gestures designed for our nonverbal behavior generation were thus labeled as deictic, emblem, iconic, metaphoric or adaptor as well. As mentioned before, gestures were extracted from our video corpus and then modeled for the virtual characters. As stated in Section 4.4, emblems rarely occurred in the video corpus and were not considered in our analysis. Thus, emblems were not selected from the video corpus to model animations for the virtual characters, too. In total, over 20 gestures were modeled to resemble a corpus gesture including each remaining category for each culture. Figure 5.8 shows an example of a beat gesture extracted from the German video corpus (left) with its corresponding animation carried out by a German looking character (right). In Figure 5.9, a metaphoric gesture is exemplified from the Japanese corpus (left) performed by a Japanese looking virtual character. Gestures that were modeled with the video corpus as a basis are considered as culture-specific and are tagged with a cultural restriction. Thus, they are only chosen for characters of the target cultural background to demonstrate culture-related differences.

Another aspect of nonverbal behavior that is investigated in this dissertation are body postures. Following the results from our corpus study, we pointed out seven postures that occur regularly in the German or Japanese cultures (see Table 4.4, Subsection 4.4.3). These postures were taken as a basis for our corpus-based posture animations. As pointed out in Subsection 4.4.3, six of these postures seem to be very well suited to show differences between the cultures. Hence, three stereotypical body postures were designed for both cultures. Figure 5.10 shows screen shots of the prototypical German body postures displayed by stereotypical German virtual characters, while Figure 5.11 shows the prototypical postures for the Japanese culture displayed by characters that simulate a Japanese cultural background. For a comparison with human participants from our video corpus performing the same postures, please see Figures 4.13 and 4.14 in Subsection 4.4.3.

Modeling nonverbal behaviors based on a video corpus as described above has the advantage that the target animation resembles the behavior of a target cultural background where it is considered appropriate. However, these gestures are not of a very general nature and can not be customized in a convincing manner, since each customization of a corpus-based animation would drift it further apart from its original. Thus, as mentioned above, the usage of corpus-based gestures and gestures of a more general nature that are customizable were combined in our approach.

Figure 5.10: Prototypical body postures for virtual characters simulating a German cultural background.

Figure 5.11: Prototypical body postures for virtual characters simulating a Japanese cultural background.

5.4 Demonstrator

In the previous sections, the integration of culture into verbal and nonverbal behavior models has been described. For demonstration purposes, these behaviors were integrated into a multiagent system to exemplify prototypical differences for the two cultures of Germany and Japan. In this section, the demonstrator is introduced with its system architecture, virtual environment as well as the process of culture-specific dialog generation for the virtual characters.

5.4.1 System Overview

To demonstrate the culture-related behavioral differences for the German and Japanese cultures investigated in this dissertation, they have been integrated to a multiagent system. Figure 5.12 shows a screenshot of the demonstrator, where two prototypical German characters (Figure 5.12 ①) and two prototypical Japanese characters (Figure 5.12 ②) interact with one another. Agents can be logged on and off via their interface (Figure 5.12 ③). The flow of conversation can be followed in a separate window (Figure 5.12 ④). For testing reasons, e.g. to easily trigger certain behaviors, the characters' behavior can also be controlled by a human user. In Figure 5.12, the male Japanese character is operated by the user, indicated by the floating shape above his head. The avatar's verbal behavior can be selected by a user interface (Figure 5.12 ⑤), while nonverbal behavior is added automatically.

The system architecture shown in Figure 5.13 integrates the models introduced earlier in this dissertation into the demonstrator. As described in the previous section, for the integration of culture-related behavior, several tasks were carried out such as planning of verbal behavior (see Subsection 5.3.1) or modeling of stereotypical nonverbal behaviors (see Subsection 5.3.2).

For the process of behavior selection in this demonstrator, we generate verbal behavior first using the planning components of each agent, and add nonverbal behavior to the generated utterances afterwards dependent on cultural background. Thus, we do not consider the choice of modalities but vary the frequency, choice and style of nonverbal behavior dependent on the selected dialog utterance. Figure 5.13 shows an overview of the system architecture.

Each of the agents holds their own planning component, which includes the agent's knowledge base and culture-specific behavioral rules. If the planning component of an agent decides to communicate with another agent, a speech act is

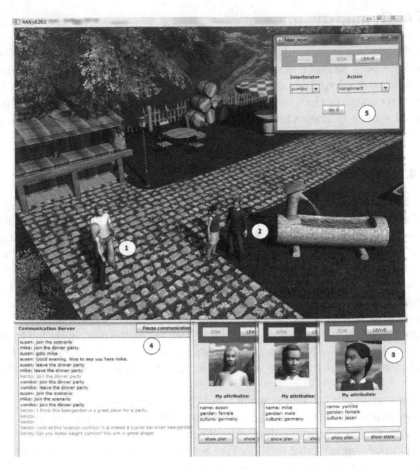

Figure 5.12: Screenshot of the demonstrator exemplifying prototypical culture-related differences in prototypical German and Japanese dialog behavior.

triggered for that agent by its planning component and sent to the agent communicator of the verbal behavior generation component. For the abstract speech act, an appropriate sentence is chosen from the verbal knowledge base and processed to the application communicator, which requests from the nonverbal behavior component whether an accompanying gesture should be performed. First, a selection mechanism decides which gesture is selected depending on cultural background, if any. As a second step, it is decided whether the selected gesture should be mod-

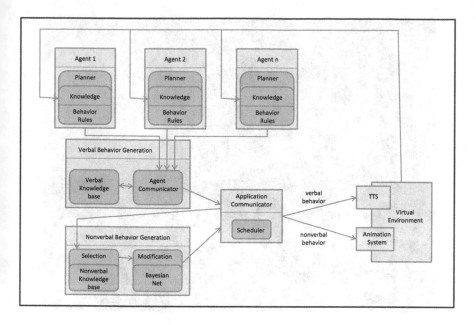

Figure 5.13: Overview of the system architecture.

ified in its expressivity, according to the cultural settings in the Bayesian network. After sending the selected nonverbal behavior to the communicator, a scheduler decides on the timing of the agent's performance, e.g. whether a pause should be inserted. Verbal behavior is sent to the text-to-speech component of the virtual environment, where different voices and languages can be set for the agents. Nonverbal behavior is processed by the animation component of the virtual environment. Finally, feedback about the behavior that was performed in the virtual environment is sent back to the agents that are either source or target of that action. The dynamic knowledge bases of the agents are updated, which in return updates their planning process.

For the system, XML based verbal and nonverbal knowledge bases were created that can easily be extended. In the current version of the demonstrator, the knowledge bases contain over 100 verbal templates and over 70 animations.

Figure 5.14: Screenshot of the Virtual Beergarden including prototypical Asian and Western characters as well as culture-related decoration.

5.4.2 Characters and Environment

For the simulation of our findings, the Virtual Beergarden scenario running in the AAA application [DEH+11] is used as a virtual environment. The scene is designed to resemble a typical Bavarian Beergarden including a bar, chestnut trees, typical Bavarian benches and tables, bistro tables and a wooden spring that give the scenario a rustic flair. Thus it is very well suited to match a typical German scenario (see Figure 5.12 of the above subsection for a screenshot of the Bavarian scenario).

To point out the multicultural aim of our project, a different scene can be loaded, including a variation of the Virtual Beergarden scenario that is decorated with Asian artifacts, which was very well received by our Japanese cooperation partners. To this end, Japanese cherry trees, stone pagodas, a gateway, Japanese lanterns and a stone fountain are added to the original scene to resemble e.g. a Japanese evening in the Bavarian beergarden. Figure 5.14 shows a screenshot of the scenario including some Asian items.

In the application, an arbitrary number of agents can be loaded that are able to move through the scenario freely and to exhibit verbal and nonverbal behaviors. For the simulation of different cultural backgrounds, culture-specific characters were created. Thus, prototypical German looking and prototypical Japanese looking characters were modeled (see Figure 5.14). To resemble different cultural backgrounds, outward aspects such as skin type, hair color, shape of the face and clothing were adapted.

Agent interaction can happen on two levels: verbally, achieved through text-to-speech, and nonverbally by applying animations such as gestures or body postures. These so-called high-level behaviors are handled by the verbal and nonverbal behavior components of our demonstrator (see Figure 5.13). Therefore, a communication protocol is provided by the virtual environment that allows to control the characters easily.

Low-level behaviors such as positioning towards each other, finding appropriate interpersonal distance or gaze behavior, vice versa, are generated by the virtual environment autonomously according to paramters that can be specified in advance [DEH+11]. If, for example, an agent should move through the scenario and approach another agent, the virtual characters will automatically detect each other when entering their social zones and react by e.g. turning their bodies in such a way that they are facing each other depending on their personal settings.

Since nonverbal behaviors could happen in an overlapping manner, e.g. a gesture should be performed while the character rests in a certain body posture, the virtual environment needs to handle animation blending as well.

Animations are annotated in a temporal manner as introduced by McNeill (see Subsection 2.2.3). Each gesture is divided into three phases: In the preparation phase, the hands are brought into the gesture space. The stroke phase carries the content of the gesture, while in the retraction phase, the hands are finally brought back into a resting position. In the Virtual Beergarden, preparation and retraction phases are used for animation blending.

Regarding the implementation of body postures, each posture contains a preparation, stroke and retraction phase as well. In comparison to gestures, posture animations have to be loop-able. Playing the stroke several times consecutively instead of just remaining in the last frame of the animation has the advantage that the character performs small idle movements instead of remaining still. To this end, the start and end frame of the stroke phase of a posture need to be exactly the same. If a gesture is selected while the character remains in a certain posture, the character goes back into the body posture that was displayed before playing the gesture animation. To avoid undesired effects caused by different initial positions, the preparation and stroke phases are used for animation blending. This allows the system to keep the stroke intact while the blend-in is happening at the preparation level and thus shows fluid motions and helps avoid going into a neutral position before exhibiting a new animation.

5.4.3 Generation of Example Dialogs

The general approach of integrating culture into the behavior of virtual characters was described earlier in this chapter. In principle, these behaviors can be combined freely. For demonstration purposes, in this subsection concrete small talk dialogs are presented including culture-specific verbal and nonverbal behaviors.

5.4.3.1 Culture-specific Small Talk

As described in Section 5.3.1, abstract dialog steps are planned by each agent individually by their planning component. After such an abstract action is triggered, natural language needs to be generated that represents the target action. A template-based verbal knowledge base is therefore stored in the verbal behavior component of the system, where a set of appropriate dialog utterances is provided for each interaction type.

To exemplify culture-related differences in small talk behavior for the German and Japanese cultures, templates for 9 different topics were created, 3 topics for each of the categories described earlier: immediate, external and communication situation (see Subsection 2.2.1 for a full description of topic categories). This number of topics appears to be sufficient to demonstrate the generation of prototypical culture-related differences in small talk. However, additional topics can easily be added to the verbal knowledge base to create more variation in the dialogs. Table 5.2 summarizes the topics. These topics were carefully chosen to assure that topics are appropriate in principal in both cultures. This is particularly important when simulating culture-related differences, since topics that are save in one culture are not necessarily save in another culture as well [ININ00]. To avoid this problem, we only took topics into account that are save in both target cultures, Germany and Japan.

For the demonstrator, topics were either chosen because they appeared in the corpus recordings of both cultures or after agreement with our Japanese coopera-

Situation	Immediate	External	Communication
# 1	location	movies	job
# 2	weather	places	origin
# 3	food	friends	hobbies

Table 5.2: Topics wand corresponding categories added to the verbal knowledge base.

tion partners. Especially for the immediate situation, we were not able to use topics that occurred in the corpus, since recordings took place indoors during an experimental setting at university, while our virtual simulation takes place outside in the Virtual Beergarden location. Therefore, we agreed on topics that appeared reasonable for the virtual surrounding. For the external and communication situation, two topics each were chosen from the corpus and one was agreed on separately, in order to ensure a smooth flow of the conversation. For example, for switching from talking about a common friend that works in the Beergarden (social) to asking whether the conversation partner has a side job, too (private).

As described in Section 5.3.1, four dialog acts are needed for each topic: (1) question, (2) answer, (3) reverse-question and (4) reverse-answer. To provide a wider variability of dialogs, three different utterances were written for each dialog act. In that manner, over 100 templates were added to the verbal knowledge base. Additional dialog acts such as greeting or farewell with corresponding utterances were created as well to simulate a complete small talk conversation. Please see Appendix C.2 for a full list of dialog templates stored in the verbal knowledge base.

In the following, two example dialogs that were generated by our system are introduced, one prototypical for the German culture and another prototypical for the Japanese culture.

Table 5.3 highlights the abstract dialog acts that are generated by the planning components of two prototypical German agents. In the example dialog, three topics are discussed, one covering the external situation and two that cover the communication situation (reflecting Tendency 1 implemented in Subsection 5.3.1). In addition, the flow of the dialog is sequential for all three topics (reflecting Tendency 2 implemented in Subsection 5.3.1).

In comparison, Table 5.4 presents a prototypical Japanese small talk conversation. As in the German version, it contains three different topics. However, for the

Agent	Action	Topic	Category
A	question	friends	external
B	answer	friends	external
B	reverse question	friends	external
A	reverse answer	friends	external
A	question	job	communication
B	answer	job	communication
B	reverse question	job	communication
A	reverse answer	job	communication
A	question	origin	communication
B	answer	origin	communication
B	reverse question	origin	communication
A	reverse answer	origin	communication

Table 5.3: Abstract representation of a prototypical German small talk dialog.

Agent	Action	Topic	Category
A	question	weather	immediate
B	answer	weather	immediate
B	reverse question	weather	immediate
A	reverse answer	weather	immediate
A	question	food	immediate
B	answer	food	immediate
A	question	places	external
B	answer	places	external
B	reverse question	places	external
A	reverse answer	places	external
B	reverse question	food	immediate
A	reverse answer	food	immediate

Table 5.4: Abstract representation of a prototypical Japanese small talk dialog.

Japanese dialog, two topics covering the immediate situation and one topic covering the external situation were selected (reflecting Tendency 1 implemented in Subsection 5.3.1). In addition, the flow of conversation differs from the German version. In the prototypical Japanese dialog, the second topic is not discussed sequentially, but finished at a later point in time (reflecting Tendency 2 implemented in Subsection 5.3.1).

After selecting appropriate verbal utterances from the verbal knowledge base for the prototypical German abstract sequence, the following dialog could be generated:

```
A: Did you know that Heidi is working in this Beergarden?
B: I did. She has been working here for a month now.
B: Heidi seems to be doing very well in her job doesn't she?
A: She likes working here very much, although she is always very busy.

A: Do you have a side job as well?
B: I do. I am working in an Italian restaurant.
B: How about you? Do you have a side job too?
A: No. I am currently not working part time.

A: Are you from this region originally?
B: I am not from here. I was born and raised in America.
B: Have you been to the US?
A: Yes I have been to New York last year.
```

For the Japanese version, the following dialog could be generated from our verbal knowledge base:

```
A: Look at the weather isn't it great?
B: Yes we do have little rain and many sunny days this year.
B: It was also nice and warm last week wasn't it?
A: Yes. It was indeed very warm.

A: Have you seen the menu in this Beergarden?
B: I did. They offer typical Bavarian food and some
   Japanese delicacies too.

A: Do you know the new Sushi restaurant that opened a few days ago?
B: I have not been there. That sounds very interesting.
B: Can you tell me where it is?
A: It is very close. If you exit this Beergarden you can see it
   on your left hand side.

B: Are you having the Japanese food today?
A: Japanese food is good. However in a Beergarden I will go
   for something typical German.
```

Besides the content of the dialog, timing is a crucial aspect of dialog behavior that varies with culture. In our literature review and corpus analysis, culture-related differences in communication management behavior such as pauses in speech and overlapping speech was described. For the integration into our demonstrator, we focused on pauses in speech as we found significant differences in our video corpus comparing the two cultures of Germany and Japan. Since we did not consider semantics but focused on a quantitative analysis, in our demonstrator pauses in speech are simply added before the start of each sentence. Taking into account the frequency of pauses observed in our video corpus (see Subsection 4.4.2), pauses are added with a higher probability to the Japanese dialogs than to the German ones.

5.4.3.2 Nonverbal Behavior Selection

In the demonstrator, nonverbal behaviors are added to the dialog to accompany verbal behavior. Thus, the frequency, choice and style of nonverbal behavior varies dependent on the selected dialog utterance and cultural background, as observed in our video corpus. The process of nonverbal behavior selection is thus speech-act as well as corpus-driven. For combination of verbal and nonverbal behaviors, approaches such as applying filter functions as introduced by Cassell and colleagues [CVB01] could be applied. However, to exemplify a possible combination of behaviors, a simple probabilistic approach was chosen.

The process of verbal behavior selection remains a task for the hierarchical planer of each agent. If a dialog utterance is triggered, the nonverbal behavior component needs to add culture-specific nonverbal behaviors to be performed by the virtual character, taking into account the frequency of gestures, the correlation of gesture-types and speech-acts as well as the expressivity of gestures. Thus, the following decisions need to be taken, considering the agent's cultural background:

1. Should the speech act be accompanied by a gesture?

2. Which gesture should be selected?

3. Should the gesture's expressivity be modified?

For the first decision of the above enumeration, whether a gesture should be performed or not, the findings from our corpus analysis are taken as a basis. For demonstration purposes a simple probabilistic approach is used to decide on speech accompanying gestures. However, more advanced techniques as described in Chapter 5.2 can be integrated as well. To determine the correlation of verbal and nonverbal behaviors, the data of Table 4.5 Section 4.4.4 is used. However, to obtain a higher frequency of nonverbal behaviors that exemplifies culture-related differences in an illustrative manner, the probabilities extracted from the video corpus have been multiplied for our demonstrator.

For the second decision, which animation is appropriate for the current speech act, the most probable gesture type according to McNeill's classification (see Subsection 2.2.3) is computed. Therefore, the distribution presented in Table 4.6 Section 4.4.4 as observed in our video corpus is taken into account. As a next step, an animation of the computed gesture type needs to be selected. Gestures that are stored in the nonverbal knowledge base of our demonstrator are tagged according to McNeill's gesture types. Following the approach of Krenn and Pirker [KP04b], we use an XML structure that comprises a form, function and possible restrictions for each animation. Please see Appendix C.3 for an overview of the nonverbal knowledge base that currently contains over 70 animations, or see our animation homepage [Aug11] where videos of selected animations are provided.

The third decision, whether the selected gesture should be modified in a culture-specific way, is dependent on the animation itself. As described in Section 5.3.2, we took into account gestures that are either corpus-based or of a general nature that can be customized.

Gestures that were modeled to resemble a gesture that was performed in our video corpus should not be customized (see Subsection 5.3.2.2). In the demonstrator, these corpus-based animations are considered culture-specific behaviors and can, thus, only be selected for a virtual character of the target cultural background.

If a gesture of a general nature is selected on the other hand, e.g. a simple beat gesture, the animation is modified in a culture-dependent way, taking into account the most probable expressiveness derived from the Bayesian network presented in Subsection 5.3.2.1. To exemplify the customization of gestural expressivity, a set of general animations was added to our nonverbal knowledge base and tagged with McNeill's gesture types (see Appendix C.3). In our demonstrator, the adaption of gestural expressivity is realized for the expressivity parameters speed and spatial extent. To customize the speed parameter, the animation is simply played faster or slower, which is realized by the number of animation frames that are played during each application frame. The spatial extent parameter is realized by animation blending to attenuate the expressivity. A gesture's spatial extent can, for example, be lowered by blending with a posture where the hands are held very close to the

Figure 5.15: Gesture played with lower (left) and wider spatial extent (right).

body. As a result, the blended gesture will be performed closer to the body than its original. Figure 5.15 exemplifies a general gesture that is performed differently taking into account cultural background, showing increased (left) and decreased spatial extent (right).

Emblems are not considered in the selection process described above, since they cannot be added randomly to accompany speech as they are highly dependent on semantics. However, to exemplify the usage of emblems in our demonstrator, certain animations have been tagged according to their content in our nonverbal knowledge base, e.g. a hand wave is labeled with *greeting*. In addition, emblems can be culture-dependent. Therefore, culture-related restrictions are added to some emblems as well. If, for example, a greeting utterance should be spoken by a virtual character that should be accompanied by a nonverbal behavior, the knowledge base is browsed for appropriate animations that are labeled with a *greeting* context. Taking into account culture-specific restrictions, for a character simulating a German cultural background a hand-wave is selected by our system, while for a Japanese cultural background a bow is considered appropriate.

In addition, culture-dependent body postures have been added to the example dialogs. Based on our findings from the corpus study, postures are restricted to culture in our nonverbal knowledge base as well (see Subsection 5.3.2.2). As described for gestures before, culturally restricted postures can only be performed by virtual characters of the target cultural background. In total, nine prototypical body postures can be selected in our demonstrator (see Subsection 5.3.2, figures 5.10 and 5.11).

5.5 Summary

In this chapter, the technical realization of this dissertation was presented. In order to simulate culture-related differences in behaviors, not only challenges that usually occur in multiagent systems had to be solved such as planning dialog behavior or the realization of realistic nonverbal behaviors. Additionally, these behaviors had to be customized to match different cultural backgrounds.

This chapter starts from an overview of the workflow that was carried out for this dissertation which combines a theory-based and corpus-driven approach to obtain behavioral tendencies from literature as well as statistical data from a corpus, which both can be used for the integration into computational models. After these models have been integrated into a multiagent system, the procedure is completed by evaluation studies that investigate the impact of the culture-related aspects of behavior on human observers from the cultural backgrounds that were simulated.

Subsequently, the general approach taken for the implementation is described, introducing the AI techniques that are used for realization. Since the aim of this dissertation is to model different culture-related aspects of behavior, instead of addressing which technique might be best suited for our aim, we follow approaches that already successfully implemented solutions to similar problems in an intuitive manner. In the domain of dialog behavior, plan-based approaches have been proven to be very well suited.

Thus, for the implementation of culture-specific verbal behavior in this dissertation, a hierarchical planner was used that is able to cope with several communication partners. Regarding the adaptation of nonverbal behavior, Bayesian networks have been used to estimate the most probable nonverbal behavior and are, thus, used in this dissertation to model culture-related differences in the expressivity of nonverbal behavior.

After introducing the general approach, the actual modeling of culture-related differences is exemplified for the two cultures of Germany and Japan, taking into account findings from literature as well a the corpus study. To model culture-specific dialogs, the domain of small talk was chosen. In particular, two tendencies were realized: (1) Less personal topics occur in Japanese dialogs than in German ones. (2) Topics are discussed in a more sequential manner in German dialogs compared to Japanese ones. Culture-specific rules have therefore been added to each agent's planning component, where topics as well as dialog utterance are selected based on cultural background.

Regarding the adaption of nonverbal behavior, Hofstede's dimensional model [HHM10] has been taken as a basis to model a Bayesian network that estimates the most probable behavioral style. Therefore, animations of a general nature were created that can be customized in order to match different levels of expressivity dependent on cultural background. Since this approach might not be suited in any case, additionally a set of animations was created by extracting video clips from the corpus and modeling the observed nonverbal behaviors.

Finally, a demonstrator is introduced that realizes example small talk dialogs along with nonverbal behaviors in a virtual environment. For the process of behavior selection, we generate verbal behavior first using the planning system. To realize agent dialogs, a template-based verbal knowledge base was created, where a set of appropriate dialog utterances is provided for each interaction type. Nonverbal behavior is added afterwards to the generated utterances dependent on cultural background, to exemplify prototypical differences for the two cultures of Germany and Japan.

6 Evaluation of Behavioral Aspects

In this chapter, we evaluate the implemented culture-related behaviors with users from either a German or Japanese cultural background. With the evaluation studies, we investigate whether human observers prefer agent behavior that is in line with observations made for their own cultural background. This was suggested by Lee and Nass [LN98] who found out that the ethnicity of an agent affects the user's attitude and that users perceive more trust towards agents with a similar cultural background.

In order to find out which of the implemented aspects of behavior have an impact on the perception of human observers, they need to be isolated for evaluation, since different aspects of human behavior are not independent from one another. Verbal and nonverbal behavior correlate, for example, since the semantics of speech has a strong impact on the selection of accompanying nonverbal behaviors and vice versa. Thus, we were not able to evaluate verbal and nonverbal behavior in a single study and had to set up individual studies separating the different aspects.

In the subsequent sections, the evaluation studies are reported. For each study, two different versions were designed, to be conducted in Germany or Japan respectively.

6.1 Small Talk Behavior

The aim of the evaluation study described in this section is to investigate whether human observers prefer agent conversations that are in line with observations made for their own cultural background, regarding the content of dialogs.

The selection of topics during small talk conversations can vary with cultural background. In typical small talk conversations, so-called safe topics occur. According to Isbister and colleagues [ININ00], the categorization into safe and unsafe topics varies with cultural background. Literature from the social sciences suggests that in prototypical Japanese conversations less personal topics occur compared to German ones (see Section 2.3).

In our corpus study, we found, in line with literature, topics covering the immediate and external situation significantly more often in the Japanese conversations compared to the German ones, while topics covering the communication situation occurred significantly more often in the German conversations. Another aspect of verbal behavior that was considered in our corpus analysis, is the sequence in which topics are discussed in a small talk conversation. A preliminary analysis of our corpus study supported our ideas derived from literature, suggesting that topics are discussed in a more sequential manner in German conversations compared to Japanese ones. However, analyzing the full data set, our previous findings were not confirmed. We thus focused on the aspect of topic choice for our verbal evaluation study and created prototypical conversations, differing the choice of topic categories only to evaluate culture-related differences in small talk behavior with virtual characters.

To test the study design and whether observers are actually able to recognize differences in the agent conversations, a preliminary study was conducted in the German culture only [ERA11]. Since results were promising, and German participants preferred agent behavior that simulates prototypical German behavior, we set up a similar study to be conducted in both cultures. Therefore, not only participants of both cultures were needed but also discussions with members of the Japanese culture, since dialogs needed to be agreed on to ensure that they were principally feasible in both cultures. In the following, the study design and results are presented (see also [ENL$^+$11]).

6.1.1 Study Design

In order to find out whether participants from Germany and Japan prefer agent conversations that reflect a choice of topic categories that was observed for their own cultural background, we set up two versions of the evaluation study to be conducted in Germany and Japan respectively. Therefore, six English dialogs were created, three of them containing a prototypical German topic distribution and three of them containing a prototypical Japanese topic distribution. Using Figure 4.9 Section 4.4 as a basis, we equally integrated the immediate and external situation into the prototypical German small talk dialogs and all three categories into prototypical Japanese conversations, with an emphasis on the external situation. In that manner, we integrated two topics covering the external situation and two topics covering the communication situation in the German dialogs, and two topics covering the external situation, one topic covering the immediate situation and one topic covering the communication situation in the Japanese dialogs, while all dialogs lasted for approximately one minute. Topics within the dialogs were carefully chosen in agreement with our Japanese cooperation partners to assure dialogs were principally appropriate in both cultures. This is particularly important, since topics that are save in one culture are not necessarily save in another culture [ININ00]. The dialogs were later translated into the German and Japanese languages for the two evaluation studies in order to avoid effects due to the language barrier or culture-specific assumptions that might have been made for English-speaking characters.

Participants watched the videos in pairs, each containing a prototypical German and a prototypical Japanese conversation in alternating order. For each pair of videos they had to judge

- (Q1) which one is more appropriate,

- (Q2) which one is more interesting,

- (Q3) which conversation they would prefer to join and

- (Q4) which pair of agents gets along with each other better,

and participants were able to either choose one of the videos or a button, indicating that none of the two videos was preferred. In addition, a comment box was provided that allowed participants to state an opinion on their choice. With it we investigate, whether participants preferred agent behavior that was in line with observations made for their own cultural background. For the two studies, we therefore state the following two hypotheses:

H1: German participants prefer the videos showing prototypical German dialog behavior over the Japanese versions.

H2: Japanese participants prefer the videos showing prototypical Japanese dialog behavior over the German versions.

For the study conducted in Germany, Western-looking characters were used, while for the study conducted in Japan, we used Asian-looking characters. In this vein, we assured that participants did not assume a cultural background different from their own. In addition, we used language-specific text-to-speech systems for the Western and Asian characters (German and Japanese). To avoid side effects evoked by gender, we chose a mixed gender combination for the agent conversations. That is, one female and one male character interacted with each other in both cultures.

Apart from the choice of topics, no other aspects of verbal behavior were taken into account. Regarding nonverbal behavior, characters maintained a body pose prototypical for their cultural background during the whole conversation, since this had influenced their acceptance positively in an earlier study [ERL+11]. Gestures were not exhibited by the characters to avoid side effects aroused by their suitability to accompany the semantics of the speech.

Since participants only saw the version of the study that was designed for their own cultural background, all participants met the same conditions.

Figure 6.1 shows a screenshot of the online evaluation study conducted in Germany. Thus, Western-looking characters and German text-to-speech are presented as well as German introduction texts and questions. Before observing the agent videos, participants were told that the two characters have met for the first-time and were introduced to each other by a common friend who left to get drinks for everybody. In that manner, we created the assumption of a first time meeting including casual small talk, similar to the setup in our corpus study.

6.1.2 Results and Discussion

With our evaluation study, we wanted to find out whether human observers prefer agent conversations that reflect their own cultural background. Thus, we expected participants in the German evaluation study to prefer dialogs that contain prototypical German small talk behaviors, while we expected Japanese participants to prefer dialogs designed to reflect prototypical Japanese small talk behavior.

German Study In the German evaluation study, 16 participants took part, six females and ten males, in an age range of 23 to 40 years. Since all participants observed three pairs of videos, we obtained a data set containing 48 judgments. For our analysis, we conducted a chi-squared (χ^2) goodness-of-fit test in order to

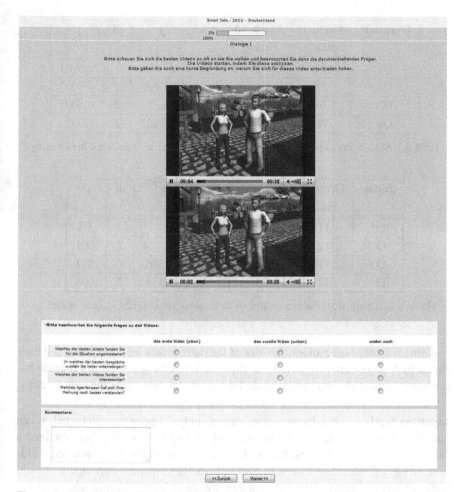

Figure 6.1: Screenshot of evaluation study to investigate culture-related verbal behavior conducted in Germany.

validate our hypothesis, stating that German participants prefer videos showing German behavior over the Japanese versions.

Our results indicate that German participants significantly prefer videos with agent conversations that reflect prototypical German topic selection for all four questions. Table 6.1 summarizes the results from the German evaluation study. Thus, participants found German conversations more appropriate and interesting, would rather like to join the conversations and think that agents get along with each other better.

Germany	German dialog	Japanese dialog	none	χ^2	df	p
Q1	33	5	10	27.875	2	< .001
Q2	37	4	7	41.625	2	< .001
Q3	34	4	10	31.5	2	< .001
Q4	28	7	13	14.625	2	.001

Table 6.1: Results from the perception study on topic selection conducted in Germany.

Japan	German dialog	Japanese dialog	none	χ^2	df	p
Q1	11	22	9	7	2	.03
Q2	12	25	5	14.714	2	.001
Q3	11	21	10	5.286	2	.071
Q4	12	23	7	9.571	2	.008

Table 6.2: Results from the perception study on topic selection conducted in Japan.

In line with our expectations, five out of ten participants who had explained their choice in the comment box, stated that they preferred the selected conversation because it was more personal and revealed more information about the interlocutors.

Japanese Study   In the Japanese evaluation study, 14 people participated, seven females and seven males, in an age range of 21 to 23 years. We thus obtained a data set containing 42 judgments. As for the German study, we conducted a chi-squared (χ^2) goodness-of-fit test to find out whether Japanese participants would prefer agent conversations that contain a prototypical Japanese topic selection over the German versions.

Our analysis revealed that the Japanese versions of small talk conversations were significantly preferred by Japanese participants for three out of the four questions. In Table 6.2, the results from the Japanese evaluation study are summarized. According to our study, Japanese participants found the Japanese versions of small talk conversations more appropriate and interesting and thought that agents were getting along with each other better. However, the study did not significantly indicate that participants would also rather like to join the Japanese conversations over the German ones. However, a trend into that direction can be observed.

Interestingly, and in line with our expectations, some Japanese participants showed that the immediate situation was of importance for them. For example, a Japanese video that included talking about the weather was judged positively by a participant because it "fit to the background image", while another participant disliked a conversation since "the content in the video does not match to the background image".

Discussion Regarding our evaluation study, the integration of different topic selections in culture-related small talk dialogs for virtual characters was very promising. Findings from literature were confirmed by our empirical study and integrated into the behavior of virtual characters. Our hypothesis that human observers prefer agent dialogs that were designed to reflect their own cultural background was confirmed. In particular, our results revealed that both, German and Japanese participants, preferred agent behavior that was in line with observations made for their own cultural background.

We thus claim that in applications where small talk is intended for virtual characters, e.g. to establish a positive personal relation with a human user, the integration of culture by selecting topics that are appropriate for the target cultural background can help improve the character's acceptance and should thus be taken into account by the designers of such a system.

6.2 Communication Management and Nonverbal Behavior

In this section, we describe our evaluation study that investigates aspects of communication management as well as nonverbal behavior for the two cultures of Germany and Japan. These aspects of behavior can be tested in a common study, since the correlation to verbal behavior needs to be carefully avoided for both aspects. In the study, each behavioral aspect is tested in isolation. Interrelations between communication management and nonverbal behavior themselves can be excluded by simply not performing them during the cases where the other aspect is focused on.

With our evaluation study, we investigate whether the culture-related differences that we found in literature and our video corpus (see Sections 2.3.2 and 4.4) have an impact on human observers during agent interaction.

As for verbal behavior, we conducted a preliminary evaluation study at an earlier point in time to test the study design and whether observers recognize differences in the agent conversations. In the study, communication management behaviors were taken into account and evaluated in the German culture only [ERA09]. Results indicate that German participants prefer agent behavior that simulates a prototypical German cultural background. We thus reused the study design to conduct evaluation studies in both cultures. In the following subsections, the study design and results are presented (see also [ERL$^+$11]).

6.2.1 Study Design

Just as in the evaluation study for verbal behavior, two versions of the study were designed. For the study conducted in Germany, German-looking characters were used and for the study conducted in Japan, we used Japanese-looking characters. Thus, participants should not assume a cultural background different from their own one.

Different aspects of behavior are not independent from one another. Thus, when investigating aspects of communication management or nonverbal behavior in agent dialogs, the semantics of speech can highly influence the perception of the observer. To avoid a preference for one of the videos due to content of the dialogs, we used Gibberish, a fantasy language that represents a language without any specific meaning of the words. To this end, words were generated that have the same statistical distribution of syllables as the words from the target language. In addition, we used language-specific text-to-speech systems for the Western and Asian characters (German and Japanese) to match the prosody of speech in the target culture.

For each behavioral dimension, participants were shown two videos with face-to-face dialogs. In one video, the characters performed prototypical German behavior, in the other one, prototypical Japanese behavior for the specific behavioral aspect. In the study, participants stated their preference by rating on a six-graded scale that contained three grades on each side, starting from "rather this video" to "by any means this video". For the two studies, we stated the following hypotheses:

H1: For each behavioral aspect, German participants prefer the videos showing prototypical German behavior over the Japanese versions.

H2: For each behavioral aspect, Japanese participants prefer the videos showing prototypical Japanese behavior over the German versions.

In order to avoid side effects evoked by gender, we showed mixed gender combinations in the videos. That is, one female and one male character interacted with each other in both cultures. The same Gibberish dialog was retained during the whole study and only aspects of communication management or nonverbal behavior were changed. Keeping the dialog consistent also assured that the users' perceptions are not influenced by other linguistic features, such as the length of the sentences.

To get participants acquainted with the situation of listening to a Gibberish dialog, we showed a neutral conversation first. In the video, the dialog was performed without any specific communication management or nonverbal behavior.

After the neutral video, six pairs of videos were shown in random order, each lasting for half a minute and containing variations in one of the following aspects of behavior, based on our literature research and corpus analysis. Please note that for the integration of communication management behavior, we had to rely on a preliminary corpus analysis, since annotations were not available for the whole data set at this point in time (see also [ERA09]).

- **Pauses in speech**: In line with research literature, we observed more pauses in the Japanese corpus. Thus, the simulated dialogs reflecting typical Japanese conversations contain more pauses compared to the German version. Taking into account our corpus findings, German agent dialogs are designed to contain one pause that lasts for one second, while Japanese dialogs contain two pauses that last one second and one pause that lasts for two seconds.

- **Overlapping speech**: Following our findings in overlapping speech, we integrated one overlap that lasts for 0.3 seconds and two overlaps that last for 0.5 seconds into the German dialog. The Japanese dialog contains three overlaps that last for 0.3 second, one that lasts for 0.5 seconds and one that lasts for one second.

- **Communication management**: Videos reflecting different communication management behaviors contain both, pauses and overlaps in speech, as described above.

- **Speed of gestures**: Our observations revealed that in the German corpus, gestures are performed faster than in the Japanese one. In the simulated dialogs, we thus customized the speed of gestures. Three gestures were shown in both videos, each played faster in the prototypical German conversation and slower in the prototypical Japanese conversation.

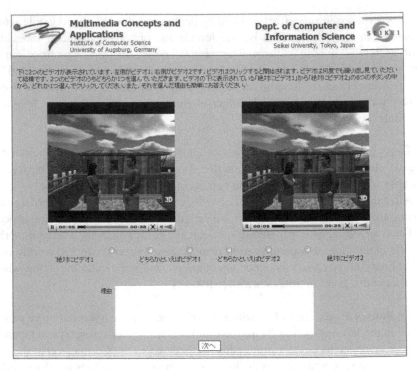

Figure 6.2: Screenshot of evaluation study to investigate culture-related differences in communication management and nonverbal behavior conducted in Japan.

- **Spatial extent of gestures**: Another pair of videos contained gestures with a different spatial extent. Based on our findings, simulated gestures have a smaller spatial extent in the Japanese conversations compared to the German ones.

- **Postures**: Our corpus findings revealed that different body postures occur in the target cultures. In the agent conversations, characters remained in a prototypical German (put hands to pockets, fold arms) or Japanese (join hands, put hand to wrist) body posture during the whole conversation.

In the two versions of our evaluation study, questions as well as instruction texts were translated in order to match the participants' mother tongues. In addition, a comment box was provided where participants were able to explain their choice. Figure 6.2 shows a screenshot of the study as it was conducted in Japan.

6.2.2 Results and Discussion

As described in the previous subsection, we designed two different versions of our evaluation study that investigate communication management and nonverbal behavior. One utilizing German-looking characters and a German text-to-speech system and another using Japanese-looking characters and a Japanese text-to-speech system, each showing both behavioral models of communication management and nonverbal behavior. In the evaluation study, participants had to decide which of the videos they liked better, assuming that participants prefer videos showing virtual characters that behave in a way that was designed to reflect their own cultural background.

German Study   In the German evaluation study, 15 participants took part (six females and nine males). With one exception, all participants were students. In a chi-squared (χ^2) goodness-of-fit test, we tested, whether the perception of the observed pattern of behavior differs statistically, in order to validate our hypothesis that German observers prefer agent behavior that reflects prototypical German behavior.

Table 6.3 summarizes the results from the evaluation study conducted in Germany. Our results reveal that significantly more than 50% of the German participants had a preference for the German version of overlapping speech and spatial extent in gestures.

For the behavioral aspects pauses in speech, communication management and posture, we almost achieved significance, suggesting that German participants prefer the German dialog versions over the Japanese ones.

For gestural speed, we did not get significant results. However, in line with our expectations, at least by trend, German participants showed a preference for the videos simulating prototypical German behavior for all aspects of behavior that were investigated.

Japanese Study   In the Japanese evaluation study, 17 people participated (three females and 14 males), of whom were all of them students. To validate our hypothesis that Japanese observers prefer agent behavior that reflects prototypical Japanese behavior, a chi-squared (χ^2) goodness-of-fit test was conducted.

Table 6.4 summarizes the results from the evaluation study conducted in Japan, where results are less distinct compared to the German study.

Germany	German dialog	Japanese dialog	χ^2	df	p
pause	11	4	3.267	1	.071
overlap	13	2	8.067	1	.005
communication management	11	4	3.267	1	.071
speed	10	5	1.667	1	.197
spatial extent	13	2	8.067	1	.005
posture	11	4	3.267	1	.071

Table 6.3: Results from the perception study on communication management and nonverbal behavior conducted in Germany.

Japan	German dialog	Japanese dialog	χ^2	df	p
pause	11	6	1.471	1	.225
overlap	12	5	2.882	1	.09
communication management	7	9	0.25	1	.617
speed	5	10	1.667	1	.197
spatial extent	7	7	0	1	1
posture	4	13	4.765	1	.029

Table 6.4: Results from the perception study on communication management and nonverbal behavior conducted in Japan.

Significantly more than 50% of the Japanese participants had a preference for the version with Japanese posture behavior. For other behavioral patterns, we cannot claim any statistically significant evidence.

Although not significant, communication management and gestural speed of the Japanese version was preferred by the Japanese participants by trend.

The results for pauses in speech and overlapping speech were a bit surprising, as participants seemed to favor the German videos over the Japanese ones (although not significant).

Discussion For the study, several aspects of human behavior were simulated with virtual characters and evaluated in isolation. Our results suggest that some of the aspects have a stronger impact on the perception of human observers than others.

Regarding communication management behaviors, pauses in speech and overlapping speech were considered. More pauses were integrated to the German version since silence generally creates tension in Western cultural backgrounds. We found a strong trend suggesting that German participants favored the German dialog versions. For the Japanese evaluation study, we did not find any meaningful results. This might be due to the missing semantics of the agent dialogs since we used Gibberish.

The results suggest that in line with literature, more pauses were perceived as disturbing by German participants, while they did not disturb the Japanese participants. We thus conclude that when including silence in conversations, cultural background should be considered, as it might be perceived as disturbing in some cultures. When integrating more silence for certain cultural backgrounds, however, the semantics of speech should be considered.

In a similar manner, we integrated more overlapping speech in the simulated Japanese conversations compared to the German ones. In our German evaluation study, we found a significant preference for the German version, suggesting that many overlaps are perceived as disturbing. In the Japanese evaluation study, we found a trend in the same direction.

Thus, just as the German participants, Japanese observers preferred the version with less overlaps. Again, this might be due to the missing semantics of speech, since it can not be assumed that the overlapping speech occurred because of feedback behavior. As discussions with our Japanese project partners showed afterwards, the use of pauses and overlaps in the Japanese language are closely related to the semantics of speech and is acceptable in one case and unacceptable in another. Thus, without having the necessary semantic clues at hand, Japanese participants might have been tempted to go for the "safe" solution and vote for the version with less pauses and overlaps.

The results highlight a very important aspect of cross-cultural studies. Despite frequent discussions and experience in the domain, the developer's own cultural expectations are always present and sometimes interfere with the development. In this case, the seemingly good solution of using Gibberish for the tests, due to the arguments given above, led us to missing an important feature of Japanese dialogs and in particular its high-context nature [Hal59].

For the integration of differences in nonverbal behavior, gestural expressivity was investigated by means of speed and spatial extent as well as body postures. Regarding gestural speed, our results indicate that at least by trend German participants preferred the faster version, while Japanese participants preferred the slower version. This suggests that the speed of gestures can be a helpful aspect when integrating cultural background. For the spatial extent of a gesture, we found a significant preference for wider gestures in the German study, while we did not find any trend in the Japanese study. Since gestures for the study were designed in Germany, it is possible that lowering the spatial extent leads to unreasonable results in other cultures.

Regarding body postures, we integrated postures that were most frequently observed in the German and Japanese corpus. Results from our evaluation study are very promising. In the German perception study, we almost achieved significance that German observers prefer prototypical German body postures. In the Japanese study, vice versa, we found a significant preference for prototypical Japanese body postures. We therefore think that modeling concrete behaviors such as body postures based on a video corpus recorded in different cultures is very well suited for the integration of cultural backgrounds into the behavior of virtual characters and can help increase a character's acceptance.

6.3 Summary

In this chapter, we described evaluation studies that were conducted in order to investigate whether human observers prefer agent behavior that was designed to reflect their own cultural background. As described in the previous chapters, culture-related differences in verbal behavior, communication management and nonverbal behavior were taken into account.

For evaluation purposes, we tested the aspects in isolation. In that manner, we were able to find out which of the implemented aspects actually have an impact on the judgment of human observers.

For evaluation, we set up two different studies, one that investigates verbal behavior and another that investigates communication management as well as nonverbal behavior. This distinction was made, since verbal and nonverbal behavior have an impact on one another and could influence the user's perception. To this end, the verbal study did not contain variations in nonverbal behavior such as gestures, while the nonverbal study contained Gibberish as a substitute for real speech to be able to integrate communication management behaviors.

For both studies, two different versions were created, one to be conducted in Germany and one to be conducted in Japan, each containing virtual characters and text-to-speech systems that match the cultural background of the observers. In each study, we hypothesized that human observers prefer agent behavior that is in line with observations made for their own cultural background. Thus, we expected German participants to prefer prototypical German agent behavior, while we expected Japanese participants to prefer prototypical Japanese agent behavior.

In the first study described in this chapter, differences in verbal behavior were taken into account. In particular, differences in topic selection were integrated into six dialogs, while prototypical German dialogs were more personal than prototypical Japanese dialogs.

Our results reveal that German observers found the German version of the dialogs significantly more appropriate and interesting, would rather like to join the conversation and think that agents get along with each other better. The Japanese part of the evaluation study reveals that Japanese participants found the Japanese versions of small talk conversations significantly more appropriate and interesting and thought that agents were getting along with each other better.

The second study described in this chapter, investigates communication management and nonverbal behaviors. To this end, differences in the usage of pauses in speech, overlapping speech, a combination of both, gestural speed, spatial extent and postures were taken into account. For the study, these aspects were tested in isolation. The evaluation conducted in Germany reveals that participants significantly preferred the version that resembled behavior observed for their own cultural background for some of the behavioral aspects (overlapping speech and spatial extent of gestures). For all other aspects, participants seemed to prefer the German versions at least by trend.

In the Japanese evaluation study, we found that Japanese participants significantly preferred postures designed for their cultural background. Only for pauses in speech and overlapping speech we observed a controversial trend. One reason for this outcome might be the missing semantics of the dialogs shown. Since the Japanese version contained both, more pauses and more overlaps in speech, but lacked the context in which they occur, participants might have chosen the safe solution, i.e. the version with less pauses and overlaps.

In sum, the evaluation studies described in this chapter suggest that human observers of different cultural backgrounds seem to prefer agent behavior that was designed to reflect their own cultural background in most cases. Thus, we think that the integration of cultural background to the behavioral models of virtual characters can lead towards a better acceptance of the characters on the user's side.

7 Generalization of the Approach

The work carried out for this dissertation can be further employed in research in different ways. On the one hand, the approach taken can be transfered to other cultures. On the other hand, the demonstrator can be used as a test bed for further research studies.

In the first section of this chapter, the transfer of the approach is demonstrated for the American and Arab cultures, investigating communication management behaviors. The second section of this chapter demonstrates how the implemented behaviors can be employed for further research studies. Although the demonstrator was also used for purposes different from cultural research, e.g. for interactive storytelling [EKM+11] [MEA11], in this dissertation the applicability is exemplified for the domain of culture, in particular, for the simulation of synthetic cultures (theory-based) and for the impact of social relationship on behavior (corpus-based).

7.1 Transferring the Approach

The workflow of this dissertation (see Section 5.1) was conducted for the two cultural backgrounds of Germany and Japan. The approach, however, is of a general nature and can be reproduced for other cultural backgrounds.

During an internship at the Institute of Creative Technologies [USC12], such a transfer has been exemplified for the Arab and American cultural backgrounds, in cooperation with researchers from the institute (see also [EHAG10]). The video

Culture / Dimension	Arab World	World Average	USA
PDI	80	55	40
IDV	38	64	91

Table 7.1: Hofstede's scores for America and Arabia on the dimensions Power Distance (PDI) and Individualism (IDV) compared to world average.

corpus used for the transfer was recorded as part of a NSF-funded project (National Science Foundation under Grant No. 0729287, and the U.S. Army Research, Development, and Engineering Command (RDECOM)), and kindly provided by the Institute of Creative Technologies [USC12]. Due to time limitations, the video corpus was not annotated. We thus focused on aspects of communication management behaviors, since they can analyzed automatically using the speech signals.

Just as in the approach taken in this dissertation, we started with an overview of behavioral tendencies described in literature, pointing out differences between the two cultures, and proceeded by grounding our expectations in empirical data by analyzing a multi-modal corpus. Findings were subsequently integrated into our demonstrator and evaluated in the target cultures to investigate their impact on the perception of human observers.

Cultural Profiles   As we pointed out in Subsection 2.2.2, communication management behaviors are considered culture-dependent [TT99]. Regarding the Arab and US American cultures, we expect rather strong differences since the cultures can be categorized very differently, using the dimensional models of culture described in Subsection 2.1.2. In particular, differences can be observed with regard to Hofstede's dimensions individualism (IDV) and power distance (PDI), see Table 7.1 for the rankings. While Arabia scores high on the PDI dimension and low on the IDV dimension, the US score low on the PDI dimension and high on the IDV dimension. Since Hofstede [HPH02] states that silence may occur in conversations in collectivistic cultures without creating tension, and the usage of pauses can be a crucial feature of their conversations, which does not hold true for individualistic cultures, we expect more pauses in Arab conversations than in American ones. In high-power cultures, interpersonal synchrony is much more important than in low-power cultures [TT99]. We therefore expect more verbal feedback in Arab conversations, as interlocutors show attentiveness while they are listening.

average occurrence (per minute)	American corpus	Arab corpus	p
silence > 0.5 sec	6.35	7.75	0.15
silence > 1 sec	1.34	2.16	0.09
same speaker	0.99	1.62	0.08
listener speech (total)	10.62	14.01	0.10
feedback <= 1 sec	8.02	10.86	0.08

Table 7.2: Differences found in the corpus analysis for the Northern American and Arab cultures.

These ideas are supported by Trompenaars and Hampden-Turner's framework [THT97], where cultures are divided into three groups: Western, Latin and Oriental cultures. While America is considered a Western culture, the Arabic world would count as an Oriental culture. Western cultures are described as verbal cultures where members get nervous and uneasy when there are long pauses. Interrupting the conversation partner is considered as impolite. Thus, turn taking is managed in a way that one starts talking after the interlocutor has stopped. In contrast, in Oriental cultures silence is much more important and, thus, does not create tension but can be considered a sign of respect.

Corpus Study To ground our expectations into empirical data, we analyzed a video corpus recorded as part of a NSF-funded effort (National Science Foundation under Grant No. 0729287, and the U.S. Army Research, Development, and Engineering Command (RDECOM)) and provided by our cooperation partners. For the acquisition of the corpus, participants were invited in pairs in the American and Arab cultures, while one watched a video in advance that he or she explained to the interlocutor during the recordings. Figure 7.1 shows example interactions from the video corpus. To assure that the listener was active, participants were told that the listener had to tell the story to the experimenter afterwards. In comparison to the work carried out in this dissertation, the videos were not annotated. Thus, whether a participant talked or not, was not calculated from the transcribed data but from the recorded audio signals. In total, 44 videos were investigated.

Table 7.2 summarizes the results of our corpus analysis. To analyze silence in speech, we computed those traces, where neither the listener nor the speaker spoke at a time. Following our analysis of communication management behavior

Figure 7.1: Example interactions from the NSF-funded video corpus (upper: Arabia; lower: Northern America).

(see Subsection 4.4.2), we sorted out brief pauses that e.g. result from breathing. Comparing the two cultures, we found a tendency that more silent traces occurred in the Arab conversations than in the American ones using the two-tailed t-test. To find out whether a pause is used as a turn-taking signal, we additionally analyzed which party breaks the silence. Comparing the two cultures, we found a tendency that it is much more common in American conversations that the same speaker breaks the silence than in the Arab conversations, where silence usually occurs between turns.

To investigate listener feedback, we analyzed the listener's audios in isolation to find out whether there are culture-related differences in the quantity of listener activity. Our analysis revealed that Arab listeners had the speaking floor more often than American listeners. To gain a deeper insight in how this tendency is related to feedback behavior, we had a closer look at very short segments of the listener's speech ($<= 1$ second). Although feedback does not necessarily have to be shorter than one second, this categorization helps filtering out short speech-segments such as "uh-huh" or "mm-hmm". Comparing the two cultures on those short segments, we found a tendency that Arab listeners were more active than American listeners (see Table 7.2). The analysis of overlapping speech did not reveal any meaningful results. We therefore did not further investigate overlapping speech.

Simulation As a next step our findings were integrated into the demonstrator described in Section 5.4. For evaluation, we used virtual agents with a culturally neutral appearance that could either be from an American or Arab cultural background. Thus, virtual characters were dark haired and not dressed in a culture-specific way. As a full body-view was shown, faces cannot be observed in enough detail to determine a certain cultural background.

Just as described in our evaluation of communication management behavior (see Section 6.2), we used Gibberish for the perception study to avoid that observers were distracted by the semantics of speech.

Using the findings from the corpus analysis, we designed agent dialogs that contain prototypical communication management behaviors and lasted for approximately one minute. More silence was integrated into the Arab dialogs compared to the American ones and pauses were positioned between turns in the Arab version and within turns in the American version. In the demonstrator, the Arab dialogs contained 3 pauses that were placed between the speaker turns and the American dialogs contained two pauses that occurred within a speaker's turn. Regarding feedback behavior, more verbal feedback was given in the Arab conversations compared to the American ones in the video corpus. In the simulated dialogs, we integrated verbal feedback twice in the American version and four times in the Arab version.

Evaluation Following our evaluation setup described in Section 6.2, we simulated the aspects of communication management in isolation as well as in combination.

Thus, in the evaluation study, participants were shown three pairs of videos in alternating order, after watching an introduction video. One pair contained the prototypical usage of pauses in speech for American versus Arab communication. Another pair contained the different usage of giving verbal feedback and a third pair contained a combination of both behaviors.

	pause		feedback		both	
	USA	Arab	USA	Arab	USA	Arab
Q1	6	2	3	5	6	2
Q2	4	4	3	5	5	3
Q3	6	2	2	6	6	2
Q4	6	2	5	3	6	2
Q5	6	2	3	5	5	3
Sum	**28**	**12**	**16**	**24**	**28**	**12**
%	70%	30%	40%	60%	70%	30%

Table 7.3: Preferences of American participants in our evaluation study.

In a preliminary study, we evaluated 10 subjects: 8 Americans and 2 Arabs, who decided which of the videos they preferred for the following five questions:

1. Q1: Which video seemed the most natural?

2. Q2: Which group of agents would you rather like to join?

3. Q3: Which video appeared more unrealistic?

4. Q4: Which pair of agents do you think liked each other better?

5. Q5: Which pair of agents was more friendly with each other?

Results from the American participants are summarized in Table 7.3. American participants significantly preferred prototypical American pause behavior (with $p < .01$, using the two-tailed t-test). For feedback behavior, American participants preferred the Arab version by trend. The combined version, however, showed exactly the same distribution as for pause behavior. This suggests that the perception of different pause behavior was dominant over feedback behavior.

Although we only had two Arab participants, interestingly both rated the Arab pause version as superior for all five questions. We take this as a first evidence that our behavior model for the usage of pauses in speech can evoke different perceptions. As for American participants, the Arab participants rated the feedback version designed for the other culture as more realistic and preferred the American version for all five questions. Another similarity can be found in the combined version, since Arab participants judged the videos showing the combined behavior the same way that they rated the videos showing the pause behavior. This strengthens the idea that pause behavior affected the participants' perceptions more than feedback behavior.

7.2 Applications

The demonstrator described in Subsection 5.4 along with its culture-specific behaviors for virtual characters holds great potential for further research studies. Therefore, it can be used as a test bed for several purposes and the implemented behaviors can be reused.

This has been exemplified successfully of synthetic cultures (theory-based) and for the impact of social relationships on behavior (corpus-based) in cooperation with our project partners in different research projects.

7.2.1 Simulation of Synthetic Cultures

The eCute project [eCu12] aims at education in cultural awareness and therefore uses synthetic cultures based on Hofstede's dimensions (see Subsection 2.1.2).

Compared to the approach carried out in this dissertation, it thus aims at a purely theory-driven approach to integrate culture. In particular, researchers from different disciplines, such as social sciences and computer science, closely work together in order to find out how cultural dimensions can be displayed with virtual characters. Therefore, cultural dimensions are integrated into the behavior of virtual characters, taking the descriptions from literature as a basis.

In the framework of the eCute project, our demonstrator was used as a test bed to simulate cultural dimensions. Although the project wants to integrate the user into the virtual scenario in order to be able to interact with the virtual characters using intuitive input devices, our non-interactive demonstrator can be used for prototyping. In addition, the behaviors modeled for our demonstrator were designed to simulate prototypical German or Japanese behavior, however, most aspects can be reused for other purposes as well, such as varying the expressivity of a gesture.

For our study, we incorporated the masculinity dimension with prototypical differences in verbal and nonverbal behavior that should resemble prototypical feminine in contrast to masculine cultures [EDH+11]. Therefore, we designed a scenario that on the one hand demonstrates differences between masculine and feminine cultures, and on the other hand leads to a conflict when members of different

Figure 7.2: Professor / student scenario simulating prototypical feminine (left) and masculine (right) cultural behavior for both characters.

cultures meet. As a showcase, we chose a conversation between a professor and a student in which the student asks for a deadline extension. In order to avoid side effects evoked by the gender of the characters, we left the genders of the virtual characters constant. Thus, only the gender-dimension of the characters' *culture* varied but not the gender of the characters itself. Figure 7.2 shows the virtual scenario including our professor-student setup with a female student and a male professor (gender), showing prototypical feminine or masculine nonverbal behavior (culture).

Each character within the scenario either has a prototypical masculine or feminine cultural background. Thus, four different scenarios where scripted. There are two major differences in the four scenarios: the student's reason for needing an extension and whether or not the professor agrees to grant an extension. The agent with the masculine script focuses on 'performance' and thus needs an extension to improve the assignment. In contrast, the agent with the feminine script focuses on 'caring' and thus needs an extension because of attending an important family event before the deadline. A masculine professor would accept the way of argumentation of a masculine student and agree to an extension. The feminine way of argumentation, by contrast, is considered as a weak excuse and leads to a conflict with no extension of the deadline. A professor from a feminine culture would understand the way of argumentation of a feminine student and extend the deadline. The conversation with a masculine student would not necessarily lead to an outwardly visible conflict but to a misunderstanding at least, since the feminine professor would not understand the student's need to improve the work. Table 7.4 outlines the four different scenarios.

Besides differences in the flow of the scenario, members of masculine and feminine cultures also differ in their choice of wording and nonverbal behavior. For

Scenario	Student	Professor	Outcome
mas. prof., fem. stud.	family event	weak excuse	conflict, extension not granted
mas. prof., mas. stud.	improvement	understands pursuit	extension granted
fem. prof., fem. stud.	family event	understands obligation	extension granted
fem. prof., mas. stud.	improvement	cares for student	misunderstanding, extension granted

Table 7.4: Flow of scenarios incorporating prototypical masculine and feminine cultural behavior.

the implementation of the different scenarios, verbal behavior was scripted based on descriptions from the literature and nonverbal behavior was added from our nonverbal knowledge base. Therefore, differences in choice of body posture and gestures as well as expressivity were taken into account.

Showing these scenarios to human observers from different cultural backgrounds, we investigated the impact on their perception. Results indicate that participants did judge the scenarios differently, but not necessarily due to the behavioral style of the characters. Thus, the scenario outcome seemed to strongly influence the perception of human observers. We think that other dimensions of culture also could have influenced the user's perceptions. On the one hand, other dimensions of the cultural background of the human participants could have influenced their judgment. We found some interesting insights distinguishing participants from individualistic and collectivistic cultures, who judged the appropriateness of the virtual characters' behavior significantly different in some scenarios. On the other hand, it is hard to exclude the other dimensions of culture from the virtual characters' behavior. The fact that we had a conversation between a student and a professor could, for example, have indicated power distance. In our future work, these issues will be addressed in further studies.

7.2.2 Impact of Social Relationship

Our demonstrator was further used to investigate other factors of human background based on the video corpus by our Japanese cooperation partners of the

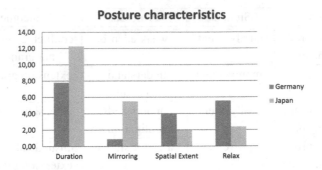

Figure 7.3: Posture characteristics in the German and Japanese corpus.

Cube-G project [Aug09]. As described in Section 4.2, the video corpus contains three prototypical scenarios: a first-time meeting, a negotiation and a meeting with someone of a higher status. For the work conducted during this dissertation, several aspects of human behavior were taken into account in the first scenario for the simulation of prototypical small talk behavior. In comparison, our Japanese colleagues focused on one aspect and compared it over two different situations. In particular, differences in body postures were investigated for the first-time meeting scenario compared to the conversation with a higher status person. In that manner, the impact of social relations on nonverbal behavior across the German and Japanese cultures was considered.

In their earlier research [LNR10], Lipi and colleagues investigated posture characteristics and in particular the impact of culture on aspects such as posture mirroring. Based on a literature study, they therefore came up with parameters which define the characteristics of posture: spatial extent, rigidness, mirroring and duration [RNA+09]. Comparing the two cultures of Germany and Japan from our common video corpus revealed culture-related differences. Figure 7.3 graphically summarizes their results. The value for duration was derived by calculating the average length of postures observed in the data. The score of mirroring reflects the total number of common posture of both interlocutors. Spatial extent and rigidness were annotated on a 7-point scale. Please note that in Figure 7.3 the opposite side of the rigidness dimension is used (relax), since a higher score indicates less rigidness. Their results indicate that Japanese participants remained in postures longer, engaged more frequently in posture mirroring, took less space and displayed more rigid postures in comparison to German participants.

Based on these differences, the impact of social relationship on posture characteristics was further investigated. Observed differences were subsequently integrated into a Bayesian network that describes the impact of culture and social relationship on their posture parameters [LNR10].

Until that point, virtual characters had not been involved in their studies. After sharing our demonstrator and some tutorial on its usage, Lipi and colleagues used the application with its culture-specific posture animations for an evaluation study that investigates culture- and relationship-related differences in posture characteristics with virtual characters [LNE+11]. Following the study designs described in Chapter 6, two different evaluation studies were created to be conducted in Germany using the German-looking characters, and to be conducted in Japan using the Japanese-looking characters. For each study, eight conditions were designed that each contained either a first-time meeting or higher status conversation and prototypical German or Japanese posture behavior observed during a first-time meeting or higher status conversation respectively. In that manner, in two out of the eight agent conversations, behavior matched the social relation and cultural background, while in the other six scenarios there was a mismatch.

In an evaluation study with eight German and 19 Japanese participants, the effect on human observers was tested along several dimensions such as naturalness or politeness. The results showed that Japanese participants prefer behavioral aspects that are in line with their own cultural background under a specified social relationship and that German participants prefer behaviors that are consistent with their own culture by perceiving interactions with a person of a higher status.

We thus think that our demonstrator qualifies as a test bed for additional studies that investigate human factors in behavior and can be used for further studies in that research area.

8 Contributions and Future Work

The first part of this chapter describes the contributions of this dissertation, taking into account the challenges that were faced as well as its benefit to the research community. First, the methodology elaborated for this dissertation contributes as a guidance for other culture-specific generation approaches. Second, the dissertation depicts a way to operationalize culture for virtual characters, provides materials and data for reproduction and identifies behavioral aspects as a foundation for culture-specific behavioral models. Finally, the technical realization of our approach provides solutions to the challenges that have to be faced when integrating culture into a computational system.

The second part of this chapter points out possible future extensions. Particularly, the workflow carried out for this dissertation can be expanded to a development cycle by using the results from the evaluation studies as an input to refine the behavioral models. Further, additional culture-related aspects of behavior can be investigated or the user can be integrated into the scenario as an active participant rather than an observer.

8.1 Contributions

The preceding chapters have presented several contributions to serve as a foundation for the integration of cultural background into a computational system.

In Section 1.3, the challenges that have to be faced when investigating culture for the behavioral models of virtual characters were outlined. These tasks were solved as follows:

8.1.1 Identify operationalizeable Models of Culture and Behavioral Differences

Literature from the social sciences was reviewed to identify appropriate theories that describe culture and corresponding prototypical behavior in Section 2.1. Dimensional models and dichotomies prove to be well suited as they take a descriptive approach to explain culture and stereotypical behavior. Different levels of human behavior are influenced by cultural background. In Section 2.2, a set of behavioral aspects was selected that can be used for the simulation of cultural background with virtual characters. In particular, aspects from verbal behavior, communication management and nonverbal behavior were considered.

Since the approach taken in this dissertation is exemplified for the German and Japanese cultures, the theories of culture introduced before were taken as a basis to construct cultural profiles for the two cultures and formulate hypotheses on the behavioral aspects pointed out as being relevant before.

8.1.2 Extract concrete Behavioral Differences from a Video Corpus

Theories from the social sciences are a good guideline to formulate hypotheses but are often too abstract to build computational models. In order to obtain statistical data on culture-related behavior, the video corpus recorded for the Cube-G project [Aug09], which constituted the frame of this dissertation, was analyzed regarding the behavioral aspects identified before (see Section 4.4).

For the corpus recordings, it was carefully assured that participants of the different cultures faced the same conditions. Therefore, each individual participated in three standardized scenarios without having prior knowledge about the recordings. Further, the conversation partners were professional actors to ensure that interlocutors have not met in advance. Also, technical issues, such as choice of camera or size of recording area, were specified for reproducibility in all recorded cultures.

To prepare the video corpus for further processing, an annotation schema was introduced in Section 4.3, based on established schemes for each of the relevant aspects. The schema contains variables and structures that are later used for the integration into computational models.

8.1.3 Build computational Models of Culture-related Behavior

Chapter 5 introduces the integration of culture-related behaviors into the behavioral models of virtual characters. Approaches were identified in Section 5.2

that had already overcome similar challenges successfully for other human factors, such as consistent dialog generation, although they have not been applied to culture yet.

To generate natural dialog behavior, a plan-based approach was employed for the production of goal-directed dialog utterances dependent on cultural background. To ensure autonomous behavior, a distributed system was implemented that generates intentional dialog behavior for each character individually.

For the realization of nonverbal behaviors, a Bayesian network was employed. The Bayesian network allowed us to deal with uncertain knowledge resulting from the fact that there is no clear mapping between cultural dimensions and nonverbal behaviors. It also enabled us to customize behaviors to a particular culture without giving up a certain amount of variability that is necessary to ensure that a character is perceived as an individual. In some cases, culture-specific behaviors cannot be generated by customizing culture-neutral behaviors because culture is reflected by specific (usually emblematic) gestures and postures that need to be accurately executed in order not to be misunderstood. To account for this fact, customizable behaviors were augmented by behaviors extracted directly from the corpus.

8.1.4 Measure Impact on Human Observers

To measure which of the implemented aspects of behavior have an impact on the perception of human observers, the aspects were tested in isolation. Therefore, separate evaluation studies were designed for the different behavioral channels to exclude correlations between different aspects of behavior, for example, by using a fantasy language to simulate communication management behaviors without adding any semantic content of speech.

To investigate whether human observers prefer agent behavior that resembles their own cultural background, two different versions of each evaluation study were designed and conducted in both target countries, Germany and Japan (see Chapter 6).

The challenges that were solved throughout this dissertation, as described above, contribute to the research area on several levels:

8.1.5 Methodical Contribution

The method used in this dissertation combines the two approaches usually taken when integrating human factors into computational systems: top-down (theory-driven) and bottom-up (corpus-driven). In that manner, the social sciences are taken as a basis to formulate hypotheses about behavioral differences, while a corpus provides statistical data on the behaviors.

The combined approach proves to be very well suited for the aim of integrating cultural background for virtual characters, as purely theory-driven approaches for example based on dimensional models sometimes cannot produce natural behavior for a given cultural background, while a purely corpus-driven approach is not general enough to be transferable to social situations differing from the context of the recordings.

In this dissertation, the integration of cultural background into the behavioral models of virtual characters was exemplified for the German and Japanese cultures. The workflow constructed for this approach, however, is of a general nature and can serve as a guidance for other culture-specific generation approaches.

For example, the general nature of our approach was used to carry out a study on the US American and Arab cultures for aspects of communication management behaviors (see Section 7.1). Following our workflow, we started with a literature research to build cultural profiles and identify prototypical behavioral tendencies. As a next step, the expectations were grounded into empirical data to obtain statistical insights into the target behavioral aspects for the two cultures. Findings were further integrated into our demonstrator to simulate prototypical culture-related behaviors with virtual characters. Following our study design to evaluate communication management behaviors using Gibberish (see Section 6.2), the implemented behaviors were investigated in perception studies with US American and Arab participants.

8.1.6 Conceptual Contribution

In the framework of this dissertation, several aspects of human behavior were integrated into the behavior models of virtual characters to exemplify culture-related differences and evaluated to investigate their impact on the perception of human observers of the target cultural backgrounds. According to Lee and Nass [LN98], users prefer virtual characters that resemble their own ethnical background. Integrating culture-related behaviors that prove to enhance the users' perceptions on a virtual character in our studies, can further improve a character's acceptance by users of the target cultural background. We, therefore, think that designers of virtual characters can use our findings to adapt relevant aspects of behavior to the desired cultural background.

To analyze the empirical data, annotation schemes were designed that capture culture-related behavioral differences. The annotation schemes, provided in Appendix A, serve as a guideline on how to structure behavioral aspects to be integrated into computational models.

Further, the findings from the corpus study can provide useful data for research in related areas. Focusing on coherent conversations in interactive systems, Breuing and Wachsmuth [BW12], for example, present a system that emulates human-like topic awareness in artificial agents. Our annotated corpus data containing topics that were discussed during the first-time meetings, will be used for a planned evaluation. In the study, dialog topics and topic shifts will be automatically identified, using their method, and compared to the annotations provided from our corpus (outlined in [BW12]) .

8.1.7 Technical Contribution

Chapter 5 describes the integration of culture-related behaviors into the behavioral models of virtual characters.

A hierarchical planner was used for the realization of natural dialog behavior to generate appropriate dialog utterances in small talk conversations and integrated into a distributed system to generate autonomous behavior for each character individually. To ensure non-monotonic behaviors, personal motivations were added to each agent's background that, in addition to cultural background, determine behavior selection.

Starting from verbal behavior, nonverbal behaviors were added to the dialogs. To customize the expressiveness of nonverbal behaviors, a Bayesian network approach was employed. To model the network, Hofstede's dimensional model [HHM10] was used as a basis, which seemed very well suited for this purpose, since the dimensions can be represented by different nodes in the network, while mappings to behaviors are available. This approach proves to be of only limited appropriateness, since national cultures do not necessarily behave prototypically for their scores on each dimension. Although, the Japanese culture scores high on the masculinity dimension, as does the Arab culture for example, it is not common for members of the Japanese culture to use wide and animated gestures, as it is suggested for prototypical masculine cultures. The theory-based approach seems to be well suited for the simulation of synthetic cultures. For the simulation of national cultures, however, findings from corpus studies can add further information on prototypical behavior.

Culture-specific behaviors cannot be generated by customization in any case, for example for emblematic gestures. To exemplify the direct extraction of nonverbal behaviors, body postures were remodeled from the video corpus to enrich our animation set, which was well received during the evaluation studies.

We see great potential for our demonstrator to serve as a test bed for research studies investigating human factors for virtual character behavior. In Section 7.2, this has been exemplified for further research on culture, namely the impact of social relationship on behavior and the simulation of synthetic cultures, by using the implemented aspects of behaviors.

8.2 Future Work

Possible extensions to the work described in this dissertation are manifold.

8.2.1 Refinement of the Models

The evaluation results for some of the culture-related aspects of behavior that were investigated in the framework of this dissertation, were meaningful and suggest that their integration can enhance the acceptance of a virtual character (see Chapter 6). For other aspects, results were less promising.

As suggested by Cassell [Cas07], findings from evaluation studies can serve as an input to refine the behavioral models of virtual characters. In this dissertation, the workflow introduced in Section 1.2 was executed only once. A refinement based on the results of the evaluation studies seems to hold great potential and is planned for our future work.

For example, observing the impact of overlapping speech across cultures did not lead to the desired effect. We think this was caused by the missing semantics of speech during our studies, which suggest that overlapping speech should not be considered on a quantitative level only but also on a qualitative level. Therefore, semantics such as feedback behavior should be taken into account, which is also supported by our analysis of verbal behavior, where we found culture-related differences in feedback behavior.

Also, the correlation to other communication management behaviors such as pauses in speech are of special interest. We aim to investigate how verbal feedback occurs, for example, after pauses, sequentially or in an overlapping manner. In addition, we want to take into account the purpose of overlaps by investigating whether it is used for example to take the floor. The same goes for pauses in speech, for which we will further explore what happens during pauses from a nonverbal point of view.

8.2.2 Training Models from Corpus Data

To model culture in this dissertation, tendencies from the literature were verified by our video corpus, and the statistical information obtained was used as a basis for computational models. For our future work, we plan to integrate findings from the corpus data directly into a model that automatically generates conversational behavior dependent on cultural background. For such an approach, Hidden Markov Models (HMM) [Rab89] seem very well suited, since they are known to cope well with temporal patterns. As a first step, we aim at predicting probable dialog sequences for a given cultural background based on our annotations of dialog utterances.

For our model of nonverbal expressivity, a Bayesian network was employed, using Hofstede's dimensional model of culture [HHM10] as a basis. As our results revealed, this approach is only suited in some cases, which points out a weakness of a purely theory-driven approach. The model was designed at an early stage of this dissertation, where analyzed corpus data had not been available yet. Modeling a Bayesian network with input from the annotated corpus data is feasible, as already exemplified for body postures by our Japanese colleagues [LNR10], see also Section 7.2. We therefore see this approach as a promising step for our future work on expressive behavior.

8.2.3 Integration of further Aspects

In this dissertation, a set of behavioral aspects was investigated that seemed to be promising for our purpose. However, the set is not complete and can be enriched by further aspects.

A possible extension includes nonverbal regulators such as head nods or eye gaze. Due to the condition of our video corpus, the analysis of head nods is feasible. In addition, head nods are considered culture-dependent. In our future work, head nods will thus be added as another aspect of culture-related conversational behavior.

In our corpus, culture-related differences in the usage of self-touching gestures were observed. These adaptor gestures are very applicable for the simulation of culture-related communicative behaviors, since they are not dependent on semantics of speech and can, thus, be used for a wide variety of dialog situations. Although adaptor gestures do not have a communicative meaning per se, they nevertheless reveal information, such as excitement or uncomfortableness.

8.2.4 Interactivity

As pointed out in Section 7.2, our demonstrator has been used for prototyping in the eCute project [eCu12]. Since the focus of the project is on education of cultural awareness, user interaction is an important aspect.

How such an interaction can be realized has been exemplified in [KED+12], where we integrated human users into our scenario using Microsoft's Kinect [Mic12]. Hence, users are able to use full-body interaction without any controller for communication with the enculturated virtual characters. Interpersonal distance behavior was investigated and our preliminary results are promising in a way that users found the interaction intuitive and that human users notice cultural differences and respond to it. We thus see great potential for controller-free interfaces for cultural learning scenarios.

Another possible integration of human users into the scenario has been outlined in [OEss], where we pointed out the potential of Augmented Reality (AR) technology for cultural education using virtual characters. We think that interacting with virtual characters in AR environments may provide a more immersive user experience than traditional virtual character interfaces such as desktop-based interfaces.

Appendix

Appendix

A Coding Schemes

In this part of the appendix, the coding schemes are provided, as they were used to annotate the video data in this dissertation. The semantics of the coding schemes is compatible for usage in the Anvil tool [Kip01]. Therefore, the head of each coding schema defines the attributes for each track that can be selected by the annotator, while in the body of the coding schemes, the annotation tracks themselves are defined. In that manner, e.g. the track "action-subject" is defined in the body, while the concrete attributes such as "info-request" or "answer" are defined in the head. In addition, tracks can be grouped into categories. Thus, e.g. a gesture's type and expressivity are grouped to "gesture".

A.1 Annotation Schema for Verbal Behavior

This part of the appendix holds our verbal coding schema.

The first group of tracks (speech), holds the participant's and actor's transliteration and translation. For these tracks no attributes are defined. Instead, a text field is provided to the annotators where the verbal behavior is written down.

The second group (communication style) holds the participant's and actor's dialog utterances as well as discussed topics. Possible dialog utterances constitute a subset of the DAMSL annotation schema [CA97] and are defined in the valueset "action-type", while possible topics are provided in the valueset "greetingphaseType". Please see Subsection 4.3.1 for further information on our annotation of verbal behavior.

```
<?xml version="1.0" encoding="ISO-8859-1"?>
<annotation-spec>
```

```
<!-- *************** HEAD ********************* -->

 <head>
  <valuetype-def>

<valueset name="actionType">
    <value-el>statement<doc>The utterance is an argument
    or another statement about the world.</doc> </value-el>
    <value-el>info request<doc>The utterance is a question
    or other form of information request.</doc> </value-el>
    <value-el>influence on future<doc>The speaker wants to
    influence to listeners future actions or his/her own
    future actions or both.</doc> </value-el>
    <value-el>agreement/ disagreement<doc>The current
    utterance indicates the speakers point of view of a
    previous action (either positive or negative).</doc>
    </value-el>
    <value-el>hold<doc>The speaker performs an act that
    leaves the decision open pending further discussion.
    </doc> </value-el>
    <value-el>understanding/ misunderstanding<doc>This
    aspect concerns the actions that speakers take in order
    to make sure that they are understanding each other,
    without stating a point of view.</doc> </value-el>
    <value-el>answer<doc>The current utterance is an answer
    to a previous information request.</doc> </value-el>
    <value-el>joke<doc>The speaker tries to be funny.</doc>
    </value-el>
    <value-el>laugh<doc>The person laughs.</doc> </value-el>
    <value-el>other<doc>The current utterance is none of the
    actions described here in its main type.</doc> </value-el>
    </valueset>

<valueset name="greetingphaseType">
    <value-el>introduction<doc>People introduce their selves
    to each other.</doc> </value-el>
        <value-el>studies subject<doc>They are talking about
        the subjects studies or job.</doc> </value-el>
        <value-el>studies actor<doc>They are talking about the
        actors studies of job.</doc> </value-el>
        <value-el>age<doc>They are talking about their age.
        </doc> </value-el>
```

```
<value-el>future plans<doc>They are talking about their
future plans.</doc> </value-el>
<value-el>going out<doc>They are talking about going
out at night.</doc> </value-el>
<value-el>task<doc>They are talking about the task that
they should solve.</doc> </value-el>
<value-el>reason<doc>They are talking about the reasons,
why they are here.</doc> </value-el>
<value-el>origin subject<doc>They are talking about
where the subject is coming from and living currently.
</doc> </value-el>
<value-el>origin actor<doc>They are talking about where
the actor is coming from and living currently.</doc>
</value-el>
<value-el>living situation<doc></doc> </value-el>
<value-el>personal habitudes subject<doc>They are talking
about the subjects personal habitudes.</doc> </value-el>
<value-el>personal habitudes actor<doc>They are talking
about the actors personal habitudes.</doc> </value-el>
<value-el>friends<doc>They are talking about their friends
/ people they know.</doc> </value-el>
 <value-el>hobbies<doc>They are talking about their hobbies.
 </doc> </value-el>
<value-el>side job<doc>They are talking about a job they
are doing/did along the way with their studies.</doc>
</value-el>
  <value-el>traveling / places<doc>They are talking about
  traveling or places they go.</doc> </value-el>
  <value-el>location of places<doc>They are talking about
  the location of places, e.g. how to get there.</doc>
  </value-el>
  <value-el>health<doc>They are talking about their/someones
  health.</doc> </value-el>
  <value-el>music / instruments<doc>They are talking about
  music.</doc> </value-el>
<value-el>topic 1<doc>They are talking about another
topic. Please note that topic into the comments field.
</doc> </value-el>
<value-el>topic 2<doc>They are talking about another
topic. Please note that topic into the comments field.
</doc> </value-el>
<value-el>topic 3<doc>They are talking about another
```

```
      topic. Please note that topic into the comments field.
      </doc> </value-el>
      <value-el>topic 4<doc>They are talking about another
      topic. Please note that topic into the comments field.
      </doc> </value-el>
      <value-el>topic 5<doc>They are talking about another
      topic. Please note that topic into the comments field.
      </doc> </value-el>
    </valueset>

  </valuetype-def>
  </head>

<!-- ************************ BODY ******************* -->

  <body>

<group name="speech">
  <track-spec name="S1: trl" type="primary">
    <doc>
      This track codes the current utterance.
    </doc>
    <attribute name="transliteration">
    </attribute>
  </track-spec>

  <track-spec name="S1: sub" type="span" ref="speech.S1: trl">
    <doc>
      This track gives an English subtitle to the current
      utterance.</doc>
    <attribute name="subtitle">
    </attribute>
  </track-spec>

  <track-spec name="S2: trl" type="primary">
    <doc>
      This track codes the current utterance.
    </doc>
    <attribute name="transliteration">
    </attribute>
  </track-spec>
```

```
<track-spec name="S2: sub" type="span" ref="speech.S2: trl">
  <doc>
    This track gives an English subtitle to the current
    utterance. </doc>
  <attribute name="subtitle">
  </attribute>
</track-spec>
</group>

<group name="communication style">
<track-spec name="action subject" type="primary">
    <attribute name="type" emptyvalue="true"
    valuetype="actionType">
    <doc>Here, the action is categorised in its main type.
    </doc>
    </attribute>
    </track-spec>

<track-spec name="action actor" type="primary">
    <attribute name="type" emptyvalue="true"
    valuetype="actionType">
    <doc> Here, the action is categorised in its main type.
    </doc>
    </attribute>
    </track-spec>

<track-spec name="greeting-phase" type="primary">
    <attribute name="phase" emptyvalue="true"
    valuetype="greetingphaseType">
    <doc>The phase indicates the pupose of the utterances.</doc>
    </attribute>
    </track-spec>
</group>

  </body>

</annotation-spec>
```

A.2 Annotation Schema for Nonverbal Behavior

In this part of the appendix, the nonverbal coding schema is provided.

As in the verbal coding schema, the first group of tracks (speech), holds the participant's and actor's transliteration and translation.

The second group (gesture) holds the participant's gestures, including a gesture's phase, type and expressivity. A gesture's phase contains preparation, stroke and retraction phases. Possible gesture types are defined in the valueset "gestureType", according to McNeill's classification [McN92]. The dynamic variation of a gesture is annotated along the expressivity parameters [Pel05] on a seven-point scale.

The third group contains the participant's arm posture. Possible values, as defined in Bull's coding schema [Bul87], are provided in the valueset "postType_arm".

Please see Subsection 4.3.2 for further information on the annotation of nonverbal behaviors.

```
<?xml version="1.0" encoding="ISO-8859-1"?>
<annotation-spec>

<!-- *************** HEAD ********************* -->

 <head>
  <valuetype-def>

   <valueset name="phaseType">
    <value-el color="#eeee00">
      preparation
      <doc>
        Preparation phase, bringing arm and hand into stroke
        position. Note that changing hand shape before/after
        moving the arm belongs to the preparation, too. Also
        code position info.
      </doc>
    </value-el>
    <value-el color="#dd0000">
      stroke
      <doc>
        The most energetic part of the gesture movement.
        <b>Encode all other attributes for this gesture phrase
        in the stroke element!</b>
      </doc>
    </value-el>
```

```
<value-el color="#ee8800">
  hold
  <doc>
    A phase of stillness just before or just after the
    stroke, usually used to defer the stroke so that it
    coincides with a certain word.
    <b>When annotating an element as "hold" do not annotate
    any other attributes!</b>
  </doc>
</value-el>
<value-el color="#00bb33">
  retraction
  <doc>
    Retraction. Movement back to rest position. In sitting
    position this is usually the arm rest, the lap or
    folded arms. <b>Encode no other attributes in a
    "retract" element.</b>
  </doc>
</value-el>
</valueset>

<valueset name="gestureType">
  <value-el color="#8cda8e">beat</value-el>
  <value-el>deictic</value-el>
  <value-el>emblem</value-el>
  <value-el>iconic</value-el>
  <value-el>metaphoric</value-el>
  <value-el>adaptor</value-el>
</valueset>

<valueset name="postType_arm">
  <value-el>none</value-el>
  <value-el>PHHd</value-el>
  <value-el>PHNk</value-el>
  <value-el>PHFe</value-el>
  <value-el>SHdH</value-el>
  <value-el>PHSr</value-el>
  <value-el>PHUAm</value-el>
  <value-el>PHEw</value-el>
  <value-el>PHLAm</value-el>
  <value-el>PHWr</value-el>
  <value-el>FAs</value-el>
```

```
      <value-el>JHs</value-el>
      <value-el>PHCt</value-el>
      <value-el>PHRs</value-el>
      <value-el>PHAn</value-el>
      <value-el>PHB</value-el>
      <value-el>PHUBs</value-el>
      <value-el>PHTh</value-el>
      <value-el>PHK</value-el>
      <value-el>PHCf</value-el>
      <value-el>PHAe</value-el>
      <value-el>PHBLs</value-el>
      <value-el>PHF</value-el>
      <value-el>PHCrAM</value-el>
      <value-el>PHCrBk</value-el>
      <value-el>PHCrSt</value-el>
      <value-el>PHTe</value-el>
      <value-el>HP</value-el>
      <value-el>PHIPt</value-el>
      <value-el>PHTr</value-el>
      <value-el>PoH</value-el>
      <value-el>HUH</value-el>
    </valueset>

  </valuetype-def>
  </head>

<!-- ************************* BODY ******************** -->

  <body>

<group name="speech">
  <track-spec name="S1: trl" type="primary">
    <doc>
      This track codes the current utterance.
    </doc>
    <attribute name="transliteration">
    </attribute>
  </track-spec>

  <track-spec name="S1: sub" type="span" ref="speech.S1: trl">
    <doc>
      This track gives an English subtitle to the current
```

```
      utterance.
    </doc>
    <attribute name="subtitle">
    </attribute>
  </track-spec>

  <track-spec name="S2: trl" type="primary">
    <doc>
      This track codes the current utterance.
    </doc>
    <attribute name="transliteration">
    </attribute>
  </track-spec>

  <track-spec name="S2: sub" type="span" ref="speech.S2: trl">
    <doc>
      This track gives an English subtitle to the current
      utterance.
    </doc>
    <attribute name="subtitle">
    </attribute>
  </track-spec>
</group>

<group name="gesture">
    <track-spec name="phase" type="primary" >
      <attribute name="type" emptyvalue="false"
      defaultvalue="stroke" valuetype="phaseType">
      <doc>
        Phase description is based on the phases postulated
        by Kendon and McNeill (1992), later on extended by
        Kita et al. (1999).
      </doc>
      </attribute>
      <attribute name="handedness" emptyvalue="false"
      defaultvalue="right" valuetype="handednessType" />
    </track-spec>

    <track-spec name="phrase" type="primary">
      <attribute name="category" emptyvalue="false"
      defaultvalue="iconic" valuetype="gestureType"
      display="true" />
```

```
      </track-spec>

    <track-spec name="expressivity" type="singleton"
    ref="gesture.phrase">
      <doc>
        This track specifies the expressivity dimensions.
      </doc>
      <attribute name="repetition" emptyvalue="false"
      defaultvalue="1" display="true" valuetype="Number(1,7)"/>
      <attribute name="fluidity" emptyvalue="false"
      defaultvalue="4" valuetype="Number(1,7)"
      display="true"/>
      <attribute name="power" emptyvalue="false"
      defaultvalue="4" valuetype="Number(1,7)"
      display="true"/>
      <attribute name="speed" emptyvalue="false"
      defaultvalue="4" valuetype="Number(1,7)"
      display="true"/>
      <attribute name="spat.exp." emptyvalue="false"
      defaultvalue="4" valuetype="Number(1,7)"
      display="true"/>
    </track-spec>
  </group>

  <group name="posture">
    <track-spec name="arm" type="primary">
  <attribute name="arm" emptyvalue="false"
  defaultvalue="none" valuetype="postType_arm"
  display="true">
    </attribute>
    </track-spec>
  </group>

   </body>

 </annotation-spec>
```

A.3 Bull's Posture Coding Schema

In [Bul87], Bull's posture scoring system is introduced. According to the system, a posture can be classified into four main types: head, trunk, arms and legs. For the work carried out in this dissertation, the arm postures are of particular interest. Thus, in Table A.1 the categories of arm positions are summarized:

Postures	Description
Hand to hand	
PHHd	Puts hand to head. The hand is placed on any part of the head excluding the face and neck.
PHNk	Puts hand to neck.
PHFe	Puts hand to face.
SHdH	Supports head on hand.
Hand to arm	
One handed	
PHSr	Puts hand to shoulder.
PHUAm	Puts hand to upper arm (between shoulder and elbow).
PHEw	Puts hand to elbow.
PHLAm	Puts hand to lower arm (between elbow and wrist).
PHWr	Puts hand to wrist.
Two handed	
FAs	Fold arms.
JHs	Join hands.
Hand to trunk	
PHCt	Puts hand to chest.
PHRs	Puts hand to ribs.
PHAn	Puts hand to abdomen.
PHB	Puts hands to back.
Hand to leg	
PHUBs	Puts hand under backside.
PHTh	Puts hand to thigh.
PHK	Puts hand to knee.
PHCf	Puts hand to calf.
PHAe	Puts hand to ankle.
PHBLs	Puts hand between legs.
PHF	Puts hand to foot.
Hand to furniture	
PHCrAM	Puts hand to chair arm.

PHCrBk	Puts hand to chair back.
PHCrSt	Puts hand to chair seat.
PHTe	Puts hands to table.
Hand to clothes	
HP	Holds pullover.
PHIPt	Puts hands into pocket.
PHTr	Puts hands to trousers.
Hand not touching	
PoH	Points hand. To score a "points hand" posture, the fingers must be in a pointing position, i.e. with at least one finger outstretched.
HUH	Holds up hand. The "holds up hand" posture refers to hand not touching positions which do not involve pointing.

Table A.1: Arm postures as described in Bull's posture scoring system.

B Frequency Data from Corpus Analysis

B.1 Topic Categories

Participant ID	Topics	Immediate	External	Communication
Japan				
2	8	3	4	1
4	17	5	8	4
5	11	2	3	6
8	9	1	5	3
9	2	0	1	1
15	6	1	4	1
19	12	4	8	0
21	13	4	7	2
23	11	4	5	2
31	14	5	9	0
32	10	4	5	1
sum	113	33	59	21
mean	10.27	3.00	5.36	1.91
SD	4.05	1.73	2.42	1.81

Table B.1: List of frequency data showing the number of topics and topic categories in the Japanese data set.

Participant ID	Topics	Immediate	External	Communication
Germany				
1	11	2	2	7
2	6	0	4	2
3	3	1	2	0
4	7	1	4	2
5	11	4	3	4
6	10	3	5	2
7	8	3	5	0
8	11	1	4	6
9	5	0	3	2
10	8	1	5	2
11	18	1	5	12
12	11	2	2	7
13	8	2	3	3
14	13	2	5	6
15	10	4	2	4
16	10	2	4	4
17	10	2	5	3
18	11	1	4	6
19	8	1	5	2
20	9	0	5	4
21	13	2	6	5
sum	201	35	83	83
mean	9.57	1.67	3.95	3.95
SD	3.16	1.15	1.24	2.77

Table B.2: List of frequency data showing the number of topics and topic categories in the German data set.

B.2 Topic Shifts

Participant ID	Different Topics	Topic Shifts
Japan		
2	5	8
4	11	17
5	8	11
8	6	9
9	2	2
15	4	6
19	5	12
21	6	13
23	6	11
31	4	14
32	7	10
sum	64	113
mean	5.82	10.27
SD	2.36	4.05

Table B.3: List of frequency data showing the number of topics and topic shifts in the Japanese data set.

Participant ID	Different Topics	Topic Shifts
Germany		
1	8	11
2	3	5
3	3	3
4	5	7
5	7	11
6	6	11
7	4	8
8	10	11
9	4	5
10	4	8
11	9	18
12	10	11
13	5	8
14	6	12
15	7	10
16	7	11
17	8	11
18	8	11
19	5	8
20	6	9
21	9	13
sum	134	199
mean	6.38	9.48
SD	2.18	3.17

Table B.4: List of frequency data showing the number of topics and topic shifts in the German data set.

B.3 Dialog Utterances

Participant ID	question	answer	statement	agreement	under-standing	hold
Japan						
2	5	8	19	1	1	3
4	18	7	17	5	24	8
5	10	16	38	3	14	13
8	6	18	24	3	6	1
9	6	12	15	1	3	4
15	14	17	30	6	13	7
19	4	6	23	4	14	5
21	9	9	20	1	14	5
23	4	7	13	3	13	1
31	11	3	39	4	13	4
32	10	10	30	1	12	16
sum	97	113	268	32	127	67
mean	8.82	10.27	24.36	2.91	11.55	6.09
SD	4.42	4.90	8.86	1.76	6.28	4.72

Table B.5: List of frequency data showing the number of dialog utterances in the Japanese data set.

Participant ID	question	answer	statement	agreement	under-standing	hold
Germany						
1	8	19	34	8	10	6
2	4	15	25	12	3	1
3	2	18	32	6	3	6
4	3	17	12	2	7	3
5	8	14	31	4	10	4
6	9	9	27	0	4	4
7	4	9	21	2	6	2
8	8	18	9	1	10	6
9	3	21	32	4	3	4
10	3	11	26	3	8	1
11	7	22	19	2	11	7
12	4	21	13	4	4	1
13	5	9	39	2	1	0
14	5	18	18	7	18	4
15	4	18	26	5	8	2
16	4	7	17	4	20	0
17	3	13	38	8	4	2
18	13	2	23	4	14	9
19	2	18	18	4	6	2
20	6	12	30	7	12	6
21	11	19	31	2	10	5
sum	116	310	521	91	172	75
mean	5.52	14.76	24.81	4.33	8.19	3.57
SD	3.01	5.35	8.47	2.85	5.01	2.48

Table B.6: List of frequency data showing the number of dialog utterances in the German data set.

B.4 Pauses and Overlaps

Participant ID	pauses > 1sec	pauses > 2sec
Japan		
2	29	19
4	27	12
5	42	11 9
8	31	9
9	31	9
15	26	9
19	26	6
21	31	13
23	19	5
31	20	4
32	26	4
sum	308	101
mean	28	9.18
SD	6.18	4.51

Table B.7: List of frequency data showing the number of pauses in the Japanese data set.

Participant ID	overlaps	overlaps > 0.5	overlaps < 0.5
Japan			
2	11	3	8
4	82	25	57
5	51	12	39
8	43	11	32
9	19	8	11
15	45	14	31
19	38	10	28
21	55	34	21
23	48	28	20
31	33	10	23
32	54	27	27
sum	479	182	297
mean	43.55	16.55	27
SD	18.98	10.08	13.43

Table B.8: List of frequency data showing the number of overlaps in the Japanese data set.

Participant ID	*pauses* > 1*sec*	*pauses* > 2*sec*
Germany		
1	7	1
2	5	0
3	12	1
4	8	0
5	3	0
6	10	1
7	6	1
8	4	0
9	6	1
10	4	0
11	11	0
12	13	3
13	12	0
14	3	0
15	2	0
16	4	0
17	7	2
18	8	1
19	3	0
20	2	0
21	1	0
sum	131	11
mean	6.24	0.52
SD	3.66	0.81

Table B.9: List of frequency data showing the number of pauses in the German data set.

Participant ID	overlaps	*overlaps > 0.5*	*overlaps < 0.5*
Germany			
1	64	22	42
2	49	32	17
3	49	16	33
4	34	18	16
5	49	25	24
6	31	14	17
7	23	5	18
8	56	21	35
9	47	15	32
10	40	16	24
11	58	22	36
12	31	10	21
13	26	6	20
14	59	22	37
15	62	16	46
16	36	9	27
17	46	11	35
18	50	18	32
19	45	15	30
20	56	16	40
21	69	25	44
sum	980	354	626
mean	46.67	16.86	29.81
SD	12.88	6.64	9.45

Table B.10: List of frequency data showing the number of overlaps in the German data set.

C Knowledge Bases

C.1 Character's Knowledge Base

For verbal behavior planning, each character is provided with an initial knowledge base, holding its personal background and motivations, categorized topics and culture-specific thresholds exemplified for Germany and Japan.

The personal motivation for a topic represents the agent's internal drive to talk about the particular topic. Each topic in the knowledge base is categorized into the following groups: immediate situation, external situation or communication situation. For simplicity reasons, the categories are referred to as immediate, social or private in the knowledge bases.

Culture-related thresholds for each topic category influence whether a topic is introduced by a character, while the culture-related thresholds for the sequence have an impact on the flow of the conversation.

Culture-specific thresholds are designed to resemble the findings from our corpus study. Personal motivations and culture-related thresholds are designed to lie in an interval between 0 and 10.

The following example shows an extraction from a character's initial knowledge base:

```
(defproblem problem mike

    (name mike)
    (gender male)
    (culture germany)

    (motivation weather 5)
    (motivation movies 7)
    (motivation job 6)
```

```
(topic weather immediate)
(topic movies social)
(topic job private)

(threshold germany immediate 8)
(threshold germany social 4)
(threshold germany private 4)

(threshold japan immediate 4)
(threshold japan social 3)
(threshold japan private 8)

(threshold germany sequence 3)
(threshold japan sequence 5)
)
```

For the process of topic selection, the following axiom determines whether a topic is appropriate to be addressed, based on the cultural background of the character. Only if a topic is considered appropriate, it is going to be introduced by the target agent.

```
(:- (appropriate ?topic)
((culture ?culture)
(topic ?topic ?category)
(motivation ?topic ?valtopic)
(threshold ?culture ?category ?valcat)

(call < ?valcat ?valtopic))
)
```

To determine the flow of a conversation, the following axiom determines whether a topic is processed sequentially or not. Only if a character's personal motivation for a topic is higher than the culture-related threshold, it will follow the prototypical sequence.

```
(:- (sequential ?topic)
((culture ?culture)
(motivation ?topic ?valtopic)
(threshold ?culture sequence ?valseq)

(call < ?valseq ?valtopic))
)
```

C.2 Verbal Knowledge Base

The verbal knowledge base contains abstract representations of the dialog acts along with templates that can be selected for the virtual characters.

For the simulation of culture-related small talk behavior, 9 topics have been investigated, three for each category: immediate situation, external situation and communication situation.

For each topic, the dialog acts ask, askback, answer and answerback are provided, each containing three possible templates. In addition, dialog acts to frame the small talk conversation were added, such as greeting or farewell, as well as speech acts that can be performed by a human user to trigger certain behaviors for testing reasons.

Topics and speech acts	Templates
small talk topics	
immediate situation	
location	
ask	So how do you like this beergarden?
	Do you enjoy this exceptional place?
	What do you think about this location?
askback	And you 'name'? Do you like it?
	And yourself? Do you like the location?
	Dont you think the same?
answer	I think it is great to go to a beergarden 'name'!
	This location is very special! A Bavarian beergarden!
	Great place 'name'. Going to a beergarden was a good choice.
answerback	It is very nice. With all the trees it is nice and shady.
	It is indeed a great place. And very well designed.
	You know 'name'. I really enjoy myself being here.
weather	
ask	We were very lucky with the weather. It rains quite often this summer doesnt it?
	Look at the weather isnt it great?
	It is a great day isnt it?
askback	It was also nice and warm last week wasnt it?
	Last summer has been very hot. Do you remember?
	Has it been sunny all week?

answer	Yes the weather is fantastic today.
	You are right. It is lovely today.
	Yes we have little rain and many sunny days this year.
answerback	Yes. It was indeed very warm.
	Yes its been very nice weather.
	Yes sunshine was very pleasant.
food	
ask	Did you try the food in here 'name'?
	Have you seen the menu in this beergarden?
	Did you see the many dishes that are lined up here?
askback	Do you like sushi 'name'?
	What do you prefer? Typical German or Japanese?
	Are you having the Japanese food today?
answer	Yes. They are having a variety of German and Japanese food.
	I did 'name'. They offer typical Bavarian food and some Japanese delicacies too.
	Its great they have sausages and sauerkraut as well as sushi!
answerback	I love sushi 'name'. But today I will go for something German.
	I like Japanese food a lot. I will order some sushi later.
	Japanese food is good. However in a beergarden I will go for something typical for that area.
external situation	
movies	
ask	Have you heard about that new alien movie on cinema?
	Are you familiar with that new alien movie?
	Did you see the alien movie that is in cinemas lately?
askback	And you 'name'? Have you seen it?
	And yourself? Did you see it already?
	How about you? Seen it?
answer	Yes! I heard about it but havent seen it.
	I heard it is good. But I did not go yet.
	Great movie 'name'.
answerback	I saw it yesterday! It was really great.
	I did see it. But I thought it was a little boring.
	I went there yesterday 'name'. I think it was decent.
places	
ask	There is also this small beergarden close by. Have you been there 'name'?
	Do you know the new Sushi restaurant that opened a few days ago?

askback	There is another place like this one. Have you heard of it 'name'?
	So where is this place 'name'?
	Do you know where that place is 'name'?
	Can you tell me where it is?
answer	No I dont know that one.
	I never heard of it.
	That sounds very interesting.
answerback	Oh it is just down the road on the left hand side.
	I dont know exactly. But I think it is in this area.
	It is very close. If you exit this beergarden you can see it already.
friends	
ask	Did you know that Heidi is working in this beergarden?
	Heidi has a new side job as a waitress in here. Have you met her yet?
	Did you know that Heidi is working in this place as a waitress?
askback	Does she like her job as a waitress?
	I think Heidi is a good waitress. Is she enjoying that job?
	Heidi seems to be doing very well in her job doesnt she?
answer	Yes I heard that she has a side job in this place.
	I did. She has been working here for a month now.
	Yes. She is serving the area next to the bar.
answerback	She likes working here very much although she is always very busy.
	I think she likes working outside with people a lot.
	Yes. She said that she enjoys working in this beergarden.
communication situation	
job	
ask	Do you have a side job as well?
	Are you working in a side job 'name'?
	Are you doing a part time job during your studies too?
askback	How about you 'name'? Do you have a side job too?
	And yourself? Are you working part time during your studies?
	Do you have a part time job as well 'name'?
answer	Oh yes. I am working in an Italian restaurant.
	Sure 'name'. I have a side job in a Cocktail bar.
	I do. I am working in a restaurant since two years.
answerback	No. I am currently not working part time.
	For my last semester I decided to not work in a side job.
	I used to work part time as well but currently do not have a side job.

origin	
ask	Are you from this region originally 'name'?
	Do you come from this area 'name'?
	Are you from around here?
askback	Have you been to the US 'name'?
	Did you ever go to America 'name'?
	Have you been there?
answer	No I am from the US originally.
	I am not from here 'name'. I was born and raised in America.
	No not originally. I moved here from the United States.
answerback	Yes I have been to New York last year.
	No I did not have the chance to go there. But I want to visit it soon.
	I did. I traveled the west coast and visited a lot of places.
hobbies	
ask	Do you enjoy traveling?
	Do you travel a lot 'name'?
	You seem to like traveling 'name' dont you?
askback	How about you 'name'? Do you like to travel?
	Do you like traveling too?
	Are you keen on traveling as well 'name'?
answer	Traveling is my major hobby. I like it a lot.
	I do 'name'. I think traveling is always a good experience.
	I do travel as much as I can.
answerback	Oh yes. I totally like traveling too.
	Absolutely. Traveling is a hobby of mine as well.
	Indeed I like to travel. I plan on going to Australia by the end of the year.
well-being	
ask	How are things 'name'?
	Hey 'name' is everything all right with you?
	How are you 'name'?
askback	How about you 'name'? How are you?
	And yourself? How are things?
	Thanks for asking! And you?
answer pos	Oh everything is just wonderful 'name'!
	Everything is great! Could not be better!
	I am good. Thanks for asking.
answer neg	Dont even ask 'name'! Life is not how it should be right now.
	I have seen better days.

answer med	I dont enjoy myself at all at the moment. I am ok 'name'! I am all right. Thanks for asking 'name'. Well everything is ok at the moment.
frame speech acts	
greeting	Hello 'name'! I have not seen you in a while. Hi 'name'. It is nice to see you again. Good evening. Nice to see you here 'name'.
farewell	You know what 'name'. I just saw a friend of mine over there! See you later! I just go over to the bar and grab a drink! It was nice talking to you 'name'.
farewell back	All right 'name'. See you later! See you 'name'.
speech acts for tests with interface	
same again	Uhm... I think you mentioned this earlier 'name'! Sure... but you are repeating yourself 'name'. Uhm... I guess I heard that from you earlier 'name'!
compliment	You look great today 'name'! What a nice outfit! Did you loose weight 'name'? You are in great shape! Did you find the fountain of youth 'name'? You look great!
thank compliment	Thanks 'name'! Thats very kind of you! You think so 'name'? Its a pleasure to hear that. You make me blush! Thanks for saying that 'name'!
block compliment	Thanks 'name'! But I know that I look awful today! Are you kidding me 'name'? I feel like the ugly duckling. Are you nuts? Look at me 'name'! I dont look good at all today.
statement location	I think this beergarden is a great place for a party. Look at this location 'name'! It is indeed a typical bavarian beergarden. We were lucky with this location. Usually it is booked out at weekends.
statement weather	We were lucky with the weather. It was supposed to rain today. It is such a warm and nice summer day today. Summer finally started. I was afraid june gloom will last forever.
location back	You are right. This is a wonderful location. Right 'name'! I like this beergarden too. This beergarden was indeed a good choice.

weather back	You are right. The weather is lovely.
	Summer at last. I love the sunshine.
	We were really lucky. Imagine it would have rained.

Table C.1: List of speech acts and corresponding templates used in our demonstrator to exemplify small talk dialogs.

C.3 Nonverbal Knowledge Base

The nonverbal knowledge base contains all animations that can be performed by our virtual characters. Table C.2 shows how the knowledge base is structured as well as the amount of animations provided for each type.

Start ID	group	number of animations
100	gestures based on German video corpus	10
200	gestures based on Japanese video corpus	13
300	non-corpus-based gestures	33
700	movement animations	8
800	body postures	7

Table C.2: Structure of the nonverbal knowledge base of our demonstrator.

In the following, the animations contained in each group are further described. To view selected animations please go to our animation website [Aug11].

For corpus-based gestures (see Table C.3), the animation lexicon provides the participant's speech, DAMSL dialog utterance [CA97] and McNeill' gesture classification [McN92], as annotated in the video corpus. Please note that corpus-based gestures are considered culture-specific and are therefore restricted to cultural background.

ID	speech	DAMSL	McNeill
Germany			
100	I uhm work here, you know.	answer	beat
101	Brings you further sure. Experience and so on. But...	statement	beat
102	it is not the case that they are only employing economists	n.a.	beat
103	in america, for pupil exchange and then meet somebody there, go there again, and meet somebody new and so on.	answer	beat
104	And what else? What do we do here? What did they say? Negotiation?	info-request	deictic
105	at the erhm university	statement	deictic

106	exactly. since my boy friend studied chemistry.	answer	deictic
107	Well I just got there and uhm, I just went straight in there.	statement	iconic
108	one club is there, but erhm...	n.a.	iconic
109	more in the direction of m m medial computing	n.a.	metaphoric
Japan			
200	In the department of education, generally, the fields are divided into three parts: pedagogy, politics of the education and psychology.	statement	beat
201	n.a.	n.a.	beat
202	n.a.	n.a.	beat
203	That German guy was telling about more and more prize money.	statement	deictic
204	Are you an undergraduate student?	info-request	deictic
205	Well, aren't you ??? at Wednesday..." (interrupted)	info-request	deictic
206	There isn't anybody who could be asked, because there's few people around here.	statement	deictic
207	For us, well in the cafeteria there is; cash you know is not valid there	statement	iconic
208	It's not far, erh it stands in this main campus, but	statement	iconic
209	Well, I take a class around the new educational psychology.	answer	metaphoric
210	Though it's okay for the exam for the cognitive Psychology,	statement	metaphoric
211	(...) for the clinical Psychology there's a great competition to enter to the faculty.	statement	metaphoric
212	n.a.	n.a.	adaptor

Table C.3: Corpus-based gestures.

Non-corpus-based gestures (see Table C.4) are of a general nature and customizable. In that manner, aspects such as speed or spatial extent can be adjusted.

However, this does not hold true for emblems, since they might lose their meaning by, e.g. changing their spatial extent.

ID	McNeill	description
300	beat	general beat gesture
301	beat	general beat gesture
302	beat	general beat gesture
303	deictic	pointing at an imaginary thing
304	metaphoric	general metaphoric gesture
305	metaphoric	general metaphoric gesture
306	metaphoric	general metaphoric gesture
307	adaptor	the character strokes its hair
308	adaptor	Scratch head
309	emblem	Becking 1
310	emblem	Becking 2
311	emblem	Becking 3
312	emblem	Big Bow
313	emblem	Small Bow
314	emblem	HeadNod
315	emblem	Stand up (move hands upwards)
316	emblem	Eat 1
317	emblem	Eat 2
318	emblem	Go away (wave hands to show s.o. to move away)
319	emblem	pointing towards oneself (German)
320	emblem	Come over here (German)
321	emblem	Tasty (character strokes its belly)
322	emblem	No (waving with index finger)
323	emblem	Stupid (waving in front of head)
324	emblem	Drink
325	emblem	No time (pointing towards imaginary wrist watch)
326	emblem	Ranicki 1 (gesture typically for a famous German TV host)
327	emblem	Ranicki 2 (gesture typically for a famous German TV host)
328	emblem	Wipe Bar
329	emblem	Pour glas
330	emblem	Drink Japanese
331	emblem	pointing towards oneself (Japanese)
332	emblem	Come over here (Japanese)

Table C.4: Non-corpus-based gestures.

Movement animations (see Table C.5) are needed on the one hand to get characters to another position within the scenario, and on the other hand to naturally orientate themselves towards each other during a conversation.

ID	description
700	Sidestep left
701	Sidestep right
702	Walk
703	Medium Step Backward
704	Small Step Backward
705	Large Step Backward
706	Skew Left
707	Skew Right

Table C.5: Movement animations.

Postures are based on Bull's coding scheme [Bul87], while prototypical postures that were frequently observed in our corpus for the German and Japanese cultures were modeled (see Section 4.4.3). Posture animations (see Table C.6) are loopable. In contrast to the performance of gestures, characters remain in a certain posture until another animation is selected.

ID	description	culture
800	Idle	
801	Fold Arms: Character folds both arms in front of its body.	Germany
802	Put Hands Into Pocket: Character puts hands on its pocket/hips.	Germany
803	Put Hand to Elbow: Character puts one hand on the other arm's elbow.	Germany
804	Put Hand to Wrist: Character brings one hand to the other hand's wrist.	Japan
805	Join Hands: Character brings together both hands.	Japan
806	Put Hands Back: Character puts both hands behind the back.	Japan

Table C.6: Posture animations.

Bibliography

[AA03]   AVRADINIS, NIKOS and RUTH AYLETT: *Agents with No Aims: Motivation-Driven Continuous Planning*. In RIST, THOMAS, RUTH AYLETT, DANIEL BALLIN and JEFF RICKEL (editors): *Proc. of 4th Int. Conf. on Intelligent Virtual Agents (IVA 2003)*, pages 269–273. Springer, 2003.

[AAG00]   AYLETT, R.S., A.M.CODDINGTON and G.J.PETLEY: *Agent-based Continuous Planning*. In *19th Workshop of the UK PLANNING AND SCHEDULING Special Interest Group (PLANSIG 2000)*, pages 14–15, 2000.

[AAL11]   ALLWOOD, JENS, ELISABETH AHLSÉN and JIA LU: *Some challenges for multimodal intercultural artificial communicators*. In *Workshop on Culturally Motivated Virtual Characters (CMVC 2011) held on IVA 2011*, 2011.

[AC97]   ALLEN, JAMES and MARK CORE: *Draft of DAMSL: Dialog Act Markup in Several Layers*. http://www.cs.rochester.edu/research/cisd/resources/damsl/ RevisedManual/, 1997. last viewed: 26.02.2012.

[AKG+00]   ANDRÉ, ELISABETH, MARTIN KLESEN, PATRICK GEBHARD, STEVE ALLEN and THOMAS RIST: *Integrating Models of Personality and Emotions into Lifelike Characters*. In PAIVA, A. (editor): *Affective Interactions*, pages 150–165. Springer, 2000.

[ALD+05]   AYLETT, R.S., S. LOUCHART, J. DIAS, A. PAIVA and M.VALA: *FearNot! - An Experiment in Emergent Narrative*. In PANAYIOTOPOULOS, THEMIS, JONATHAN GRATCH, RUTH AYLETT, DANIEL BALLIN, PATRICK OLIVIER and THOMAS RIST (editors): *Proc. of 5th Int. Conf. on Intelligent Virtual Agents (IVA 2005)*, pages 305–316. Springer, 2005.

[APV+09]   AYLETT, R., A. PAIVA, N. VANNINI, S. ENZ, E. ANDRÉ and L. HALL: *But that was in another country: agents and intercultural empathy*. In SIERRA, CARLES, CRISTIANO CASTELFRANCHI, KEITH S. DECKER and

JAIME SIMAO SICHMAN (editors): *Proc. of 8th Int. Conf. on Autonomous Agents and Multiagent Systems (AAMAS 2009)*, Budapest, Hungary, 2009.

[Arg75]   ARGYLE, M.: *Bodily Communication*. Methuen & Co. Ltd., London, 1775.

[ARM99]   ANDRÉ, E., T. RIST and J. MUELLER: *Employing AI Methods to Control the Behavior of Animated Interface Agents*. Applied Artificial Intelligence, 13(4 & 5):415 – 448, 1999.

[ARvM⁺00]   ANDRÉ, E., T. RIST, S. VAN MULKEN, M. KLESEN and S. BALDES: *The Automated Design of Believable Dialogues for Animated Presentation Teams*. In CASSELL, J., J. SULLIVAN, S. PREVOST and E. CHURCHILL (editors): *Embodied Conversational Agents*, pages 220–255, Cambridge, United States, 2000. MIT Press.

[Aug09]   AUGSBURG UNIVERSITY: *CUBE-G: CUlture-adaptive BEhavior Generation for interactions with embodied conversational agents*. http://mm-werkstatt.informatik.uni-augsburg.de/projects/cube-g/, 2009. last viewed: 26.02.2012.

[Aug11]   AUGSBURG UNIVERSITY: *Culture Specific Animation*. http://www.hcm-lab.de/projects/animations/, 2011. last viewed: 26.02.2012.

[Bal02]   BALL, EUGEN: *A Bayasian Heart: Computer Recognition and Simulation of Emotion*. In TRAPPL, ROBERT, PAOLO PETTA and SABINE PAYR (editors): *Emotions in Humans and Artifacts*, pages 303–332. MIT Press, 2002.

[BC99]   BICKMORE, T. and J. CASSELL: *Small Talk and Conversational Storytelling in Embodied Conversational Interface Agents*. In *Proceedings of the AAAI Fall Symposium on Narrative Intelligence*, pages 87–92, 1999.

[BDS⁺05]   BARBA, C., J.-E. DEATON, T. SANTARELLI, B. KNERR, M. SINGER and J. BELANICH: *Virtual Environment Composable Training for Operational Readiness (VECTOR)*. In *25th Army Science Conference*, 2005.

[Bic03]   BICKMORE, T.: *Relational Agents: Effecting Change through Human-Computer Relationships*. PhD thesis, Media Arts & Sciences, Massachusetts Institute of Technology., 2003.

[BK09]   BERGMANN, K. and S. KOPP: *Bayesian Decision Networks for Iconic Gesture Generation*. In RUTTKAY, ZSOFIA, MICHAEL KIPP, ANTON NIJHOLT and HANNES-HÖGNI VILHJÁLMSSON (editors): *Proc. of 9th Int. Conf. on Intelligent Virtual Agents (IVA 2009)*, pages 76–89. Springer, 2009.

[BPI09]   BREITFUSS, W., H. PRENDINGER and M. ISHIZUKA: *Automatic Generation of Non-verbal Behavior for Agents in Virtual Worlds: A System for Supporting Multimodal Conversations of Bots and Avatars*. In OZOK, A.-A. and P. ZAPHIRIS (editors): *Online Communities and Social Computing*, pages 153–161. Springer, 2009.

[Bre00]   BRETT, J. M.: *Culture and Negotiation*. International Journal of Psychology, 35(2):97–104, 2000.

[Bul87]   BULL, P.E.: *Posture and Gesture*. Pergamon Press, Oxford, 1987.

[BW12]   BREUING, ALEXA and IPKE WACHSMUTH: *Let's Talk Topically with Artificial Agents! Providing Agents with Humanlike Topic Awareness in Everyday Dialog Situations*. In *Proc. of 4th Int. Conf. on Agents and Artificial Intelligence*, pages 62–71, 2012.

[Byr71]   BYRNE, D.: *The attraction paradigm*. Academic Press, New York, 1971.

[BZ03]   BATEMAN, JOHN and MICHAEL ZOCK: *Natural Language Generation*. In MITKOV, R. (editor): *Oxford Handbook of Computational Linguistics*, chapter 15, pages 284–304. Oxford University Press, Oxford, 2003.

[CA97]   CORE, MARK and JAMES ALLEN: *Coding Dialogs with the DAMSL Annotation Scheme*. In *Working Notes of AAAI Fall Symposium on Communicative Action in Humans and Machines*, Boston, MA, 1997.

[Cas07]   CASSELL, J.: *Body Language: Lessons from the Near-Human*. In RISKIN, J. (editor): *Genesis Redux: Essays in the History and Philosophy of Artificial Intelligence*, pages 346–374. University of Chicago Press, Chicago, 2007.

[CBB+99]   CASSELL, J., T. BICKMORE, M. BILLINGHURST, L. CAMPBELL, K. CHANG, H. VILHJÁLMSSON and H. YAN: *Embodiment in Conversational Interfaces: Rea*. In WILLIAMS, MARIAN G. and MARK W. ALTOM (editors): *Proc. of Int. Conf. on Human Factors in Computing Systems (CHI 99)*, pages 520–527, Pittsburgh, 1999.

[CdICT10]   CAVAZZA, MARC, RAUL SANTOS DE LA CAMERA and MARKKU TURUNEN: *How was your day?: a companion ECA*. In HOEK, WIEBE VAN DER, GAL A. KAMINKA, YVES LESPÉRANCE, MICHAEL LUCK and SANDIP SEN (editors): *Proc. of 9th Int. Conf. on Autonomous Agents and Multiagent Systems (AAMAS 2010)*, 2010.

[CNB+01]   CASSELL, J., Y. NAKANO, T. BICKMORE, C.-L. SIDNER and C. RICH: *Non-verbal Cues for Discourse Structure*. In *Annual Meeting of the Association for Computational Linguistics (ACL 2001)*, 2001.

[CPC+09]   CHARLES, FRED, DAVID PIZZI, MARC CAVAZZA, THURID VOGT and ELISABETH ANDRÉ: *EmoEmma: Emotional Speech Input for Interactive Storytelling*. In DECKER, SICHMAN, SIERRA and CASTELFRANCHI (editors): *Proc. of 8th Int. Conf. on Autonomous Agents and Multiagent Systems (AAMAS 2009)*, pages 1381–1382, Budapest, Hungary, 2009.

[CSPC00]   CASSELL, J., J. SULLIVAN, S. PREVOST and E. CHURCHILL: *Embodied Conversational Agents*. MIT Press, 2000.

[CVB01]   CASSELL, JUSTINE, HANNES VILHÁLMSSON and TIMOTHY BICKMORE: *BEAT: The Behaviour Expression Animation Toolkit*. In *Proc. of 28th Annual*

Conf. on Computer Graphics (SIGGRAPH 2001), pages 477–486. ACM, 2001.

[Dec07]   DECISION SYSTEMS LABORATORY: GeNIe and SMILE. http://genie.sis. pitt.edu/, 2005-2007. last viewed: 26.02.2012.

[DEH⁺11]   DAMIAN, IONUT, BIRGIT ENDRASS, PETER HUBER, NIKOLAUS BEE and ELISABETH ANDRÉ: Individualized Agent Interactions. In Proc. of 4th Int. Conf. on Motion in Games (MIG 2011), 2011.

[DP05]   DIAS, J. and A. PAIVA: Feeling and reasoning: a computational model. In 12th Portuguese Conference on Artificial Intelligence, EPIA, pages 127–140. Springer, 2005.

[eCu12]   ECUTE PROJECT: eCute: Education in Cultural Understanding, Technologically-Enhanced. http://ecute.eu/, 2012. last viewed: 26.02.2012.

[EDH⁺10]   ENDRASS, BIRGIT, IONUT DAMIAN, PETER HUBER, MATTHIAS REHM and ELISABETH ANDRÉ: Generating Culture-Specific Gestures for Virtual Agent Dialogs. In ALLBECK, J.-M., N.-I. BADLER, T.-W. BICKMORE, C. PELACHAUD and A. SAFONOVA (editors): Proc. of 10th Int. Conf. on Intelligent Virtual Agents (IVA 2010), pages 329 – 335, 2010.

[EDH⁺11]   ENDRASS, BIRGIT, NICK DEGENS, GERT JAN HOFSTEDE, ELISA-BETH ANDRÉ, JOHN HODGSON, SAMUEL MASCARENHAS, GREGOR MEHLMANN, ANA PAIVA, CHRISTOPHER RITTER and ALEKSANDRA SWIDERSKA: Integration and Evaluation of Prototypical Culture-related Differences. In Workshop on Culturally Motivated Virtual Characters (CMVC 2011) held on IVA 2011, 2011.

[EHAG10]   ENDRASS, B., L. HUANG, E. ANDRÉ and J. GRATCH: A data-driven approach to model Culture-specific Communication Management Styles for Virtual Agents. In HOEK, WIEBE VAN DER, GAL A. KAMINKA, YVES LESPÉRANCE, MICHAEL LUCK and SANDIP SEN (editors): Proc. of 9th Int. Conf. on Autonomous Agents and Multiagent Systems (AAMAS 2010), pages 99–108, 2010.

[Ekm92]   EKMAN, PAUL: Telling Lies - Clues to Deceit in the Marketplace, Politics, and Marriage, volume 3rd edn. Norton and Co., New York, 1992.

[EKM⁺11]   ENDRASS, BIRGIT, CHRISTOPH KLIMMT, GREGOR MEHLMANN, ELIS-ABETH ANDRÉ and CHRISTIAN ROTH: Exploration of User Reactions to Different Dialog-based Interaction Styles. In SI, MEI, DAVID THUE, ELISA-BETH ANDRÉ, JAMES C. LESTER and JOSHUA TANENBAUM ANDVERON-ICA ZAMMITTO (editors): Proc. of 4th Int. Conf. on Interactive Digital Storytelling (ICIDS 2011), pages 243–248. Springer, 2011.

[ENL⁺11]   ENDRASS, B., Y. NAKANO, A. LIPI, M. REHM and E. ANDRÉ: Culture-related topic selection in SmallTalk conversations across Germany and

Japan. In VILHJÁLMSSON, HANNES HÖGNI, STEFAN KOPP, STACY
MARSELLA and KRISTINN R. THÓRISSON (editors): *Proc. of 11th Int.
Conf. on Intelligent Virtual Agents (IVA 2011)*, pages 1–13. Springer, 2011.

[ERA09] ENDRASS, BIRGIT, MATTHIAS REHM and ELISABETH ANDRÉ: *Culture-
specific Communication Management for Virtual Agents.* In SIERRA, CAR-
LES, CRISTIANO CASTELFRANCHI, KEITH S. DECKER and JAIME SIMAO
SICHMAN (editors): *Proc. of 8th Int. Conf. on Autonomous Agents and Multiagent Systems (AAMAS 2009)*, Budapest, Hungary, 2009.

[ERA11] ENDRASS, B., M. REHM and E. ANDRÉ: *Planning Small Talk Behavior
with Cultural Influences for Multiagent Systems.* Computer Speech and Language, 25(2):158–174, 2011.

[ERL+11] ENDRASS, B., M. REHM, A.-A. LIPI, Y. NAKANO and ELISABETH AN-
DRÉ: *Culture-related Differences in Aspects of Behavior for Virtual Char-
acters across Germany and Japan.* In SONENBERG, LIZ, PETER STONE,
KAGAN TUMER and PINAR YOLUM (editors): *Proc. of 10th Int. Conf. on
Autonomous Agents and Multiagent Systems (AAMAS 2011)*, pages 441–448,
2011.

[Gal92] GALLAHER, P. E.: *Individual Differences in Nonverbal Behavior: Dimensions of Style.* Journal of Personality and Social Psychology, 63(1):133–145,
1992.

[GRA+02] GRATCH, J., J. RICKEL, E. ANDRÉ, N. BADLER, J. CASSELL and
E. PETAJAN: *Creating Interactive Virtual Humans: Some Assembly Required.* IEEE Intelligent Systems, 17(4):54–63, 2002.

[Hal59] HALL, EDWARD T.: *The Silent Language.* Doubleday, 1959.

[Hal66] HALL, EDWARD T.: *The Hidden Dimension.* Doubleday, 1966.

[Hal83] HALL, E.-T.: *The Dance of Life.* Doubleday, New York, 1983.

[HFF+08] HENDERSON, J., P. FISHWICK, E. FRESH, R. FUTTERKNECHT and B.-
D. HAMILTON: *Immersive Learning Simulation Environment for Chinese
Culture.* In Interservice / Industry Training, Simulation, and Education Con-
ference (I/ITSEC 2008), paper no. 8334, 2008.

[HH87] HALL, E.-T. and M. HALL: *Hidden differences: Doing buisness with the
Japanese.* Anchor Press / Doubleday, New York, 1987.

[HHM10] HOFSTEDE, GEERT, GERT-JAN HOFSTEDE and MICHAEL MINKOV: *Cultures and Organisations. SOFTWARE OF THE MIND. Intercultural Cooperation and its Importance for Survival.* McGraw Hill, 2010.

[HMP06] HARTMANN, BJORN, MAURIZIO MANCINI and CATHERINE PELACHAUD:
*Implementing Expressive Gesture Synthesis for Embodied Conversational
Agents.* In GIBET, S., N. COURTY and J.-F. KAMP (editors): *Gesture Work-
shop (GW 2005)*, number 3881 in LNAI, pages 188–199. Springer, 2006.

[HNJT11]   HERRERA, DAVID, DAVID NOVICK, DUSAN JAN and DAVID TRAUM: *Dialog Behaviors across Culture and Group Size*. In *Proc. of 6th Int. Conf. on Universal access in HCI, Part II (HCII 2011)*, number 6766 in *LNCS*, pages 450–459. Springer, 2011.

[Hof91]   HOFSTEDE, G.: *Cultures and Organisations - Intercultural Cooperation and its Importance for Survival, Software of the Mind*. Profile Books, London, Great Britain, 1991.

[Hof01]   HOFSTEDE, GEERT: *Culture's Consequences - Comparing Values, Behaviours, Institutions, and Organizations Across Nations*. Sage Publications, 2001.

[Hof03]   HOFSTEDE, G.: *Cultures and Organisations - Intercultural Cooperation and its Importance for Survival, Software of the Mind*. Profile Books, Great Britain, 2003.

[Hof12]   HOFSTEDE, GEERT. http://www.geert-hofstede.com/, 2012. last viewed: 26.02.2012.

[HPH02]   HOFSTEDE, GERT J., PAUL B. PEDERSEN and GEERT HOFSTEDE: *Exploring Culture - Exercises, Stories and Synthetic Cultures*. Intercultural Press, Yarmouth, United States, 2002.

[IC07]   IACOBELLI, FRANCISCO and JUSTINE CASSELL: *Ethnic Identity and Engagement in Embodied Conversational Agents*. In PELACHAUD, C., J.-C. MARTIN, E. ANDRÉ, G. CHOLLET, K. KARPOUZIS and D. PELÉ (editors): *Proc. of 7th Int. Conf. on Intelligent Virtual Agents (IVA 2007)*, pages 57–63. Springer, 2007.

[IKE12a]   IKEA GERMANY: *IKEA*. http://www.ikea.com/de/, 2012. last viewed: 26.02.2012.

[IKE12b]   IKEA UK: *IKEA*. http://www.ikea.com/gb, 2012. last viewed: 26.02.2012.

[ININ00]   ISBISTER, K., H. NAKANISHI, T. ISHIDA and C. NASS: *Helper agent: Designing an assistant for human-human interaction in a virtual meeting space*. In TURNER, THEA and GERD SZWILLUS (editors): *Proc. of Int. Conf. on Human Factors in Computing Systems (CHI 2000)*, pages 57–64, New York, United States, 2000. ACM.

[Jen01]   JENSEN, FINN V.: *Bayesian Networks and Decicion Graphs*. Springer, 2001.

[JHM⁺07]   JAN, D., D. HERRERA, B. MARTINOVSKI, D. NOVICK and D. TRAUM: *A Computational Model of Culture-Specific Conversational Behavior*. In PELACHAUD, CATHERINE, JEAN-CLAUDE MARTIN, ELISABETH ANDRÉ, GÉRARD CHOLLET, KOSTAS KARPOUZIS and DANIELLE PELÉ (editors): *Proc. of 7th Int. Conf. on Intelligent Virtual Agents (IVA 2007)*, pages 45–56. Springer, 2007.

[JMV04]   JOHNSON, W.-J., S. MARSELLA and H. VILHJÁLMSSON: *The DARWARS Tactical Language Training System*. In *Interservice / Industry Training, Simulation, and Education Conference*, 2004.

[Joh10]   JOHNSON, W.-L: *Using Immersive Simulations to Develop Intercultural Competence*. In ISHIDA, T. (editor): *Culture and Computing*, number 6259 in *LNCS*, pages 1–15. Springer, 2010.

[JTN08]   JONSDOTTIR, G.-R., K.-R. THORISSON and E. NIVEL: *Learning Smooth, Human-Like Turntaking in Realtime Dialogue*. In PRENDINGER, H., J.-C. LESTER and M. ISHIZUKA (editors): *Proc. of 8th Int. Conf. on Intelligent Virtual Agents (IVA 2008)*, pages 162–175. Springer, 2008.

[JV08]   JOHNSON, W.-L. and A. VALENTE: *Tactical Language and Culture Training Systems: Using Artificial Intelligence to Teach Foreign Languages and Cultures*. In *Innovative Applications of Artificial Intelligence (IAAI 2008)*, pages 1632–1639. Association for the Advancement of Artificial Intelligence (AAAI), 2008.

[KED+12]   KISTLER, FELIX, BIRGIT ENDRASS, IONUT DAMIAN, CHI TAI DANG and ELISABETH ANDRÉ: *Natural Interaction with Culturally Adaptive Virtual Characters*. Special Issue of the Journal on Multimodal User Interfaces: Interacting with Embodied Conversational Agents (JMUI), 4, 2012.

[Ken91]   KENDON, A.: *Conducting Interaction: Patterns of Behavior in Focused Encounters*. Cambridge University Press, Cambridge, 1991.

[KGWW08]   KANG, S., J. GRATCH, N. WANG and J. WATTS: *Agreeable People Like Agreeable Virtual Humans*. In PRENDINGER, II., J. LESTER and M. ISHIZUKA (editors): *Proc. of 8th Int. Conf. on Intelligent Virtual Agents (IVA 2008)*, pages 253–261, Tokyo, 2008. Springer.

[KHD+09]   KIM, J., R.-W. HILL, P. DURLACH, H.-C. LANE, E. FORBELL, M. CORE, S. MARSELLA, D. PYNADATH and J. HART: *BiLAT: A game-based environment for practicing negotiation in a cultural context*. International Journal of Artificial Intelligence in Education, 19:289–308, 2009. IOS Press.

[Kip01]   KIPP, M.: *Anvil - A Generic Annotation Tool for Multimodal Dialogue*. In *Eurospeech 2001*, pages 1367–1370, 2001.

[KNA07]   KIPP, M., M. NEFF and I. ALBRECHT: *An Annotation Scheme for Conversational Gestures: How to economically capture timing and form*. Journal on Language Resources and Evaluation - Special Issue on Multimodal Corpora, 41(3-4):325–339, 2007.

[KNKA07]   KIPP, MICHAEL, MICHAEL NEFF, KERSTIN-H. KIPP and IRENE ALBRECHT: *Towards Natural Gesture Synthesis: Evaluating gesture units in a data-driven approach to gesture synthesis*. In PELACHAUD, CATHERINE, JEAN-CLAUDE MARTIN, ELISABETH ANDRÉ, GÉRARD CHOLLET,

KOSTAS KARPOUZIS and DANIELLE PELÉ (editors): *Proc. of 7th Int. Conf. on Intelligent Virtual Agents (IVA 2007)*, pages 15–28. Springer, 2007.

[KP04a] KELLERMANN, K. and NICHOLAS A. PALOMARES: *Topical Profiling: Emergent, Co-Occurring, and Relationally Defining Topics in Talk*. Journal of Language and Social Psychology, 23(3):308–337, 2004.

[KP04b] KRENN, BRIGITTE and HANNES PIRKER: *Defining the Gesticon: Language and Gesture Coordination for Interacting Embodied Agents*. In *Proceedings of the AISB-2004 Symposium on Language, Speech and Gesture for Expressive Characters*, pages 107–115, University of Leeds, UK, 2004.

[KRA08] KODA, T., M. REHM and E. ANDRÉ: *Cross-Cultural Evaluations of Avatar Facial Expressions Designed by Western Designers*. In PRENDINGER, H., J. LESTER and M. ISHIZUKA (editors): *Proc. of 8th Int. Conf. on Intelligent Virtual Agents (IVA 2008)*, pages 245–252. Springer, 2008.

[KRNT10] KODA, TOMOKO, ZSOFIA RUTTKAY, YUKA NAKAGAWA and KYOTA TABUCHI: *Cross-Cultural Study on Facial Regions as Cues to Recognize Emotions of Virtual Agents*. In ISHIDA, TORU (editor): *Culture and Computing*, pages 16–27. Springer, 2010.

[KS61] KLUCKHOHN, K. and F. STRODTBECK: *Variations in value orientations*. Row, Peterson, New York, United States, 1961.

[Lin12] LINDEN RESEARCH, INC.: *SecondLife*. http://secondlife.com/, 2012. last viewed: 26.02.2012.

[LM06] LEE, J. and S. MARSELLA: *Nonverbal Behavior Generator for Embodied Conversational Agents*. In GRATCH, J., M. YOUNG, R. AYLETT, D. BALLIN and P. OLIVIER (editors): *Proc. of 6th Int. Conf. on Intelligent Virtual Agents (IVA 2006)*, pages 243–255. Springer, 2006.

[LMP+05] LAMOLLE, MYRIAM, MAURIZIO MANCINI, CATHERINE PELACHAUD, SARKIS ABRILIAN, JEAN-CLAUDE MARTIN and LAURENCE DEVILLERS: *Contextual Factors and Adaptative Multimodal Human-Computer Interaction: Multi-level Specification of Emotion and Expressivity in Embodied Conversational Agents*. In A. DEY ET AL. (editor): *CONTEXT 2005*, LNAI 3554, pages 225–239. Springer, 2005.

[LN98] LEE, EUN-JU and CLIFFORD NASS: *Does the ethnicity of a computer agent matter? An experimental comparison of human-computer interaction and computer-mediated communication*. In PREVOST, S. and E. CHURCHILL (editors): *1st Workshop of Embodied Conversational Characters (WECC'98)*, 1998.

[LNE+11] LIPI, AFIA AKHTER, FUMIE NORI, BIRGIT ENDRASS, YUKIKO NAKANO and ELISABETH ANDRÉ: *How Culture and Social Relationship Affect the Perception of Agent's Nonverbal Behaviors?* In *Workshop on Culturally Motivated Virtual Characters (CMVC 2011) held on IVA 2011*, 2011.

[LNR10]   LIPI, A.-A., Y. NAKANO and M. REHM: *Culture and Social Relationship as Factors of Affecting Communicative Non-verbal Behaviors*. Japanese Society of Artificial Intelligence, 25(6):712–722, 2010.

[MA07]   MARCUS, AARON and CHAVA ALEXANDER: *User Validation of Cultural Dimensions of a Website Design*. In AYKIN, N. (editor): *Usability and Internationalization, Part II, HCII 2007*, pages 160–167. Springer, 2007.

[MAD⁺05]   MARTIN, JEAN-CLAUDE, SARKIS ABRILIAN, LAURENCE DEVILLERS, MYRIAM LAMOLLE, MAURIZIO MANCINI and CATHERINE PELACHAUD: *Levels of Representation in the Annotation of Emotion for the Specification of Expressivity in ECAs*. In PANAYIOTOPOULOS, T., J. GRATCH, R. AYLETT, D. BALLIN, P. OLIVIER and T. RIST (editors): *Proc. of 5th Int. Conf. on Intelligent Virtual Agents (IVA 2005)*, pages 405–417. Springer, 2005.

[McN92]   MCNEILL, DAVID: *Hand and Mind - What Gestures Reveal about Thought*. University of Chicago Press, Chicago, London, 1992.

[MDA⁺09]   MASCARENHAS, SAMUEL, JOAO DIAS, NUNO AFONSO, SIBYLLE ENZ and ANA PAIVA: *Using Rituals to Express Cultural Differences in Synthetic Characters*. In SIERRA, CARLES, CRISTIANO CASTELFRANCHI, KEITH S. DECKER and JAIME SIMAO SICHMAN (editors): *Proc. of 8th Int. Conf. on Autonomous Agents and Multiagent Systems (AAMAS 2009)*, pages 305–312, Budapest, Hungary, 2009.

[MEA11]   MEHLMANN, GREGOR, BIRGIT ENDRASS and ELISABETH ANDRÉ: *Modeling parallel state charts for multithreaded multimodal dialogues*. In *Proc. of 13th Int. Conf. on Multimodal Interaction (ICMI 2011)*, pages 385–392. ACM, 2011.

[Mic12]   MICROSOFT DEUTSCHLAND GMBH: *Xbox 360 + Kinect*. http://www.xbox.com/de-DE/kinect, 2012. last viewed: 29.02.2012.

[MS02]   MATEAS, M. and A. STERN: *Towards Integrating Plot and Character for Interactive Drama*. In *Working notes of the Social Intelligent Agents: The Human in the Loop Symposium*. AAAI Press, 2002.

[NCLMA99] NAU, DANA, YUE CAO, AMNON LOTEM and H. MUNOZ-AVILA: *SHOP: Simple Hierarchical Ordered Planner*. In *Proc. of 16th Int. Joint Conf. on Artificial Intelligence (IJCAI 1999)*, pages 968–973, 1999.

[NMAC⁺01] NAU, DANA, H. MUNOZ-AVILA, YUE CAO, AMNON LOTEM and STEVEN MITCHELL: *Total-Order Planning with Partially Ordered Subtasks*. In *Proc. of 17th Int. Joint Conf. on Artificial Intelligence (IJCAI 2001)*, 2001.

[NRSC03]   NAKANO, Y., G. REINSTEIN, T. STOCKY and J. CASSELL: *Towards a model of face-to-face grounding*. In *Annual Meeting of the Association for Computational Linguistics (ACL 2003)*, pages 553–561, 2003.

[OCC88]   ORTONY, A., G. CLORE and A. COLLINS: *The Cognitive Structure of Emotions*. Cambridge University Press, UK, 1988.

[OEss]   OBAID, MOHAMMAD and BIRGIT ENDRASS: *Culturally Aware Virtual Characters in Augmented Reality Environments*. Interfaces (The Quarterly Magazine of BCS Interaction Group), 89, in press.

[PCdC⁺02]   PELACHAUD, C., V. CAROFIGLIO, B. DE CAROLIS, F. DE ROSIS and I. POGGI: *Embodied contextual agent in information delivering application*. In *Proc. of 1st Int. Conf. on Autonomous Agents and Multiagent Systems (AAMAS 2002)*, pages 758–765. ACM, 2002.

[PCLC07]   PIZZI, D., F. CHARLES, J.-L. LUGRIN and M. CAVAZZA: *Interactive Storytelling with Literary Feelings*. In PAIVA, A., R. PRADA and R.-W. PICARD (editors): *Proc. of Int. Conf. on Affective Computing and Intelligent Interaction (ACII 2007)*, pages 630–641, Heidelber, Germany, 2007. Springer.

[Pea93]   PEASE, ALLAN: *Body Language: How to read other's thoughts by their gestures*. Sheldon Press, London, 1993.

[Pel05]   PELACHAUD, CATHERINE: *Multimodal expressive embodied conversational agents*. In *Proc. of 13th annual ACM Int. Conf. on Multimedia*, pages 683–689, 2005.

[Pro11]   PROCEDURAL ARTS: *Facade: a one-act interactive drama*. http://www.interactivestory.net/, 2005-2011. last viewed: 26.02.2012.

[Rab89]   RABINER, LAWRENCE R.: *A tutorial on Hidden Markov Models and selected applications in speech recognition*. IEEE, 77(2):257–286, 1989.

[RAB03a]   RIST, T., E. ANDRÉ and S. BALDES: *A Flexible Platform for Building Applications with Life-Like Characters*. In JOHNSON, W. L., E. ANDRÉ and J. DOMINGUE (editors): *Proc. of Int. Conf. on Intelligent User Interfaces (IUI 2003)*, pages 158–165. ACM Press, 2003.

[RAB⁺03b]   RIST, T., E. ANDRÉ, S. BALDES, P. GEBHARD, M. KLESEN, M. KIPP, P. RIST and M. SCHMITT: *A Review on the Development of Embodied Presentation Agents and their Application Fields*. In PRENDINGER, H. and M. ISHIZUKA (editors): *Life-Like Characters: Tools, Affective Functions and Applications, Cognitive Technologies*, pages 377–404, Heidelberg, Germany, 2003. Springer.

[RAB⁺09a]   REHM, MATTHIAS, ELISABETH ANDRÉ, NIKOLAUS BEE, BIRGIT ENDRASS, MICHAEL WISSNER, YUKIKO NAKANO, AFIA-AKHTER LIPI, TOYOAKI NISHIDA and HUNG-HSUAN HUANG: *Creating Standardized Video Recordings of Multimodal Interactions across Cultures*. In KIPP, MICHAEL, JEAN-CLAUDE MARTIN, PATRIZIA PAGGIO and DIRK HEYLEN (editors): *Multimodal Corpora*, number 5509 in *LNAI*, pages 138–159. Springer, 2009.

[RAB+09b] REHM, MATTHIAS, ELISABETH ANDRÉ, NIKOLAUS BEE, BIRGIT EN-
DRASS, MICHAEL WISSNER, YUKIKO NAKANO, AFIA AKHTER LIPI,
TOYOAKI NISHIDA and HUNG-HSUAN HUANG: *Multimodal Corpora*,
chapter Creating Standardized Video Recordings of Multimodal Interactions
across Cultures. Springer, 2009.

[RAN+07] REHM, MATTHIAS, ELISABETH ANDRÉ, YUKIKO NAKANO, TOYOAKI
NISHIDA, NIKOLAUS BEE, BIRGIT ENDRASS, HUNG-HSUAN HUAN and
MICHAEL WISSNER: *The CUBE-G approach - Coaching culture-specific
nonverbal behavior by virtual agents*. In MAYER, IGOR and HANNEKE
MASTIK (editors): *ISAGA 2007: Organizing and Learning through Gaming
and Simulation*, 2007.

[RBA08] REHM, M., N. BEE and E. ANDRÉ: *Wave Like an Egyptian - Accelerometer
Based Gesture Recognition for Culture Specific Interactions*. In *HCI 2008
Culture, Creativity, Interaction*, 2008.

[RDMH05] RAYBOURN, E.-M., E. DEAGLE, K. MENDINI and J. HENEGHAN: *Adaptive Thinking & Leadership simulation game training for Special Forces Of-
ficers*. In *Interservice/Industry Training, Simulation, and Education Conference (I/ITSEC)*, paper no. 2370, 2005.

[RN96] REEVES, B. and C. NASS: *The Media Equation - How People Treat Com-
puters, Television and New Media Like Real People and Places*. Cambridge
University Press, Cambridge, 1996.

[RNA+09] REHM, M., Y. NAKANO, E. ANDRÉ, T. NISHIDA, N. BEE, B. ENDRASS,
M. WISSNER, A.-A. LIPI and H.-H. HUANG: *From observation to simu-
lation: generating culture-specific behavior for interactive systems*. AI &
Society, 24(3):267–280, 2009.

[RNKWT12] REHM, MATTHIAS, YUKIKO NAKANO, TOMOKO KODA and HEIKE
WINSCHIERS-THEOPHILUS: *Culturally Aware Agent Communication*. In
ZACARIAS, M. and J.V. DE OLIVEIRA (editors): *Human-Computer Inter-
action*, number 396 in *SCI*, pages 411–436. Springer, 2012.

[RW05] REHM, M. and M. WISSNER: *Gamble - A Multiuser Game with an Embodied Conversational Agent*. In *Entertainment Computing - ICEC 2005: 4th
International Conference*, pages 180–191. Springer, 2005.

[Sch88] SCHNEIDER, K. P.: *Small Talk: Analysing Phatic Discourse*. Hitzeroth,
Marburg, 1988.

[SHT+02] SATO, R., R. HIGASHINAKA, M. TAMOTO, M. NAKANO and K. AIKAWA:
Learning decision trees to determine turn-taking by spoken dialogue systems.
In *ICSLP 2002*, pages 861–864, 2002.

[SKLL04] SIDNER, C., C.-D. KIDD, C. LEE and N. LESH: *Where to Look: A Study of
Human-Robot Engagement*. In *Proc. of Int. Conf. on Intelligent User Interfaces (IUI 2004)*, pages 78–84. ACM Press, 2004.

[TH96]   TRAUM, D. and P. HEEMAN: *Utterance Units and Grounding in Spoken Dialogue*. In *ICSLP 96*, 1996.

[The12]   THE UNIVERSITY OF CHICAGO: *McNeill Lab: Center for Gesture and Speech Research*. http://mcneilllab.uchicago.edu/, 2012.   last viewed: 26.02.2012.

[THT97]   TROMPENAARS, FONS and CHARLES HAMPDEN-TURNER: *Riding the waves of culture - Understanding Cultural Diversity in Business*. Nicholas Brealey Publishing, London, 1997.

[TT99]   TING-TOOMEY, S.: *Communicating across cultures*. The Guilford Press, New York, 1999.

[Uni]   UNIVERSITY OF MARYLAND: *SHOP: Simple Hierarchical Ordered Planner*. http://www.cs.umd.edu/projects/shop/. last viewed: 26.02.2012.

[USC12]   USC INSTITUTE FOR CREATIVE TECHNOLOGIES: *ICT: Institute for Creative Technologies*. http://ict.usc.edu/, 2012. last viewed: 26.02.2012.

[WM10]   WU, PEGGY and CHRISTOPHER MILLER: *Interactive Phrasebook - Conveying culture through etiquette*. In BLANCHARD, E.-G., W.-L JOHNSON, A. OGAN and D. ALLARD (editors): *3rd Int. Workshop on Culturally-Aware Tutoring Systems (CATS2010) held on ITS2010*, pages 47–55, Pittsburg, USA, 2010.

[YBC10]   YIN, LANGXUAN, TIMOTHY BICKMORE and D.-E. CORTÉS: *The Impact of Linguistic and Cultural Congruity on Persuasion by Conversational Agents*. In ALLBECK, J.-M., N.-I. BADLER, T.-W. BICKMORE, C. PELACHAUD and A. SAFONOVA (editors): *Proc. of 10th Int. Conf. on Intelligent Virtual Agents (IVA 2010)*, pages 343–349. Springer, 2010.

The Author

Birgit Endrass studied Informatics and Multimedia at Augsburg University, Germany, where she obtained her doctoral degree in 2012. For her thesis "Cultural Diversity for Virtual Characters: Investigating Behavioral Aspects across Cultures", supervised by Prof. Elisabeth André, she received the certificate *summa cum laude* and was rewarded with the Research Award of Augsburg University (Wissenschaftspreis der Universität Augsburg) and the prestigious IFAAMAS-12 Victor Lesser Distinguished Dissertation Award.

For her work experience she completed internships at some well-known research institutes: INESC-ID (Lisbon, Portugal), National Institute for Informatics (Tokyo, Japan) and Institute for Creative Technologies (Los Angeles, USA) and actively participated in several international projects.

As a faculty member of Augsburg University, she extended her research on culture-specific behaviors to other human factors, e.g., age differences. For intuitive interaction she explores novel interfaces such as humanoid robots as social companions for elderly people, or touch-based interaction in serious learning games for children.

The Author